Legacy and Illusions

Abstract and Artistic Photography

by

Klaus Bohn, MPA, F/SPPA, A

Feeling more deeply about photography

www.photographicartvictoria.com

CCB Publishing
British Columbia, Canada

Legacy and Illusions: Abstract and Artistic Photography

ISBN-13: 978-1-927360-19-4
First Edition

Library and Archives Canada Cataloguing in Publication
Bohn, Klaus
Legacy and illusions : abstract and artistic photography / by Klaus Bohn.
ISBN 978-1-927360-18-7 (bound).--ISBN 978-1-927360-19-4 (pbk.)
Also available in electronic format.
1. Photography, Artistic.
2. Photography, Abstract.
3. Composition (Photography).
I. Title. II. Title: Abstract and artistic photography.
TR642.B64 2012 771 C2012-901566-0

Publisher: CCB Publishing
British Columbia, Canada
www.ccbpublishing.com

I dedicate this book…

To those who have made a difference in photography

This includes those who are known and have made a difference, and those who have shared one-to-one with other photographers; not as famous or well-known, and yet made a difference in kind – those who will make a difference to the art of photography.

Photography is a growing art and yet the reality is still the same. It won't matter if an image was made by Ansel Adams long ago. The longevity of its beauty is still the same. To study and learn from the past has a present influence and a future benefit to the art of photography. We can learn by studying their books, like the ones by Erving Penn or Richard Avedon. They were perhaps controversial in their day, and yet now we value them for their input to our current day photography; history becomes our teacher and the present will become the past. May we value the past, the greats.

Yousuf Karsh's work has a profound influence on portraiture with a message in the expressions of the famous and not so famous. His photographs have a stunning effect for us even today, and will last into tomorrow. For this cause we learn from others, and the greats as our mentors, to influence our own work to pass on to our clients – even if it isn't known to them. I long to savour their talents, their ability and creativity on my work, may it last in such a way to pass it on – everlasting. May it be our burning desire to leave an imprint from our work in this world!

Klaus Bohn

Other books by Klaus Bohn

50 Principles of Composition in Photography
Published 2006

"Fantastic book!"
Clay Blackmore Photographer LLC

The Art Within Portrait Photography
Published 2007

"Klaus produced a great body of work,
and has also developed the talent to put into
words the deeper meaning of his photographs."
Ken Whitmire, M.Photog., CR, FASP

Giclee Prints by Klaus Bohn

*Giclee prints of the images presented in this book
may be purchased directly through Klaus Bohn's web site:*

www.photographicartvictoria.com

Foreword

I have known Klaus since I was in high school back in 1983. I had a huge love for photography and wanted to learn as much as I could from him. I took several classes from Klaus and spent many hours at his studio in Moose Jaw. Klaus became more than a teacher, he became my friend and mentor.

Klaus taught me much more than photography, he taught me how to think. As my life has evolved from photographer to business owner to hairstylist to husband to a father, Klaus' teachings have been very influential.

Over the almost three decades I have known Klaus his life has seen many twists and turns in the road but the core of the man, his very essence, has not changed. He thinks on a different plane than most people do. Even though I am not creating many images these days I have purchased all of Klaus' books. His teachings go beyond photography; I still use his teachings in cutting hair and other aspects of my life every day.

Allow Klaus' teachings in, don't accept or reject, just let them in.

Shawn Dreger

Preface

Artistic Perception and Interpretation

Concealed Illusions – *The Photographer's Unknown Resource*

Ninety-five percent of everything we do is unconscious. Consider this for a moment. We eat, dress, drive, and perform hundreds of other daily activities without much conscious thought at all. It's like we're on autopilot. Our actions and reactions, likes and dislikes, and most of our decision-making operate at this unconscious level.

Most lifelong patterns are imprinted on our subconscious minds at a very young age, usually before seven. These patterns influence our thoughts and emotions. They colour how we perceive the world and our place in it. In essence, we have unconscious filters through which all incoming sensual data are processed.

How does all of this apply to you as a photographer?

Although your conscious mind plays an important role in how and what you photograph or edit, your subconscious patterns play a far greater role than you might realize. When you concentrate on a subject, you may or may not notice the smells and sounds around you. And you are certainly not aware of what your peripheral vision is picking up. In fact, your subconscious mind is pulling in millions of bits of information every second. Most is discarded, but much of it is processed through those filters mentioned above.

These unobserved inputs are constantly swaying your choices of f-stop, composition, angle, focus, cropping, and hundreds of other essentials. As a professional, you make many of these decisions instantly.

Cognitive & Perceptive Cycles

There is a biorhythm that operates 24/7 in our body known as the *Basic Rest-Activity Cycle* (*BRAC*). While some biological cycles last for many days, the BRAC oscillates consistently at between 90 and 120 minutes. During the **Active phase** of the cycle, we tend to be more logical, more detail-oriented, and take a black and white (all or nothing) approach to everything. Conversely, the **Rest segment** is typified by being holistic, creative, and we like to consider the *big picture*.

So, how does this influence taking or editing that photo? Just being aware of this psychological cycle, you will be better equipped to know what biases are influencing your decisions. Whether setting up a shot or editing, you may be either logical and rational on one extreme, or highly creative and imaginative on the other. Of course, you may also be between cycles. Do what you have to do, and then give it a review in another thirty minutes. You will be critiquing the job with a new mind!

Are you Visual, Auditory, or Kinesthetic?

Although each of us is a blend of these three profiles, some people live, learn, and communicate in a dominant one. Since you're a photographer, you must have some visual tendencies. If you also happen to be somewhat kinesthetic, a hands-on approach will be evident in how you view and ultimately present your subject matter. A kinesthetic inclination might also include emotional considerations. Being aware of your unique style will enhance your decision making, whether conscious or unconscious.

Brian Walsh, PhD

Brian Walsh, PhD is the author of numerous books on self-empowerment, interpersonal communications, and enriched learning. He is a Master Practitioner of Neurolinguistic Programming, a Clinical Hypnotherapist, an Emotional Freedom Technique Practitioner, and an Acupuncture Detoxification Specialist.

Contents

Introduction

A Love for Life

I love life. I have experienced life and want to experience more of life in every safe and interesting way, to stretch my experiences to the limit; to love all that there is to love in this life. I have had the opportunity to fly with the Snowbirds Demonstration Team (431 Squadron) as a photographer... so many privileges have been afforded to me in my profession, to travel all over the world and make a living in photography since I was 25 years old.

Portraits are my passion, to create an image from reality to art. To communicate verbally is an art, but to stretch oneself and speak with photographic art, my business name "www.photographicartvictoria.com", has been my joy and delight. To share and be passionate, my brand FDP – *feeling more deeply about photography* – has also extended to my personal and professional relationships. As the saying goes, we live life once, and I feel like I have lived many lifetimes worth of experiences, and will continue to endeavour moment by moment in this pursuit. So hang on and feel the wind and enjoy the sun, experience the present moment in life! Every minute in which we are awake and experience it fully is being born again anew. What more can I say but that is what life means to me and relationships must mean and do mean, in the most fulfilled lives and fully awakened experiences.

When you look at my work I hope you can see my passion and feel my heart beating with joy and excitement right to the pit of one's stomach, and if you miss this experience then perhaps you could read my books *50 Principles of Composition in Photography* and *The Art Within Portrait Photography*. This current work about "the illusion in photography" that is currently in your hands is presented for you to explore and enjoy a different aspect of my life's work, abstract and artistic photography.

My love for photography is filled with passion, but what is greater than making images from a camera is the continual process that affords the artistic liberty to create our own expressions so an individual is born, with each unique artist being akin to an unicorn, one of a kind and that is what I prize most highly above any measure, to make an image so original that it begs comparison! I value what is possible today by printing Giclees on watercolour paper and then continue the process by painting my added impressions.

Art is the "feeling" one is given, the talent to produce in a most unique way – extremely personal – that can't be copied because it is from the heart. I don't mean documentary but beyond one's visual capability – the interpretation of the recorded or embellished finished image.

More than that – to have a vision – to see from the heart that each image can impart feelings that surge though your veins when the art piece is complete. Taking the photo is only part of the experience; Photoshop can add to the outcome, hand embellishments add one's own hand at painting on a photograph, especially if it is put on canvas. Giclee finishes have been my bestsellers because of its long endurance over time.

Photography has always been an expression of my vision – not merely documentation. The *art in photography* goes beyond what is in front of the camera – what has been within the photographer's mind and imagination. How do you accomplish this with an apparatus we call a camera – a mere machine? The answer is to focus on the result, the outcome, the end product. A chef once stated that when he makes a new dish he can taste it before it is made. As a photographer my vision is the end result – how I achieve it makes it ART.

These are my favourite photographs for me to produce, not only do I have a vision of what I want to finish with but it has also given me the opportunity to envision the end from the beginning! To capture the raw material one must have an insight of what we want to produce like any artist; then work on it. Nowadays Photoshop has afforded me additional possibilities. It is easy to create the outcome I desire. Embellishment is now possible because of the paper and the way one can still work on the image after it has been printed, with other mediums like coloured pencils, watercolour paints, and I have even used oil paints on canvases.

Photographic art lends itself to wall decor for homes and offices. It is possible to hang an artistic image practically everywhere, one that speaks to the viewer or at least can enhance the area and enable the environment to be more hospitable; incorporating it into a space to enjoy and make it more friendly, even in an office.

I wish this to be my legacy, what I will be remembered for and to move others in a similar manner.

There is so much to say. Please read my photographs with this in mind.

Some of the images in this book have been reproduced from the original framed photograph.

Depending on the photograph's final finish, be that on canvas, watercolour paper or other unique substrate, this will impact the texture revealed within the images illustrated in this book.

My Style

People need to realize that words are like tools, and how you use your tools will make your talent and ability more viable. A sculptor reveals what he saw in the marble and releases the hidden beauty within the stone. The use of tools makes this possible, but it is the vision that enables the image to become a reality. Tools for painting, brushes, pallet knives and other tools that have been used are only tools, but one needs to know how to use them effectively. In photography it is the same, one's vision – interpreted with the camera, filters, and in working with the equipment of today including Photoshop or other programs.

A story to illustrate this point…

A wood chopper was chopping wood and a person came to speak with the wood chopper:

"Your axe must be why you can chop so well."

"Yes," said the man, "the head is the right weight and the handle is the right length so the balance is just right for me to chop wood with just one blow."

"You are so lucky to have the right equipment," said the other man.

"No," said the wood chopper, "I chose the right tools and learned how to use them by practicing regularly; my ability to produce my *style*. The axe is not my style – I have the style and know how to use it well."

We must all develop this uniqueness from within. It can't be taught; instead it needs to be practiced with the heart – from within is what makes us all different and unique. In one of my classes I said even the great Orville Ottenbreit can't produce a Klaus Bohn original.

Passion + Vision = Results

If we only have passion it will take us only so far – as long as the passion lasts.

Vision without passion fizzles in time because there is nothing to drive the vision.

Passion with vision has a lasting effect on the person possessing just that – the drive to continue until it brings the results.

Movement

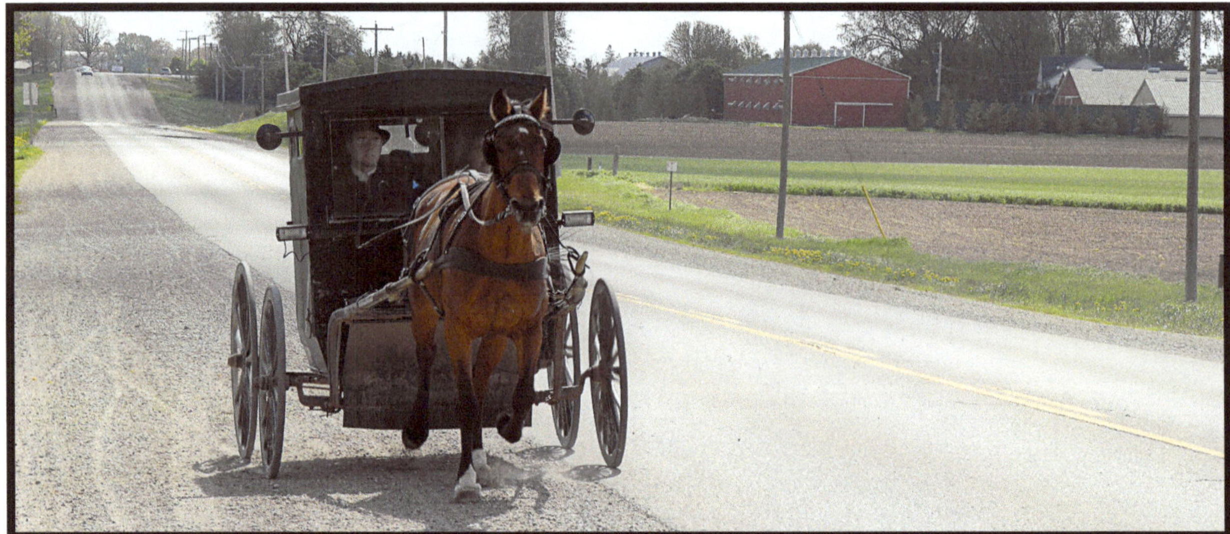

Amish Time

As the buggy drifted to the modern road I could see the car would take them over. The signal lights are modern and the drift can even be seen in the photo. Time changes everything a little at a time…

As One

Perfect flying pattern
with two kites – amazing.

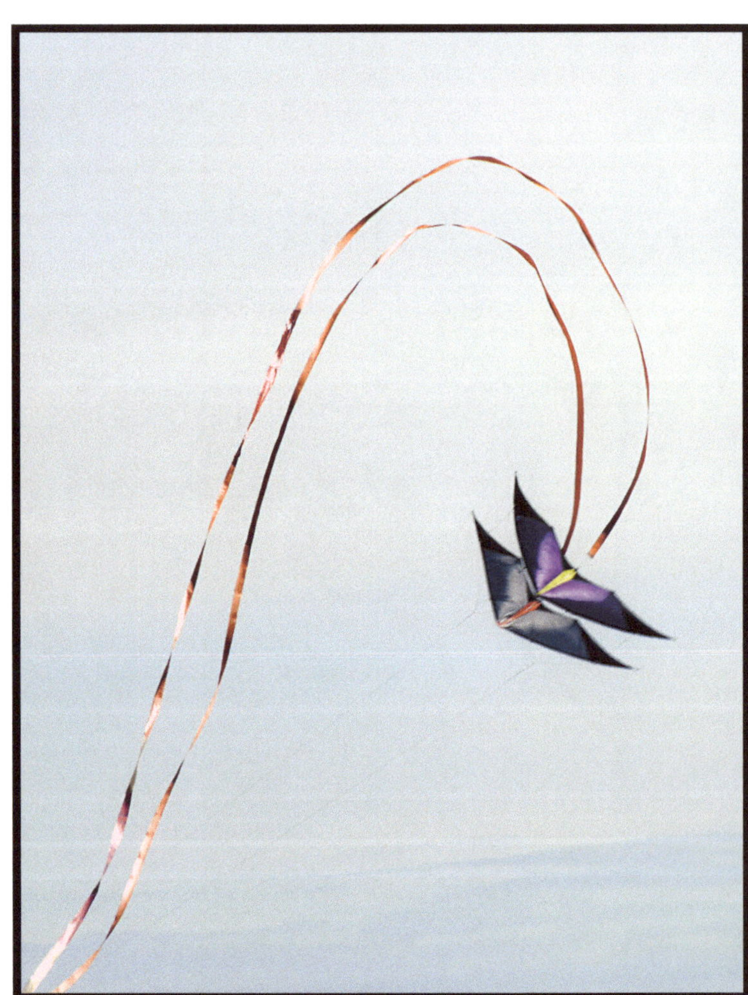

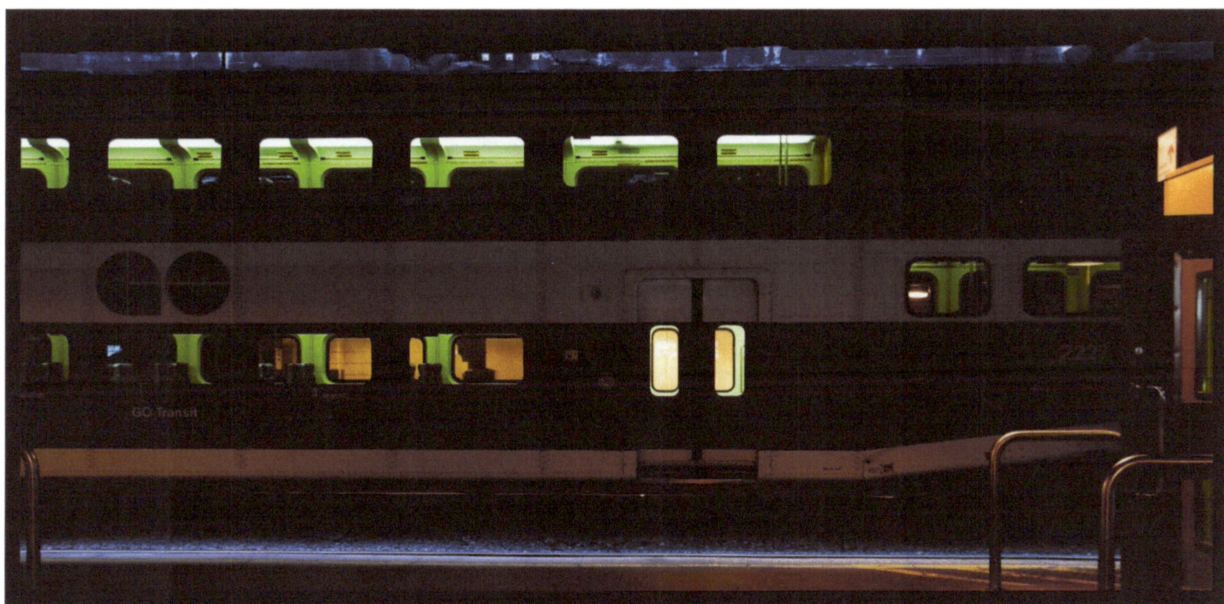

Cartoon Train

This cartoon-like image gave me a new insight to an illusion and yet it captures my attention as I photographed what seemed to me more of a dream-like image. I like to think outside the box. I find if that is what I do then I am in a bigger box and this keeps on going and I never leave the box. I found a way for me to escape this phenomenon is to look up and avoid any fence or restrictions. By looking up into my imagination it no longer restricts my creativity. Looking up brings me into my subconscious were I am free and allowed to be myself and not influenced by the work of others.

I feel the need to surround myself with images that can influence my imagination. I need to see my work on my walls in my office and home so my imagination evolves and becomes new to me…

There are new ways of enhancing wall decor in homes and offices to create a warm and positive feeling to the environments in which we live and work. Like looking through a window the beauty of nature is stimulating to the senses; as we create our environment, photographs can add to this pleasure when nature is not available, choosing inspiration, beauty and comfort through art photographs of one's choice.

Our senses are so finely tuned by past experiences that we can imagine what we see with all our senses, seeing, feeling... My brand is FDP, *feeling more deeply about photography.* For me it is all about the feeling I get when I enjoy and study a fine piece of art, being moved by its beauty.

Wall decor has enchanted many cultures from the beginning of time. Wall paintings and drawings were part of their living space for enjoyment and decor for coming generations. The saying that we become what we think about perhaps is indeed true. We become influenced by what we see every day. Our environment plays a large part in our lives. So growth is in my future... **I want to see what I haven't seen before.**

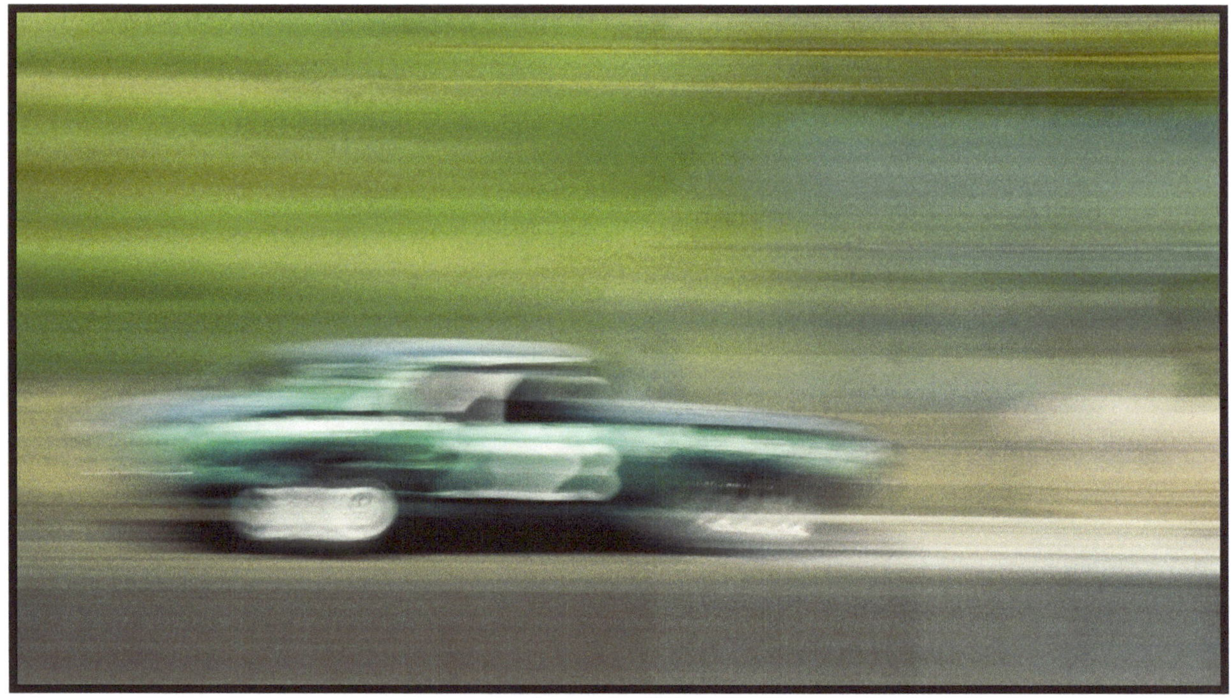

Counter Pan

Most of us are familiar with the term panning – when we drag the shutter a bit and move the camera with the subject – we want to stay in reality sharpness and blur everything else. Drag the shutter just means to slow down the shutter's time, for instance setting it at ¼ of a second or slower and increasing the blurriness of all that surrounds the subject you are trying to keep in focus.

Counter panning is the opposite. Instead of following the subject we move the camera in the opposite direction with a slow shutter speed, perhaps 1/30 of a second or slower. The challenge is to keep both eyes open so we can see in this case the car coming from the left and going to the right. My camera was moving from right to left, the opposite way the car was travelling. I hand held the camera and held my breath; timing of course means everything, so as you see the car coming you squeeze the button and keep the camera moving left past the car, do not stop moving the camera after the shutter is pressed.

The image has a unique feeling in relationship to the movement of the car, it stretches and duplicates as you can see in the number 23 blurred and stretched. The wheels have been increased as if there were a number of wheels front and back. The soft blur gives the car a feeling of tremendous speed, with just enough information in the car to see what it is and its purpose, which is to race.

A good friend of mine, Greg, told me that this is one of the best photographs I ever made, and he should know since he is a very good photographer from Regina, Saskatchewan.

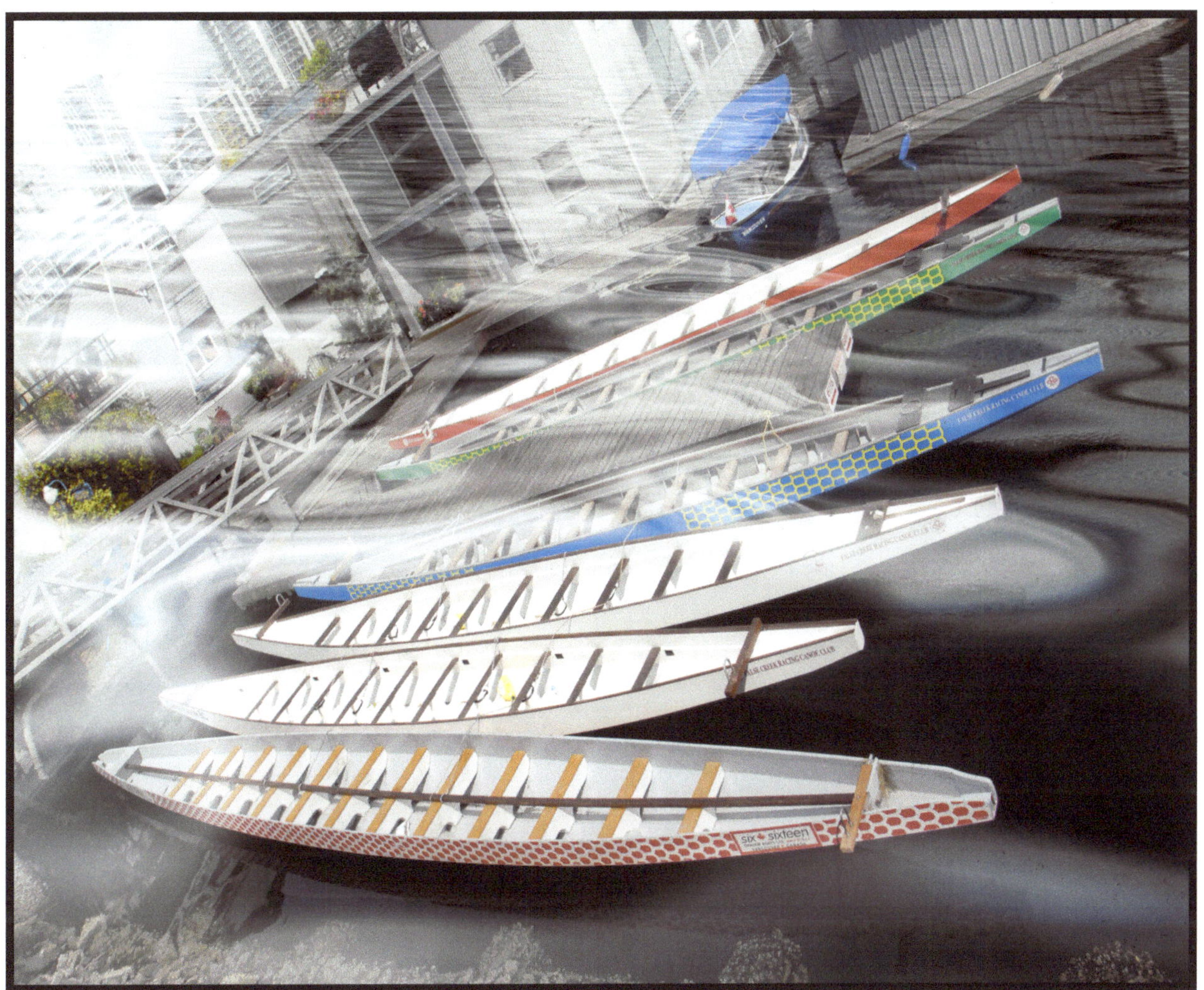

Crashing Boats

Crashing boats became real. I looked at the photograph but it was still missing something, so I added the feeling of crashing in a storm. I like the feel of movement and action. For me every image needs to impart a message and add a little drama to the scene.

Praise received:
The above image was submitted and approved in the Inspired Art Group on RedBubble.

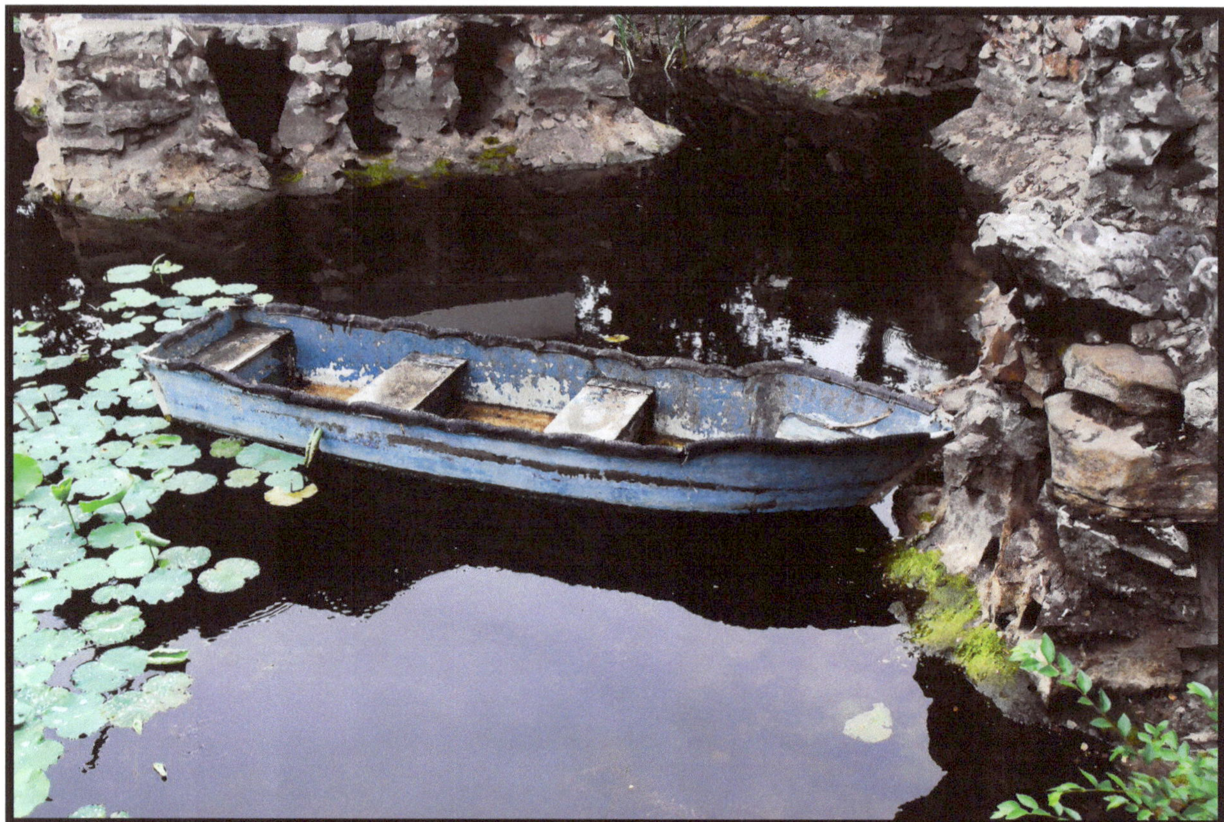

Enchanted Boat

Photograph of an enchanted boat I took while travelling in China. The mood wasn't there until I did some work on the image. I feel the magic adds to the photograph!

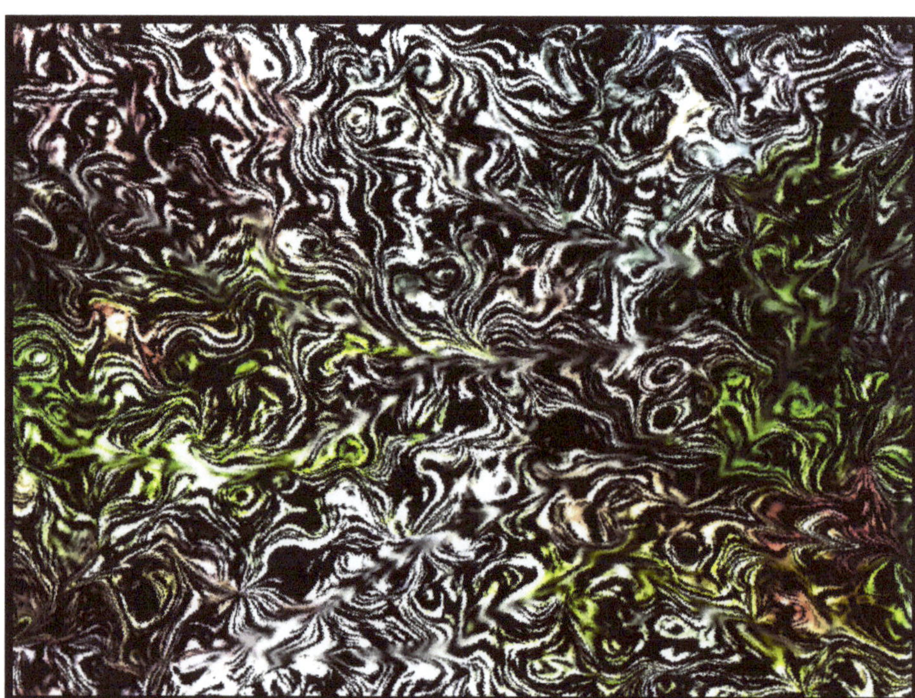

Liquefy

A design of lines and patterns to mesmerize the eyes and mind!

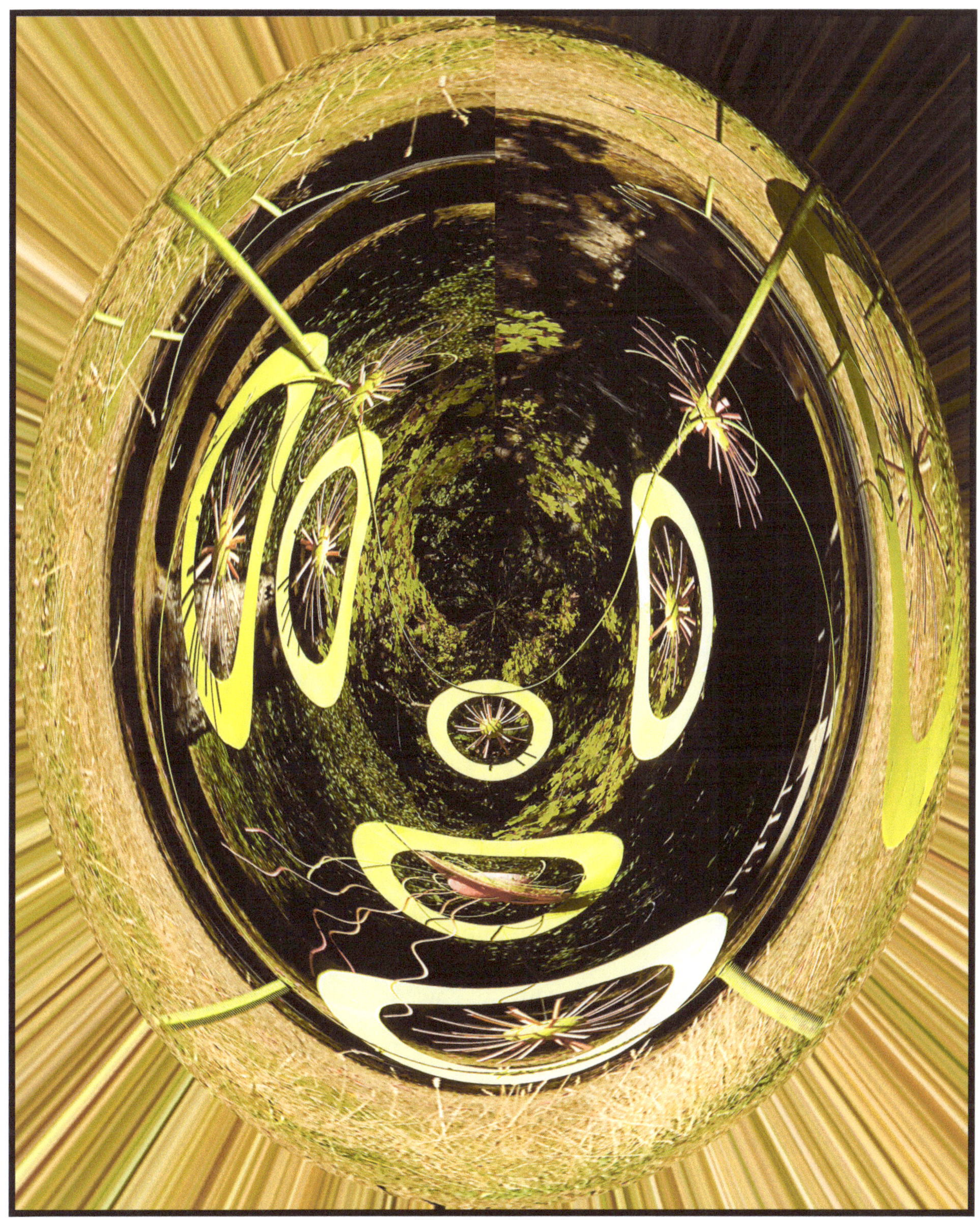

Moving Mask

We seem to hide behind what makes our true reality; what we don't want others to see or even as we look at ourselves, there are hidden pieces. Moving mask just spoke to me; as our timelines change with age, it moves to more illusions of grandeur – what we think we are or want to have others see – as we see ourselves behind a masked reality.

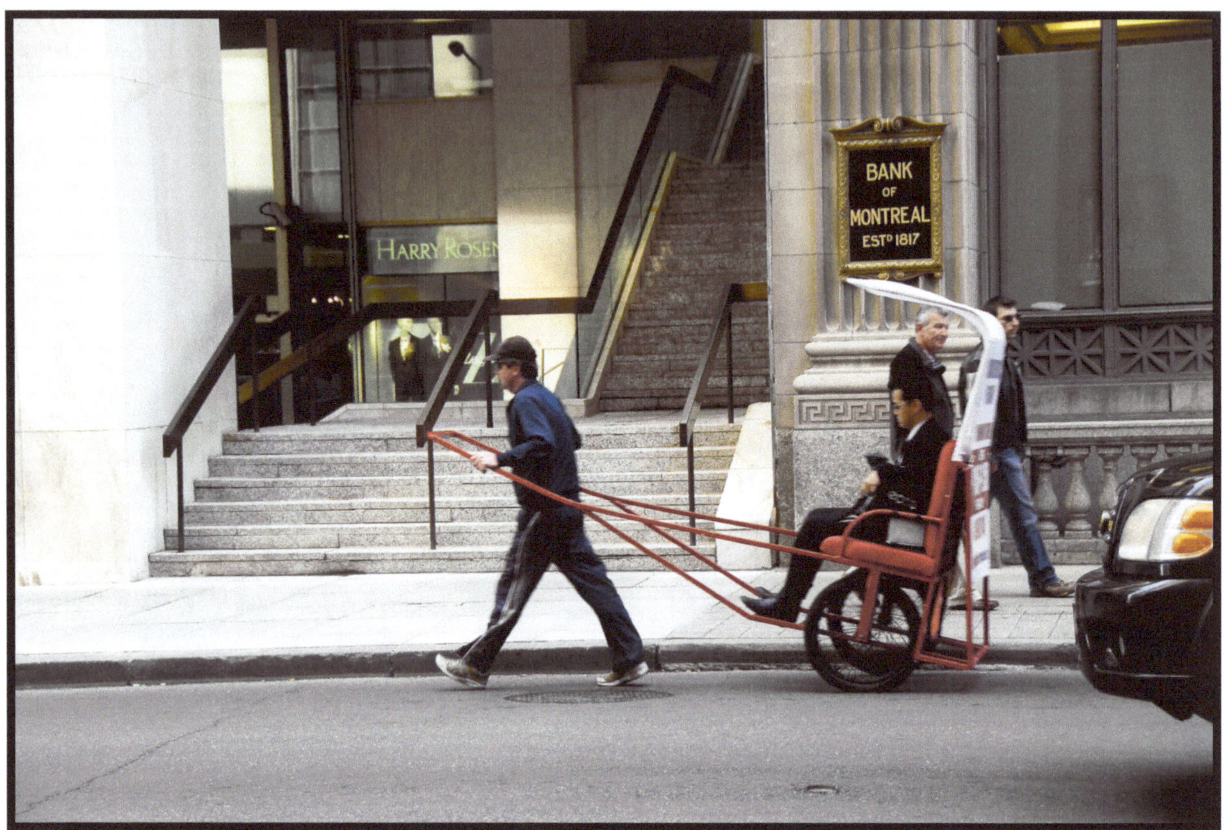

Pull

This was very unusual to see in downtown Toronto, so I anticipated the action. The person pulling another and in the background the bank – money – it is just out of time and out of place.

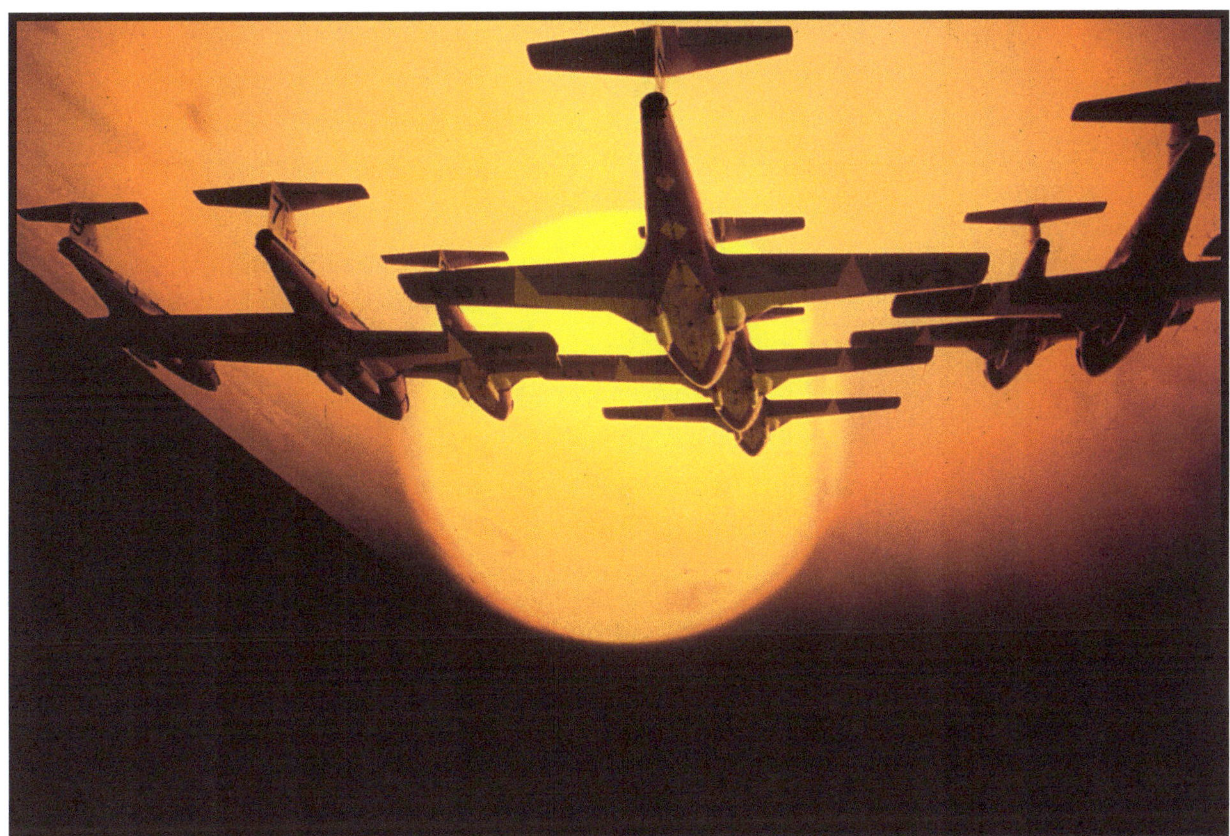

Snowbirds

I had the privilege to go up with the Snowbirds Demonstration Team (431 Squadron); it is nothing short of miraculous. I photographed on slide film then went further and added another slide with a yellow button, the sun. Sandwiching them together for the effect as you see above is the end result: Flying into the sun…

I was asked to go up with them as a photographer since I had my studio in Moose Jaw, Saskatchewan at the time. It was scary but also a privilege to be in one of the crossover planes and pulling so many G-forces I had a hard time lifting the camera to my eyes. Then flying down to earth seemed like we would not be able to make the turn up in time, the light was nice and I am still alive.

The image of the Snowbirds flying into the sun – a trick I learned from Rocky Gunn – he used buttons and sandwiched slides together to give the three dimensional illusion of flying into the sun. The sun is so big that I could never have captured its size in relationship to the planes. The pilots loved the image so much that each one wanted a copy.

<u>Praise received</u>:

"Oh my word, WOW this is such an exciting image! What a great opportunity to be up there with them! I love the vibrancy of the orange glow, adds magic to the feeling this evokes in me. I really feel I'm there too!"

Keith: "This is awesome Klaus… The two images were great photos on their own but then putting them together like this… brilliant!"

Double Vision

There are things we perceive as our own reality and then there is that which is filled with our imagination; that which is just our perception, our imagination, our desire for what we would like to have in our life. Movement is necessary in that perception because nothing is stationary; the flux of change is ever around us and constantly in motion – as I studied this phenomenon my reality shifted from the obvious to the sublime or should I say to that which I have focused on sublimely and with my six senses that I am aware of, at least in part.

To describe something that perhaps in itself is indescribable with mere words is a task befitting those who have travelled to the other side and back again; I know of no one today with these credentials. The saying goes, "Fools rush in where angels fear to tread!" Please do not expect a revelation because revelations go within from the Universal Mind, from that which the sixth sense is in connection with, greater than we, and are yet affordable to each one of us. The price is not out of reach, but costly; to those who don't have it and the ones who have the uncanny sense of how blessed and adventurous they can become, like explorers travelling alone without companionship for the most part; may I suggest men like Van Gogh and in our day, the person not yet know, undiscovered like voyages of the universe, within our subconscious.

I am asked most often what I think of someone else's work. How foolish it would be if I tried to stand in their place to expound their virtues; by their own expressions they stand or fall. It is not me but they who express their imagination in a visionary way, most often unexplored by the viewer, otherwise they would need no explanation!

People will often say, "I am a student, and therefore I need a teacher." No, no, no... you need someone to educate you, not a teacher. Education comes from the ones who ask the right questions so you will, in time, be able to reach inside yourself, from within, for the answer; only you have the answer for yourself. There are always the fundamentals and we might say the essentials to begin with; I am thankful for those who are so able without any instruction from another, those whose talent, ability and skill seem to be born from within, like Beethoven who is without equal, wrote his symphonies perfectly without corrections the first time. Let us be thankful and appreciate individuals who were born to create, regardless of their creative outlet or endeavour.

May we learn to see with our naked eyes that which is so obvious when we see it – also with the eye of intuition, or perhaps even an altered reality – to what we perceive as real. Awaken a dream-like state, the alpha level so to speak, which is there for us to explore and learn from and live in a greater percentage of time. Create that which hasn't been done before, the impossible made possible so it can be seen.

Nature

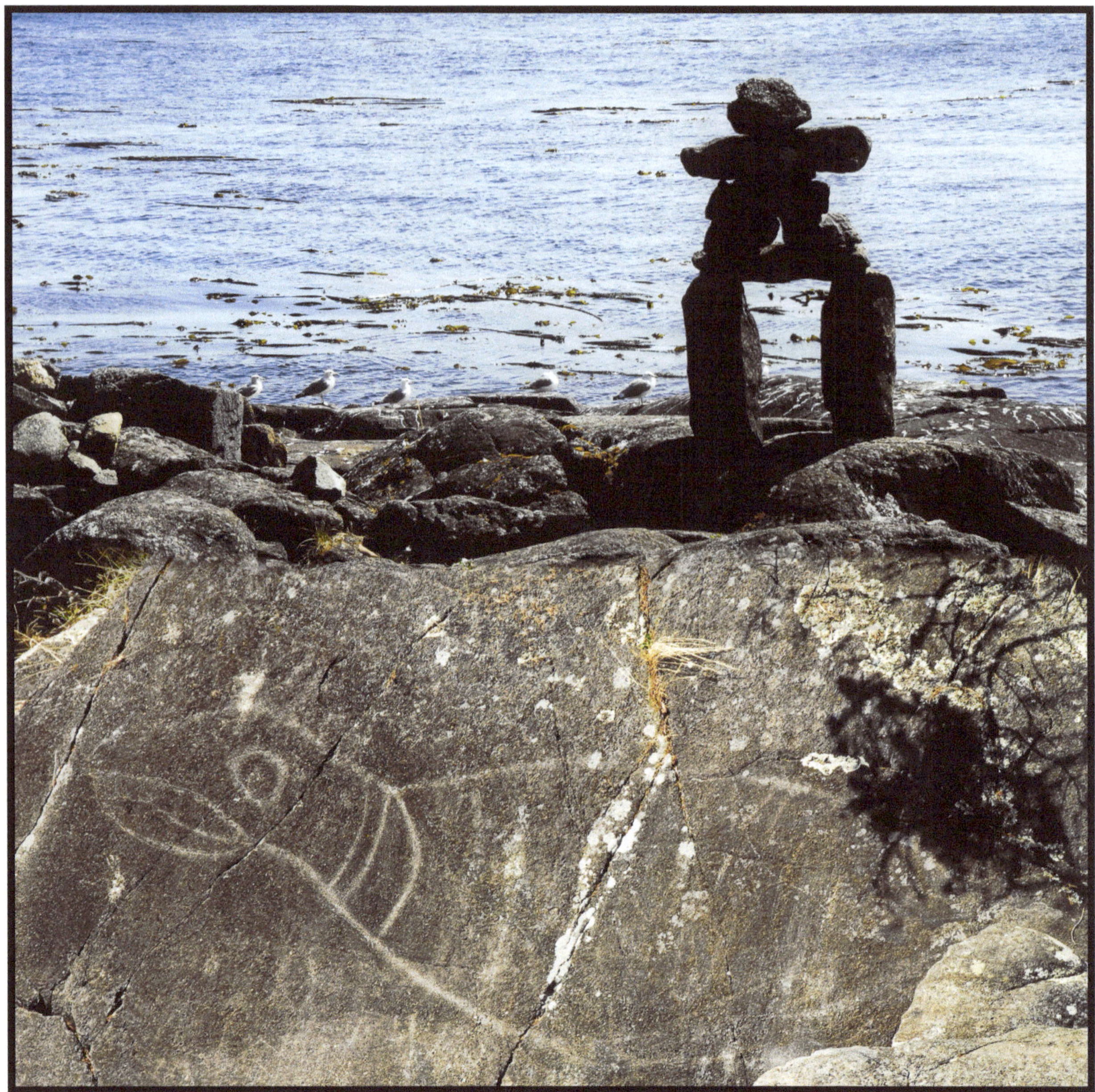

2 in 1: Inuksuk

This is from the cover of a coffee table book I had published. I dedicated the book to the 2010 Olympic Winter games which promoted the Inuksuk. This image is actually two different images pulled together because I liked the painting on the rock and the sculpture was in another place so I put the two together. To show, speak and give us the history of their culture.

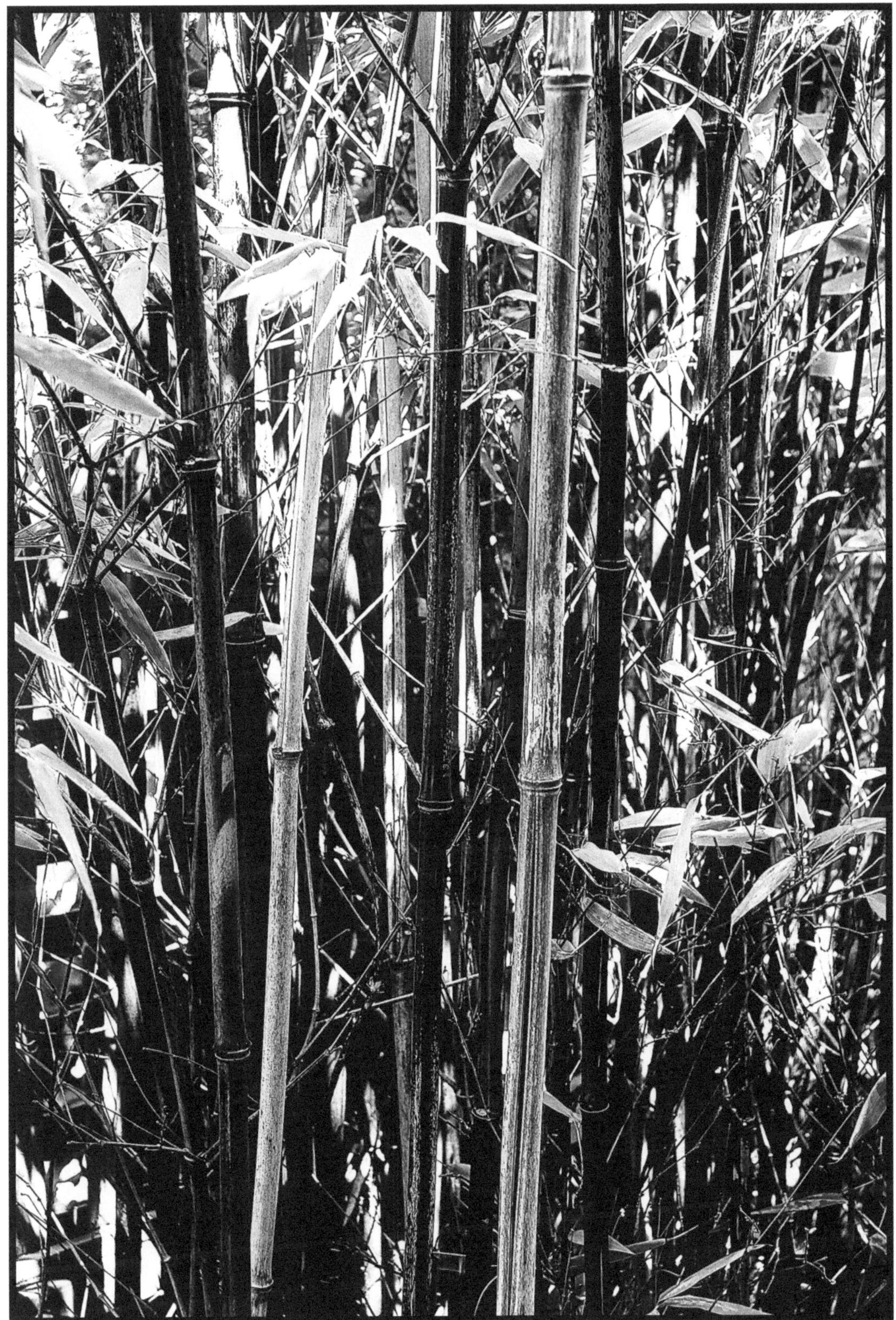

Bamboo

This image was taken in my family's yard so I enhanced the outcome by changing the end result to black and white. Bamboo is strong and bendable like an image should be to the viewer; flexible but strong in composition and design.

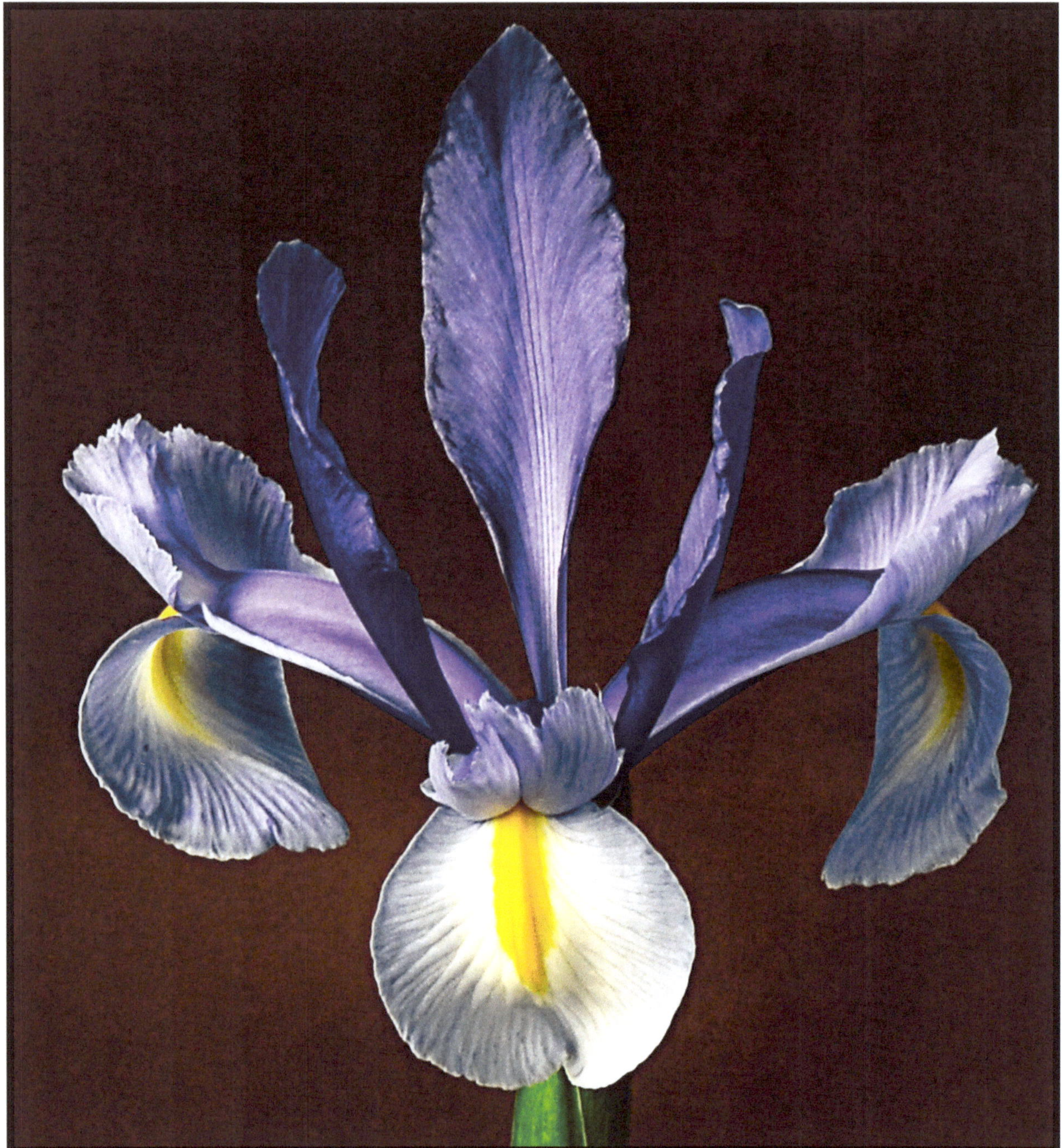

Blue Iris

I photographed the iris in my studio. I felt this beautiful flower needed to be preserved in an image for the future.

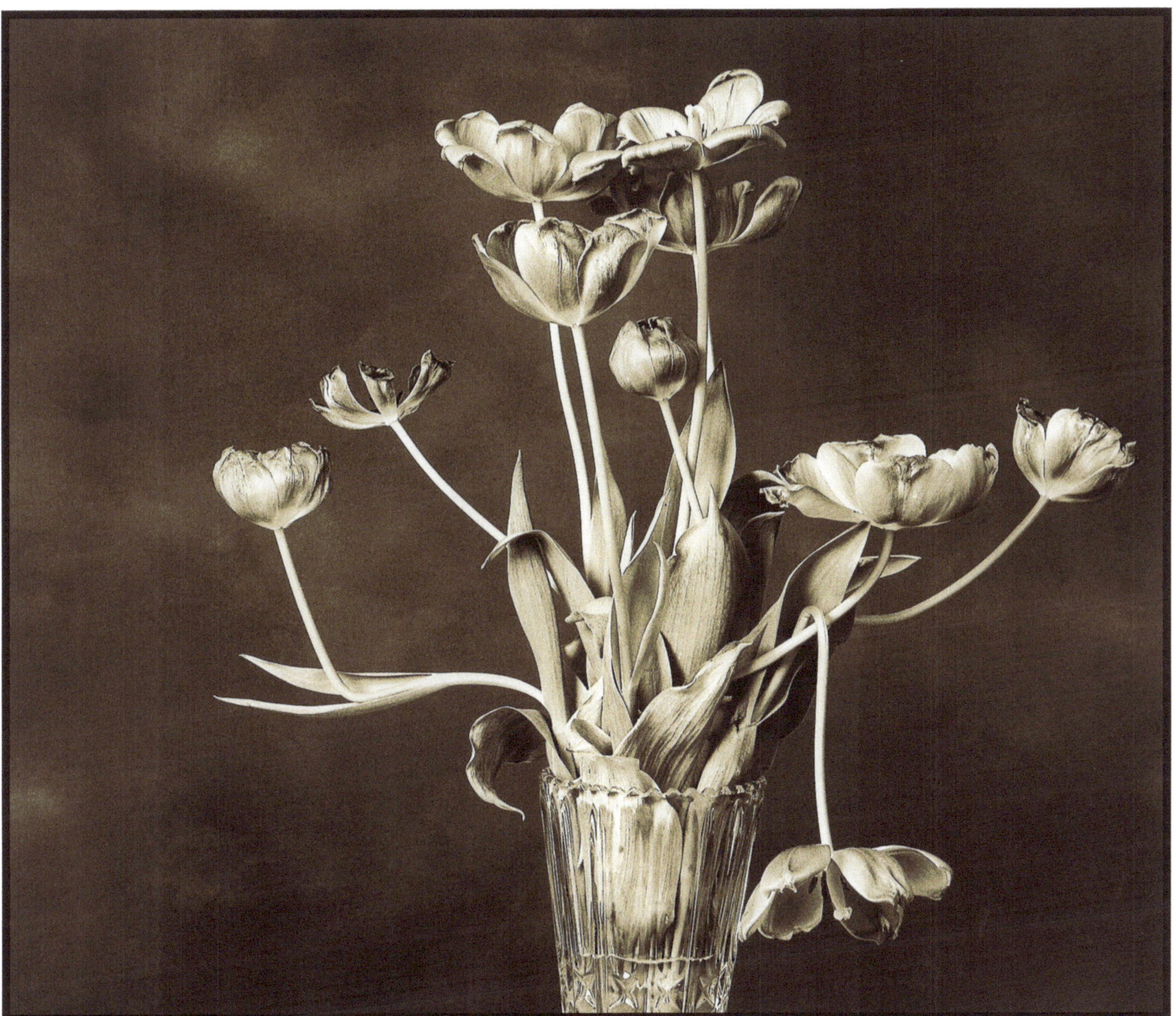

Bronzed

It like these flowers as a sculpture. My beloved mother was going to throw away the dying flowers, but I remembered seeing a book by Irving Penn in which he photographed dying flowers. I asked her for the flowers and she thought it was brazen of me to want to photograph them. I took a shot of them in color but it was a no go, so I photographed them in black and white – still nothing I liked. Then I uploaded the file and tried a sepia tone, but it was still a no go. I worked with darker and golden brown shades until I saw what looked like a sculpture in bronze. That was it, the feeling I got was what I had in mind. Composition purposely off-centered – a reality of life now almost gone but preserved in bronze. As in a sculpture as in a photograph, lasting for many years, still there to be viewed and studied.

My source of inspiration came from Irving Penn and seeing the flowers in their last stage of life I was inspired to photograph something that we don't see very often in a photograph; that is more than just a normal photograph, it is an art piece because of studying the work of others and going beyond. Art is our intuition, what we feel, and can put together in a meaningful way.

Praise received:

"Klaus, you are a great addition to the We Sell Art Group, Fine Arts & Photography."

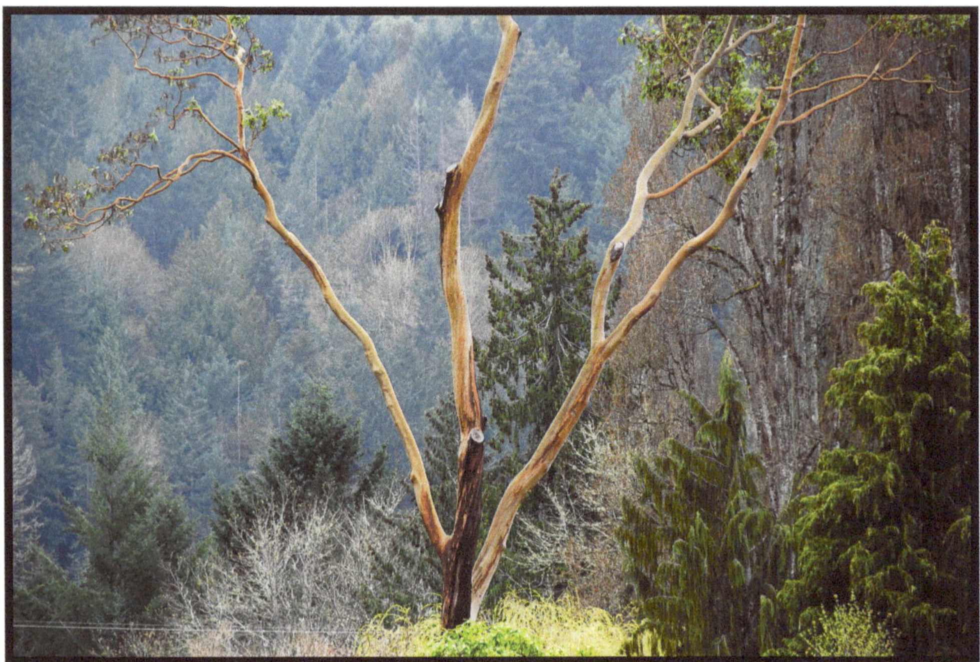

Butchart Gardens #1

I like the nakedness of the tree in the foreground. Arbutus trees shed their bark each year. Three folded branches coming out from the main part of the tree, sculpturing its beauty in contrast with the surrounding full foliage.

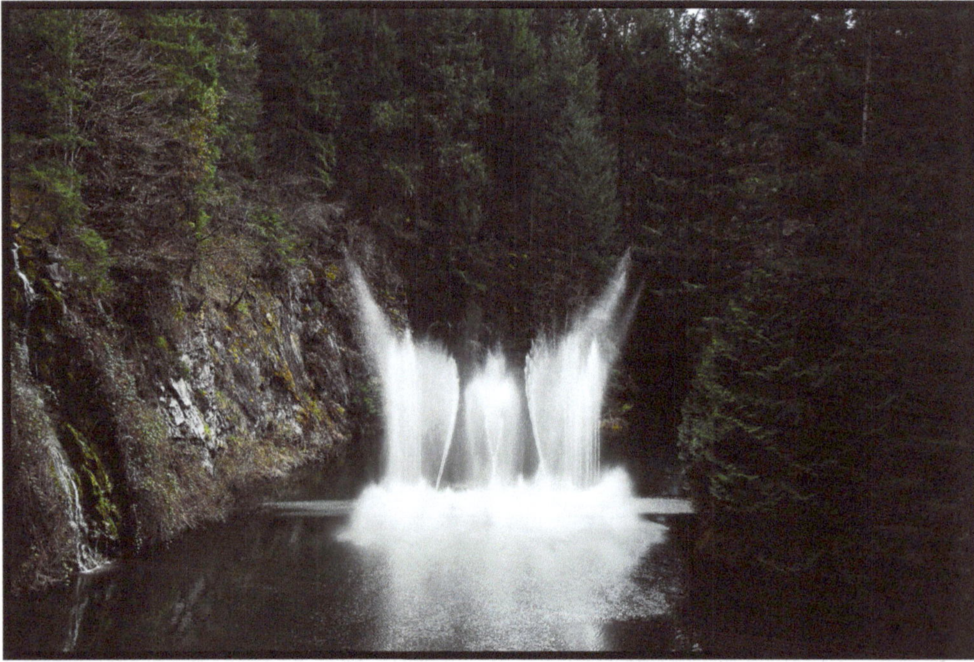

Butchart Gardens #2

The fountains have been programmed to give a vision of angelic imagery. They are wonderful to look at and use our imagination when envisioning our creativity.

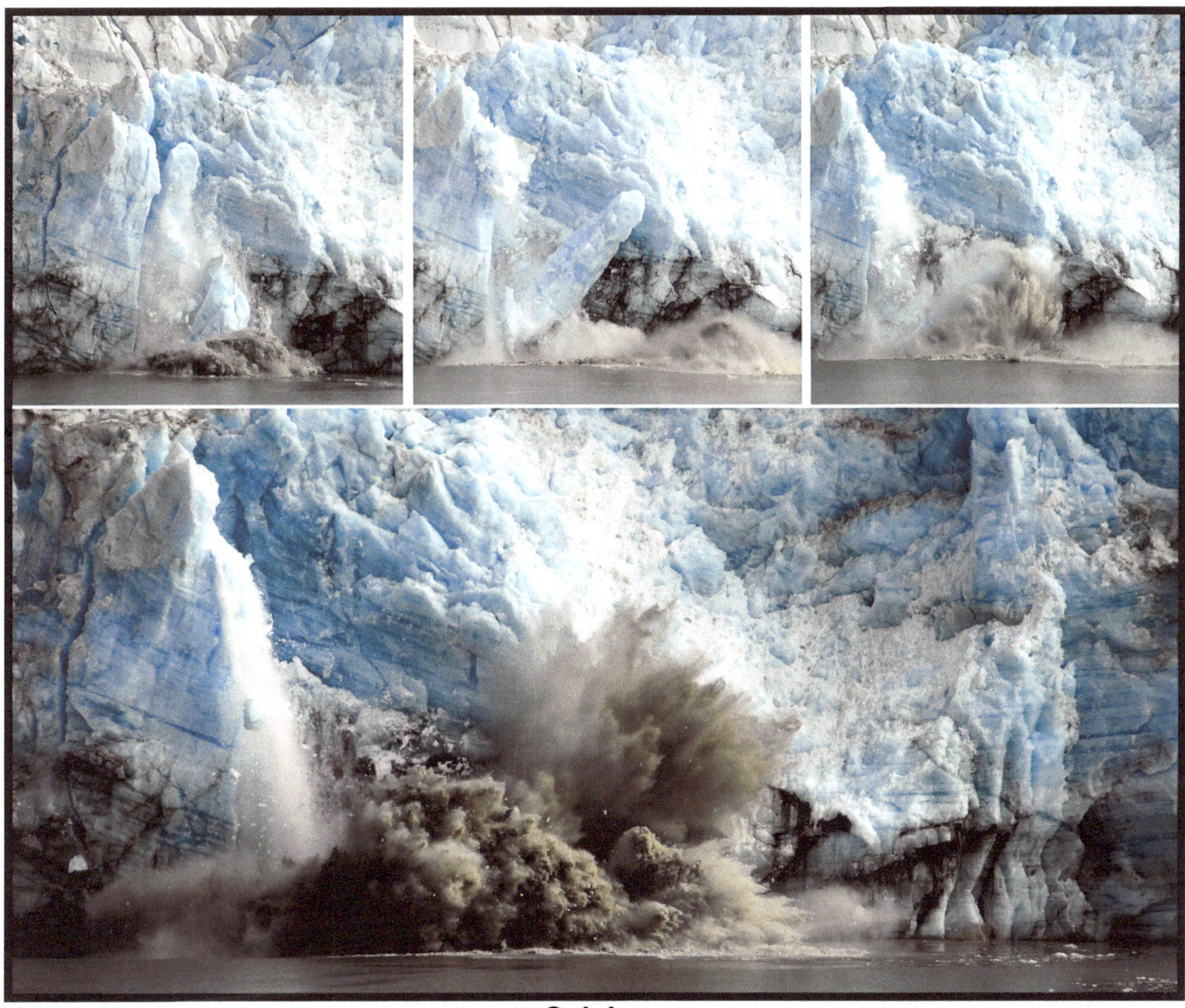

Calving

Alaskan calving ice – as I saw it breaking away I took shots in succession. When I viewed the images I could see that the story needed more than one image. To enjoy this event I chose three smaller images showing the progression, and then the big splash – the final event. I used a digital camera plus a filter. It is a great seller.

Praise received:

Submitted and approved in the Inspired Art Group on RedBubble.

"This has the WOW factor! Beautiful work!"

"Terrific! Nicely designed storytelling collage, beautiful colours."

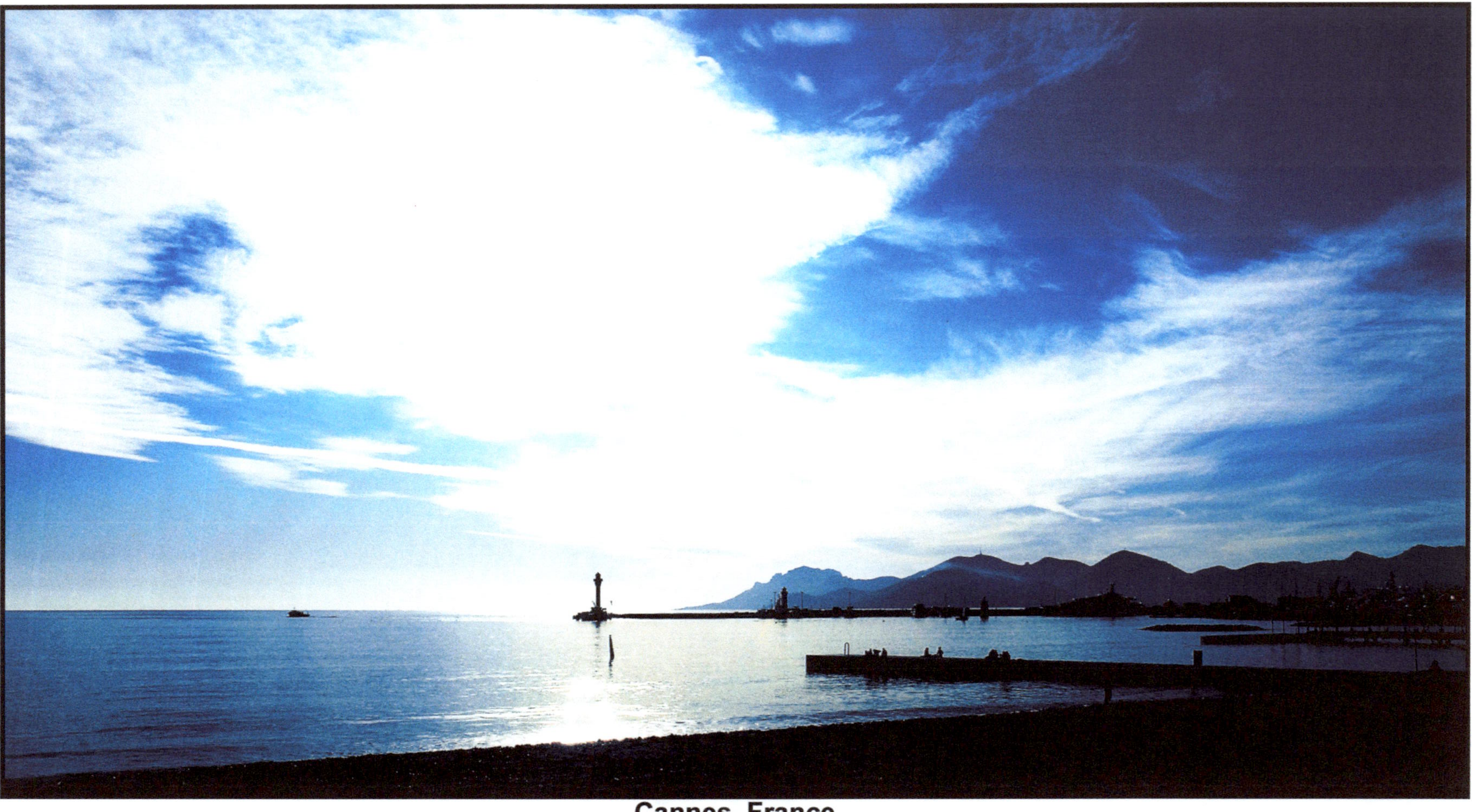

Cannes, France

To the image I added x-process to make the feeling more unique and a flavour of blue. Heavenly blues is my coveted colour and it stimulated the feeling from within. I was motivated to change the exact color; it added to the experience having visited there.

Praise received:
"You enhanced the beauty of this fabulous place, Klaus.
Cannes is one of my favourite places... I adore it! Definitely a favourite!"

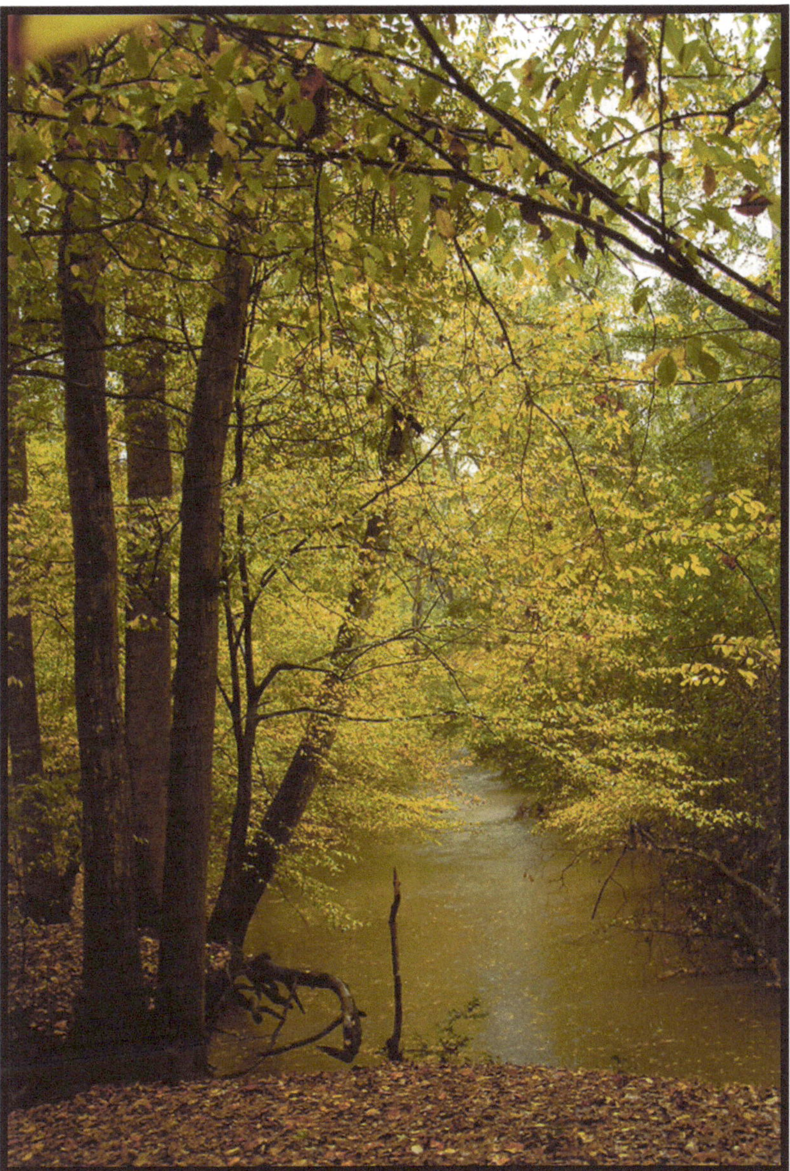

Carolina Creek

The walk I took with my friend in South Carolina enabled me to make this photograph. Lovely soft rain came down and I enjoyed my walk with a friend in another land. I like the feeling it gave me and the effect was overwhelming to be there.

Praise received:

"It's beautiful. I think photographers can be so in love with a particular moment in time that we want to capture it to savour later on. We hope we can look upon the photo and perhaps it will trigger that feeling once again."

Carol: "I think as photographers and artists we develop a special way of seeing and perhaps a special appreciation for the beauty and composition in nature and everything else… gorgeous light and tones in this lovely shot, Klaus… it's a very beautiful image."

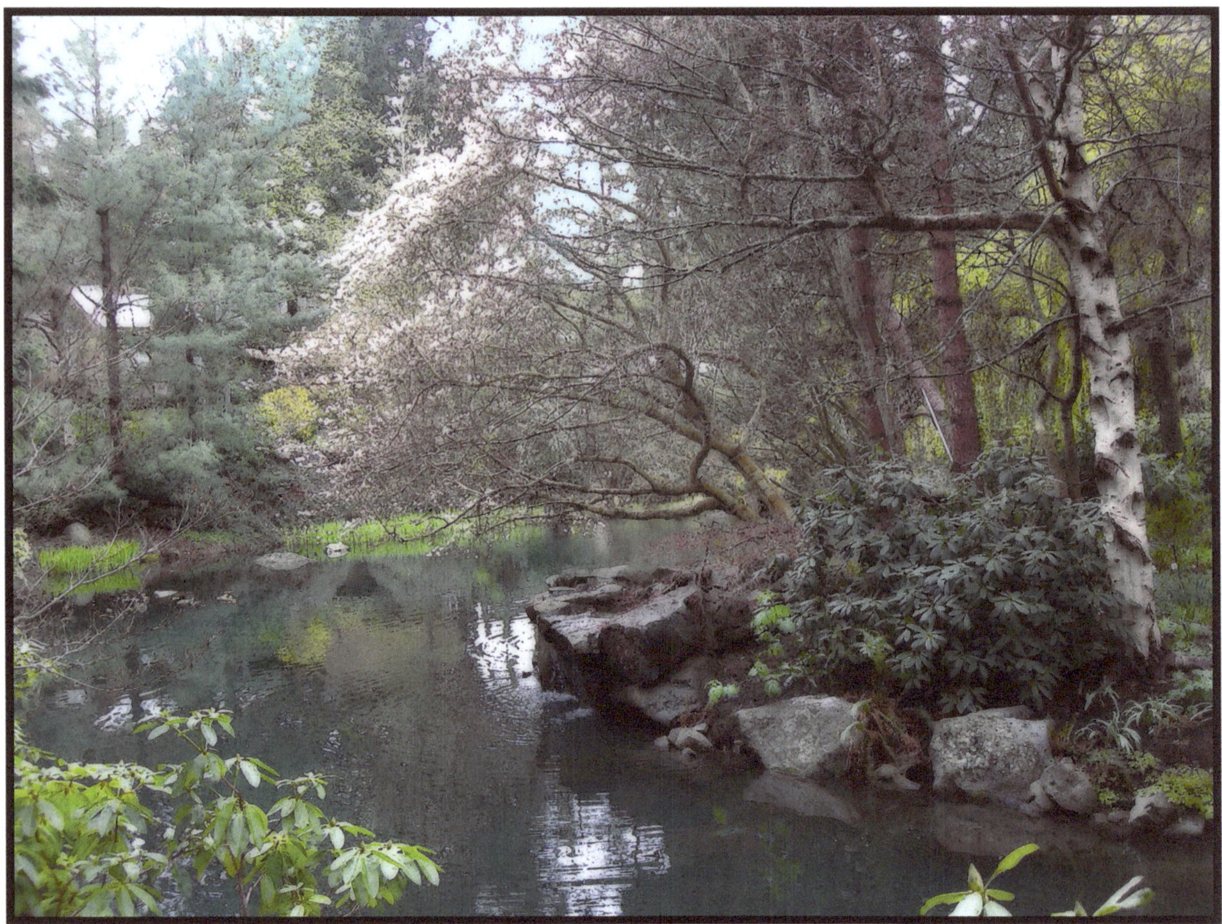

Dry Brush Walk

It is my favourite place to walk and be alone. This is a manmade lake, not very large but tranquil because very few people walk this path. I added a dry brush effect from Photoshop to add a mystic quality. Simple and yet with feeling.

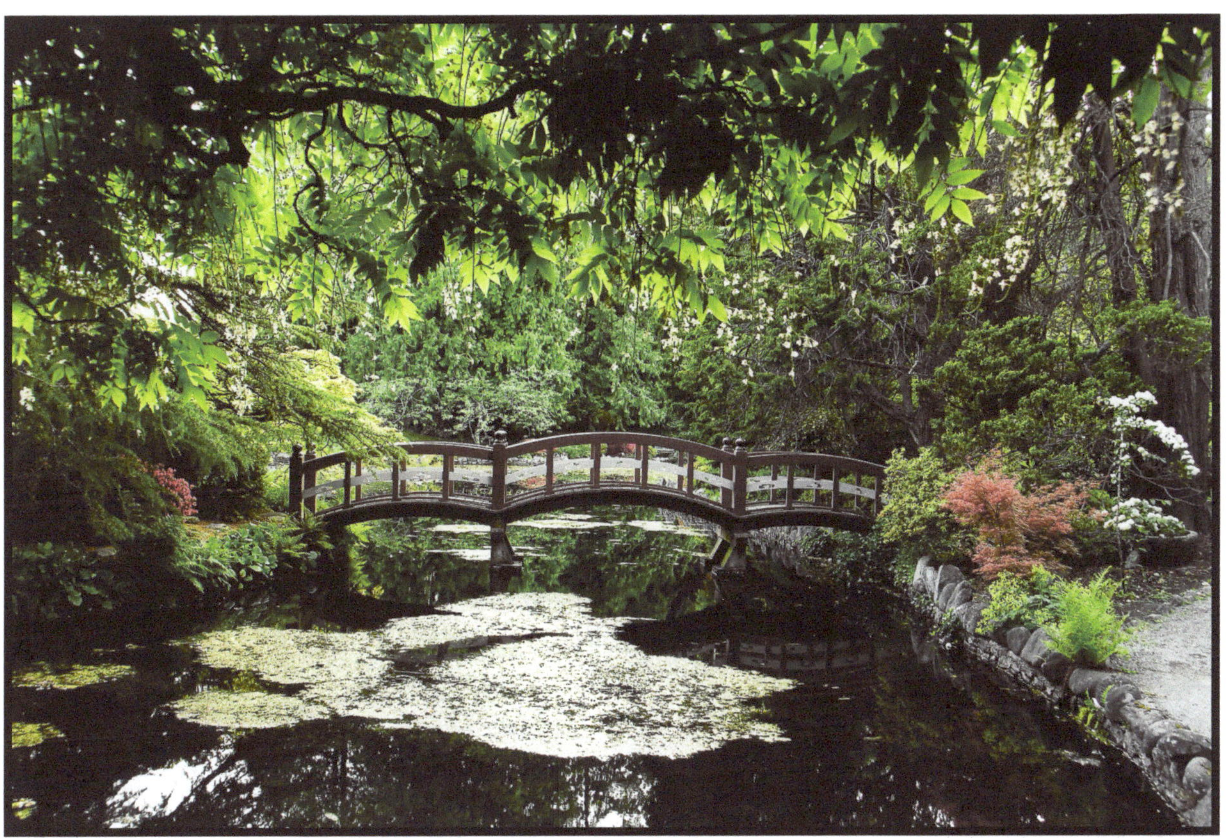

Enchanted

A bridge, a dream place, a place of peace and tranquility. I love to go there and meditate – Royal Roads, a university now, with a large garden and places for people to go and find peace, within. The site was so arresting, all I needed to find was the right angle; up about four feet above my height to block out the sky and a filter that enhanced the vibrant colours. Feeling that invitation to cross the bridge and yet I want to stay just where I am – this perfect space, spellbound and somehow kept from leaving. There may be many places we have had this experience but this is one of my favourite. It is near to my heart and close to where I live.

<u>*Praise received*</u>*:*

"Congratulations! Your photo has been featured in 'A Garden Somewhere.' This photo was chosen because it was of a very high quality and it captured exactly the sort of work we are looking for in this group."

"This place looks extremely peaceful and comfortable! Thanks for sharing it with us all. I also like your approach to art."

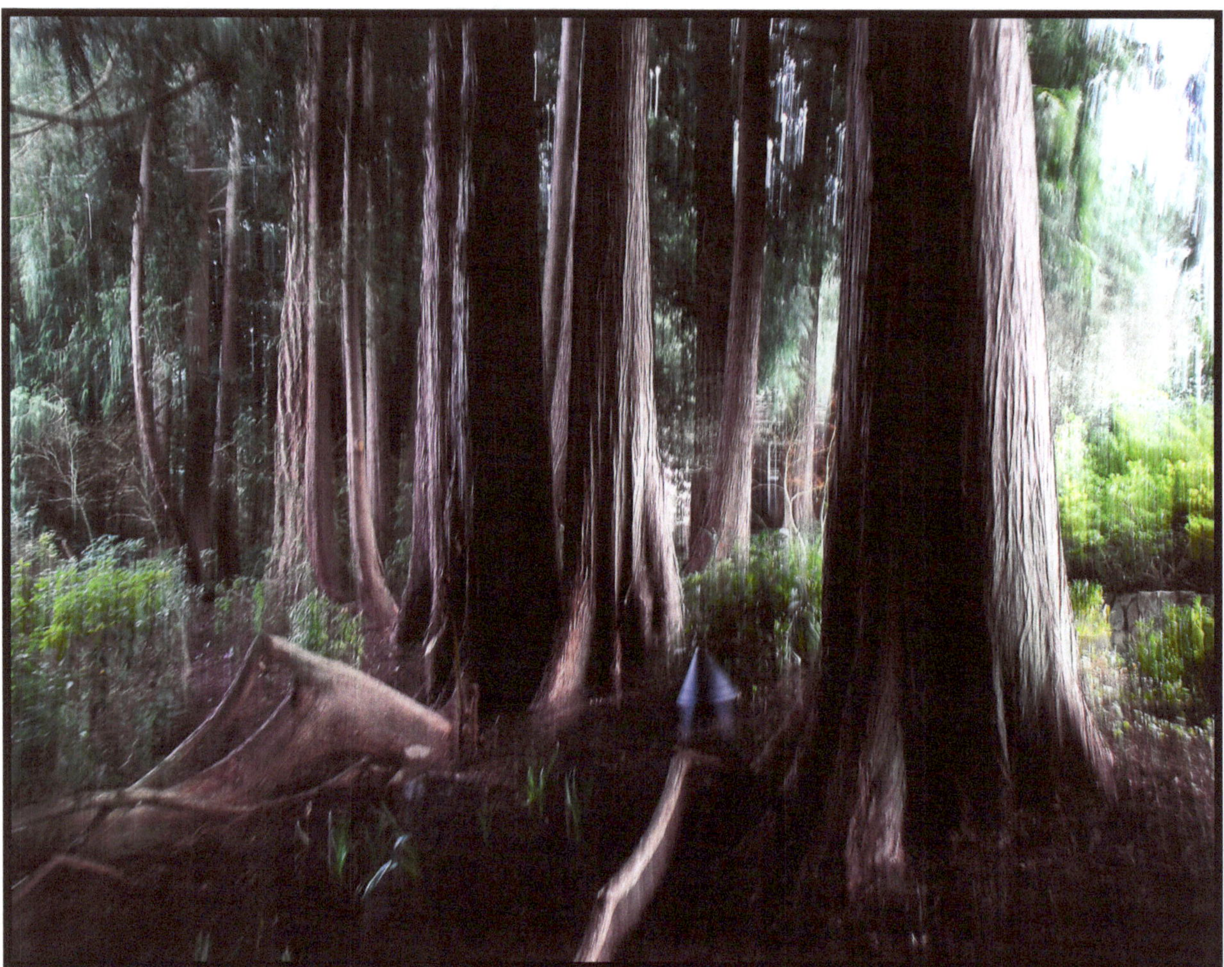

Fear Factor

There are times when what we don't understand can stand in the way of learning more about ourselves, and to capture that emotion in a photograph is perhaps unrealistic, but nevertheless something we should attempt, like a poetic expression from the heart! Capturing these images in an unreal way not only gave me a vision into the subconscious mind, but a dream of an interpretation of reality. The trees are barren and yet there exists life around them in the distance, with motion and strong dark colours with splashes of green but not on the trees in front; a strong spooky feeling but not alive to our sense of reality, there's movement and yet somehow it seems dead.

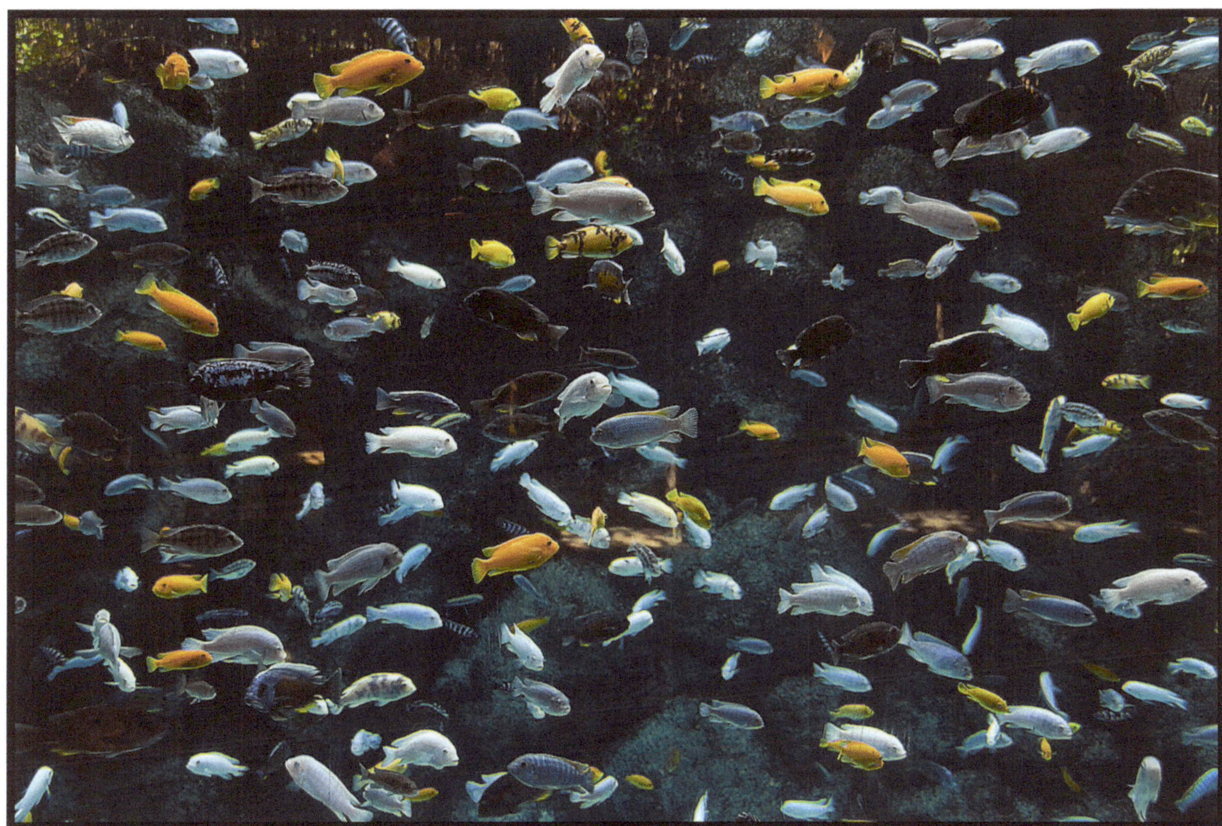

Fish

I thought the movement and colour design added to the photograph's final outcome. A large image of this is on the wall in many places. It gives the appearance that one is looking into an aquarium to feel nature in an office or home, for beauty and reality of life lies before our eyes – experience and imagination fills in the gap of reality.

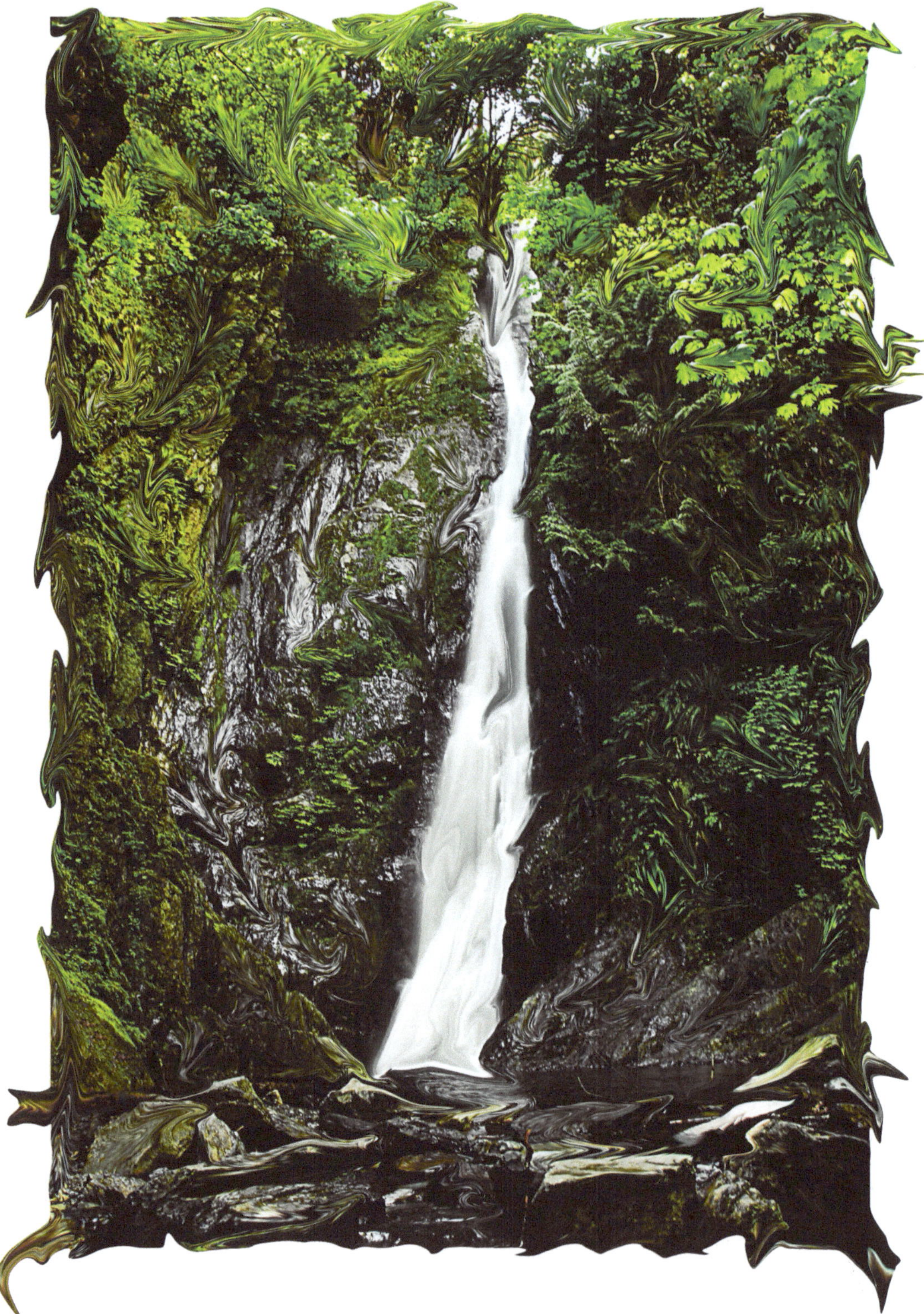

Full Waterfall Fantasy

I was working on a children's book for my grandchildren, so I embellished the waterfall to provide a feeling of imagination intertwined with the reality of flowing water. I used Photoshop for the design and imagination.

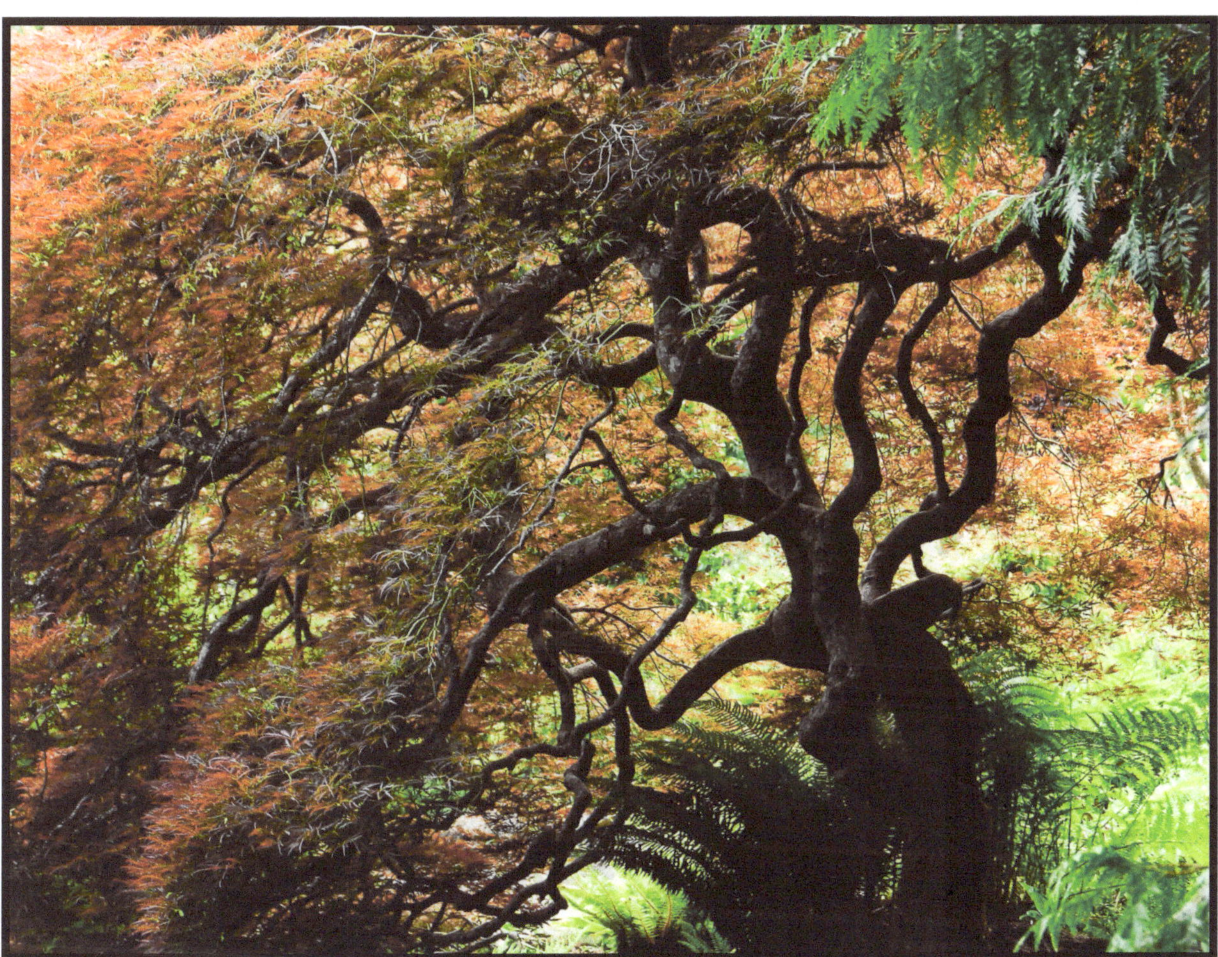

Gnarly Tree

I found this amazing tree in the Royal Roads garden. Magnificent, outstanding, designed by nature – I had the privilege to record it for people to see and appreciate the twists and turns of this unique tree. The composition enabled me to crop as it suited me at the time. It truly reveals the artistic design of nature.

<u>Praise received</u>:

Joseph: "Very impressive how you captured the colours which are intertwined throughout the piece. The tree not only catches my eye, but also how the colours are so integrated within the piece, yet slowly encapsulating the dead tree. In this shot, life is surrounding death. This is outstanding."

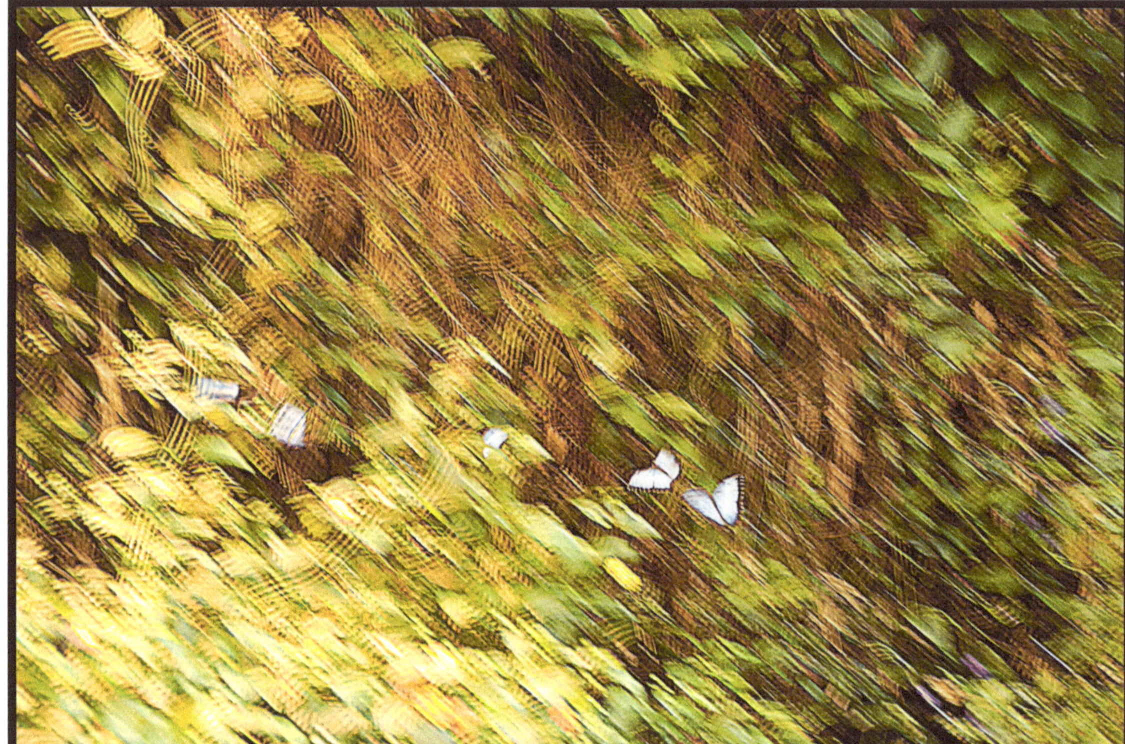

In Pursuit

In Pursuit is one of my favourite images because I probably will never be able to reproduce this photograph again. There is movement in all things; sometimes we see it, sometimes we don't. In this photograph the movement is continual until the viewer takes their focus away from the image.

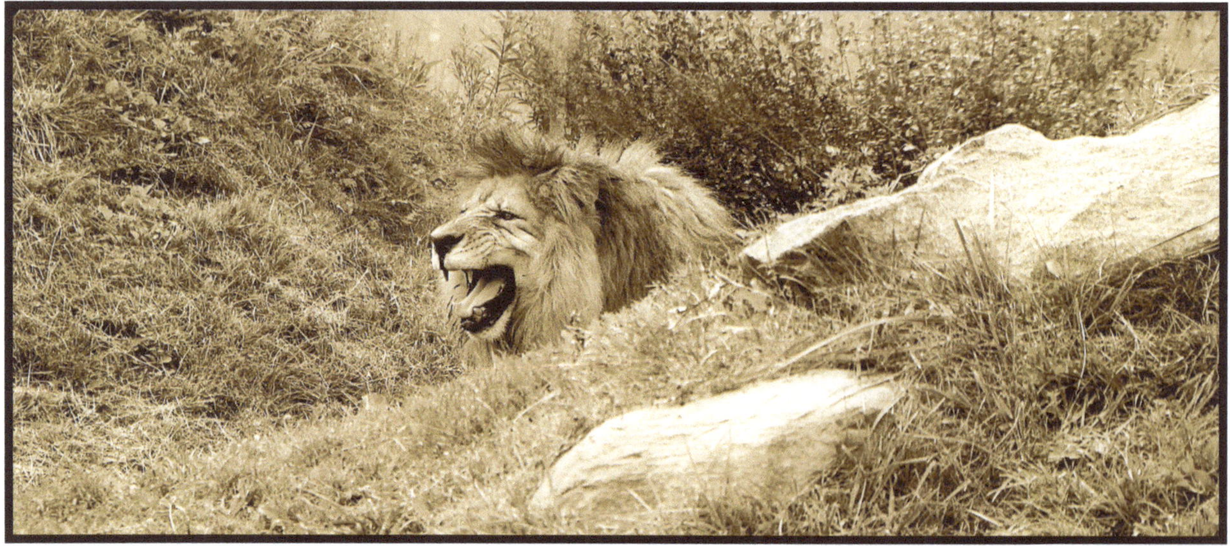

Lion's Roar

I just saw the lion peek around the rock and heard it roar. I like brown tone because it gives a different feeling to the outdoors, and it adds to the imaginary roar we can hear in our minds.

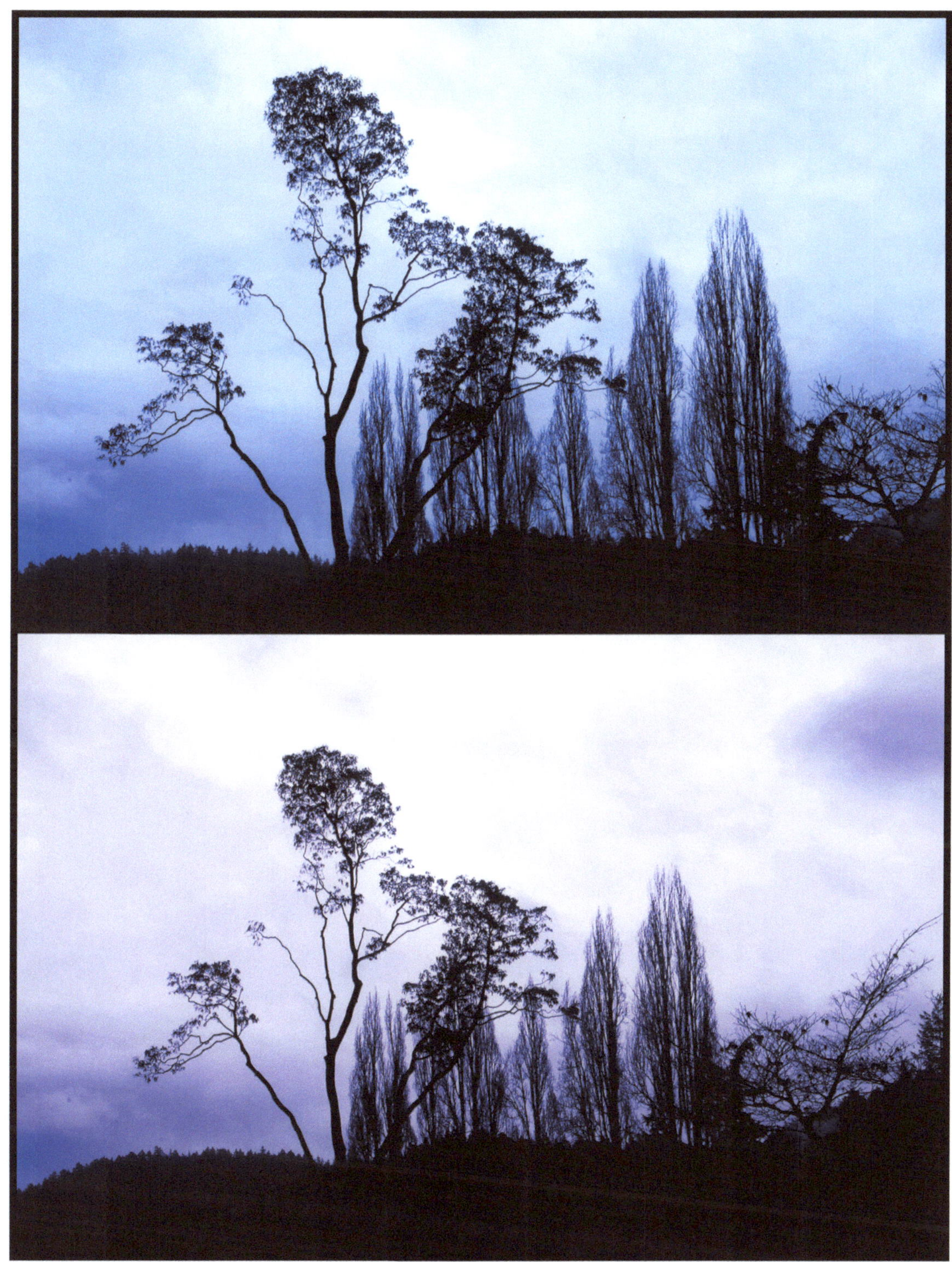

Monochrome

Blues and purples entice our imagination's appetite to feast upon these hues. We have a tendency to look for reality as we think we see it, but there are visions of grandeur beyond the perception that exists within our imagination. If you are given the privilege to see as you've never seen before, it opens up a new reality which perhaps we have not even imagined. Let the artist in our imagination shine forth even if you can't put it into words, but maybe with your art.

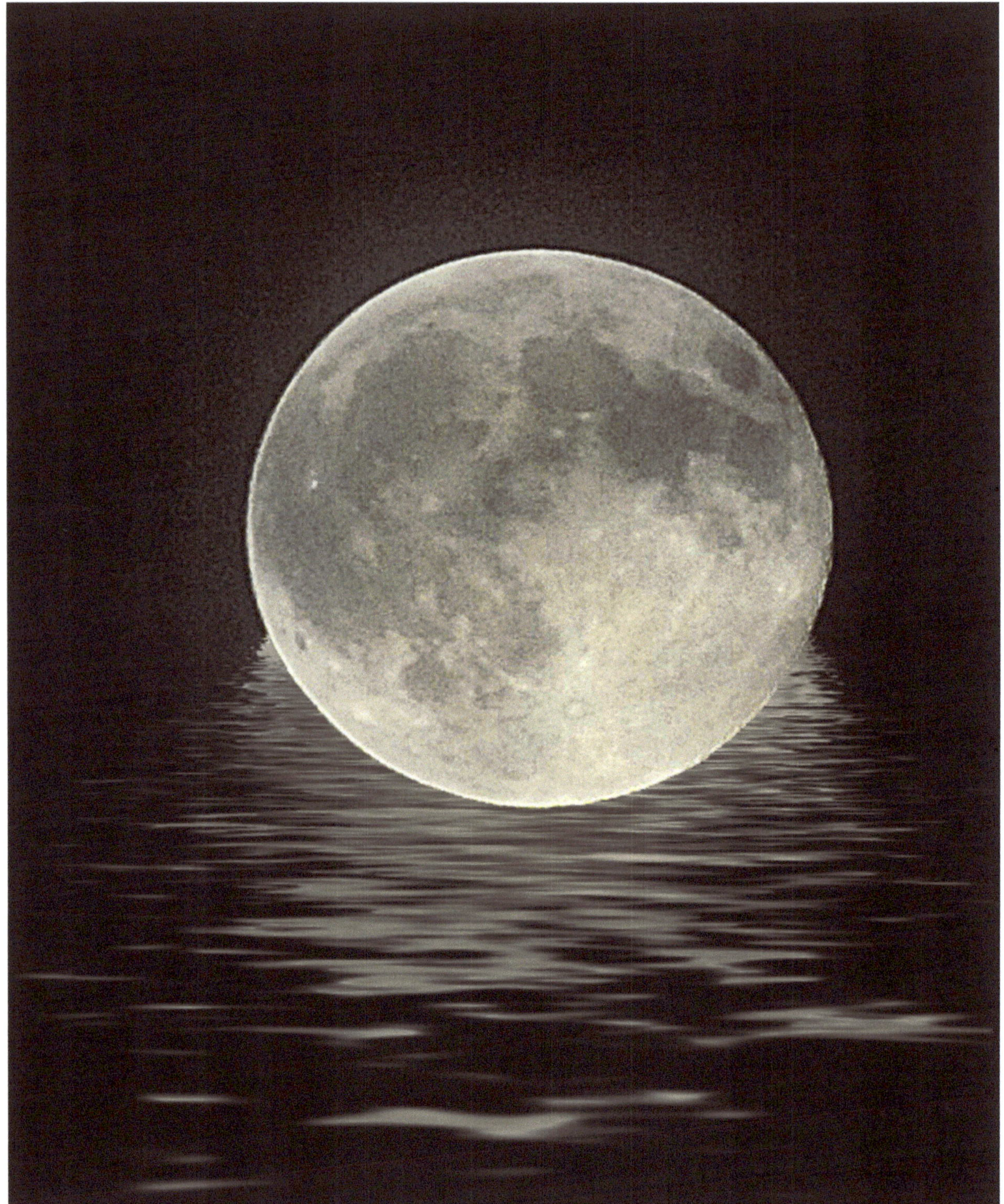

Moon Power

To the moon and back – the power of the moon on the water and on our lives. Living on Vancouver Island has a great effect on some people when the moon is full. It seems to have a draw because of the water. One can see the effect on the water even in the above art piece.

Moon Rise

New moon March 19, 2011 – on Saturday evening I went out to the ocean to photograph the moon. That day the moon was only 221,565 miles (356,575 kilometres) away – the closest it's been in almost 20 years. It appeared 14 percent larger and 30% brighter than usual. It was so thrilling to see the moon rise so spectacularly. I photographed some more close-ups but felt this one told the story best. The moon was moving somewhat so the image is not razor sharp, yet this was all in my imagination as I saw it.

Praise received:

"Splendid composition, colours and the light - so very beautiful. Thank you for sharing this artwork."

Carol: "Your shot came out absolutely beautifully. It's a wonderful composition and the vertical crop is PERFECT, Klaus!"

Bill: "The moon casting a spun gold reflection is tremendous!"

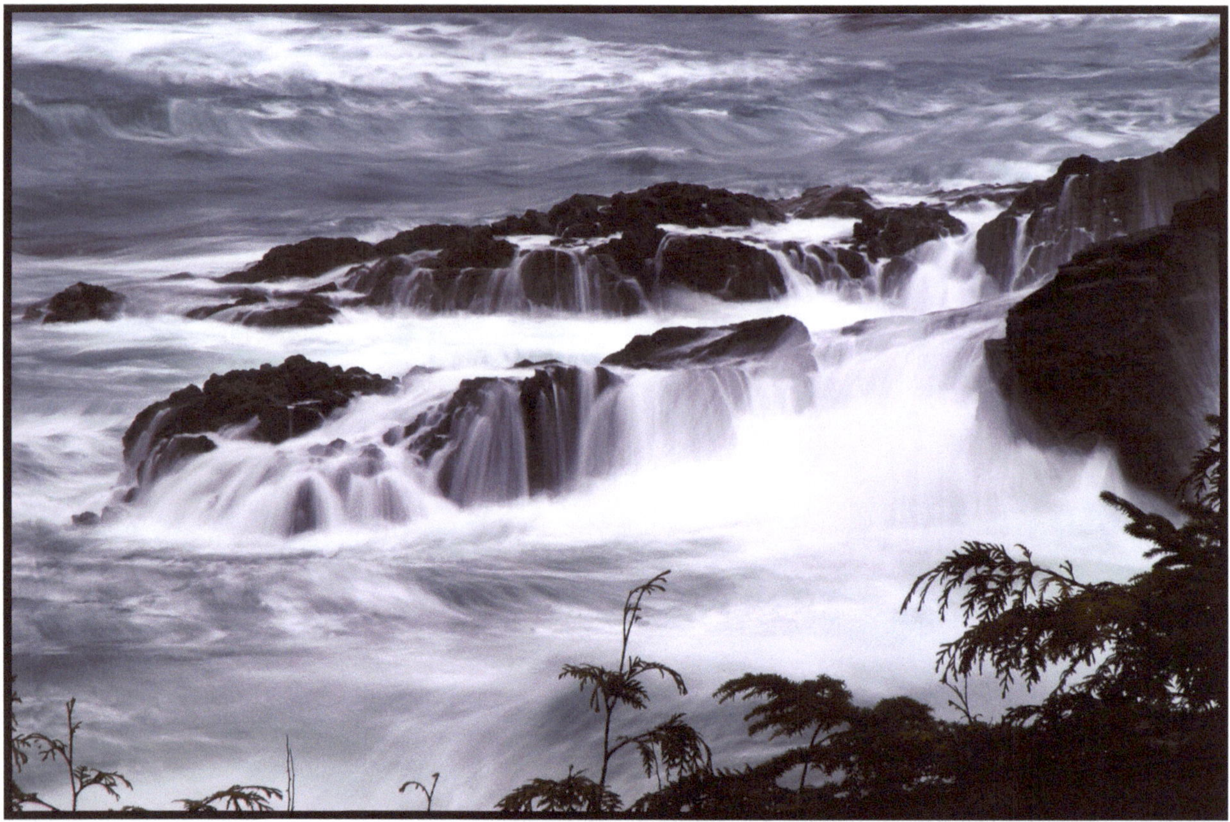

Moving Sound

The ocean was outside my window and I felt its call. I put my camera on my tripod and went outside on my balcony. Perfect place – the rush energized me. I wanted to share my feelings and what this experience meant to me; I dragged the shutter on my camera so it would look more as it is movement personified. Yes, I used my digital camera.

Praise received:
Submitted and approved in the Inspired Art Group on RedBubble.

"Will need to study your work more, as you are able to make a still image move!"

Kathy: "Wow... I SO love this one! I love the sound of crashing waves at the ocean... such a calming effect. This makes me feel like I am there!"

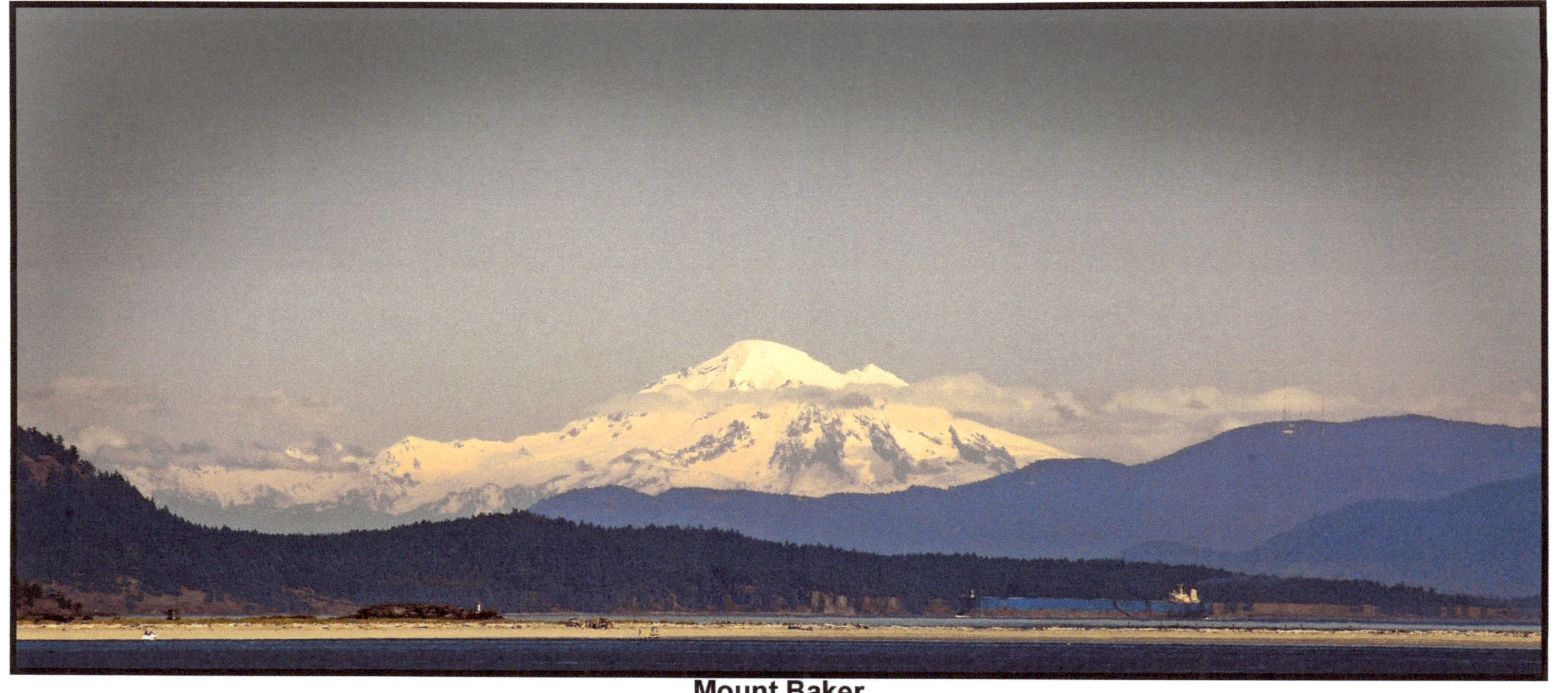

Mount Baker

I took this image of Mount Baker from my sister's balcony. I have tried to photograph this scene many times before – this is my best result so far. I live on Vancouver Island in the city of Victoria. The mountain is in the U.S. for those who may not know this. I like the lighting that brings feeling and warmth to the snow-capped mountain. I've had the privilege to see the mountain with many different looks. A few times a week I visit my family – we are close and every time we eat out on their balcony I am drawn to this wonderful majestic mountain. The thrill of having so many opportunities – to see it in all seasons – thrills my mind and touches my heart!

Praise received:

Carol: "Beautiful with the cloud passing in front of the mountain peak Klaus. I have been to Victoria on Vancouver Island… a wonderful place! How wonderful to be able to sit out there on the balcony enjoying this view."

Joseph: "The shot is outstanding. What impresses me is how you were able to capture the various shadings from ground level to the sky. You are fortunate to have access to such a view on a regular basis. Well done Klaus, a fav."

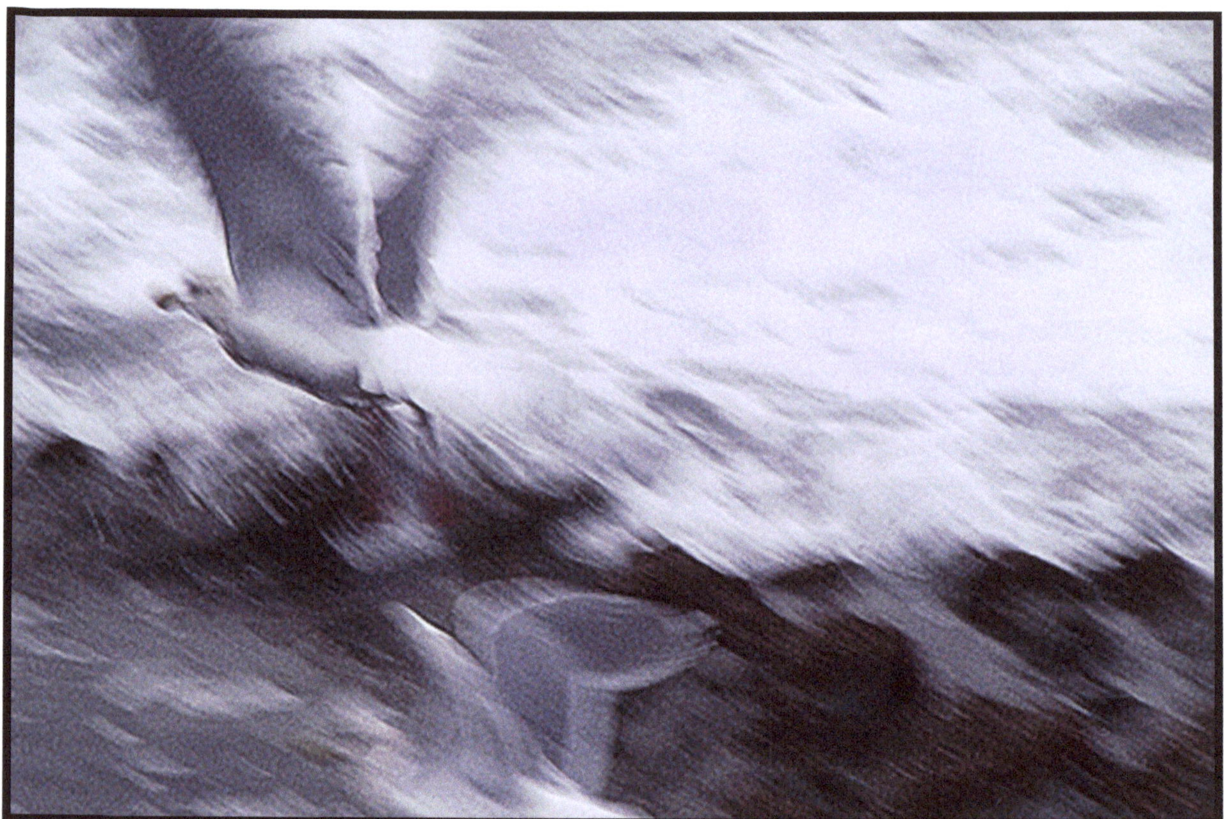

Music in Nature

The seagulls almost drowned out the sound of the ocean waves. Like music, the songs of the birds and the sound of the ocean are different and yet in harmony. A sound that was pleasant to my ears even if somewhat loud.

Praise received:

Bill: "Klaus, I adore the movement in this piece. One can feel the power of the ocean here and almost hear the squawking of the seagulls. Great stuff!"

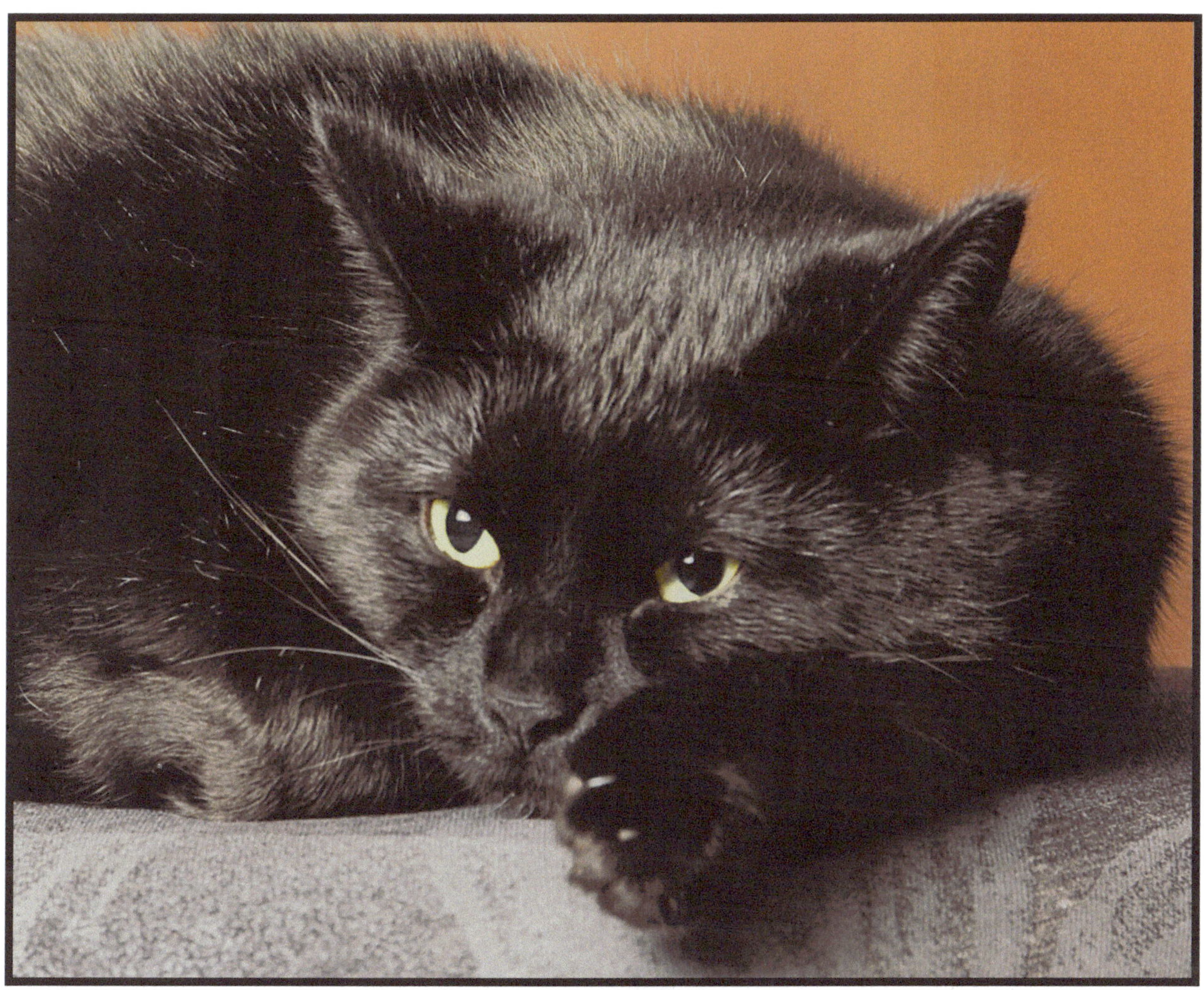

My Cat Billy

Billy is my daughter's cat that she gave to me to babysit – and eventually he became my cat. We are great friends even though I am really a dog lover. I truly learnt so much from Billy. He brings me many gifts, even little bunny rabbits, and lets them go in the house for me to play with. Other little things as well, such as birds, which he never harms.

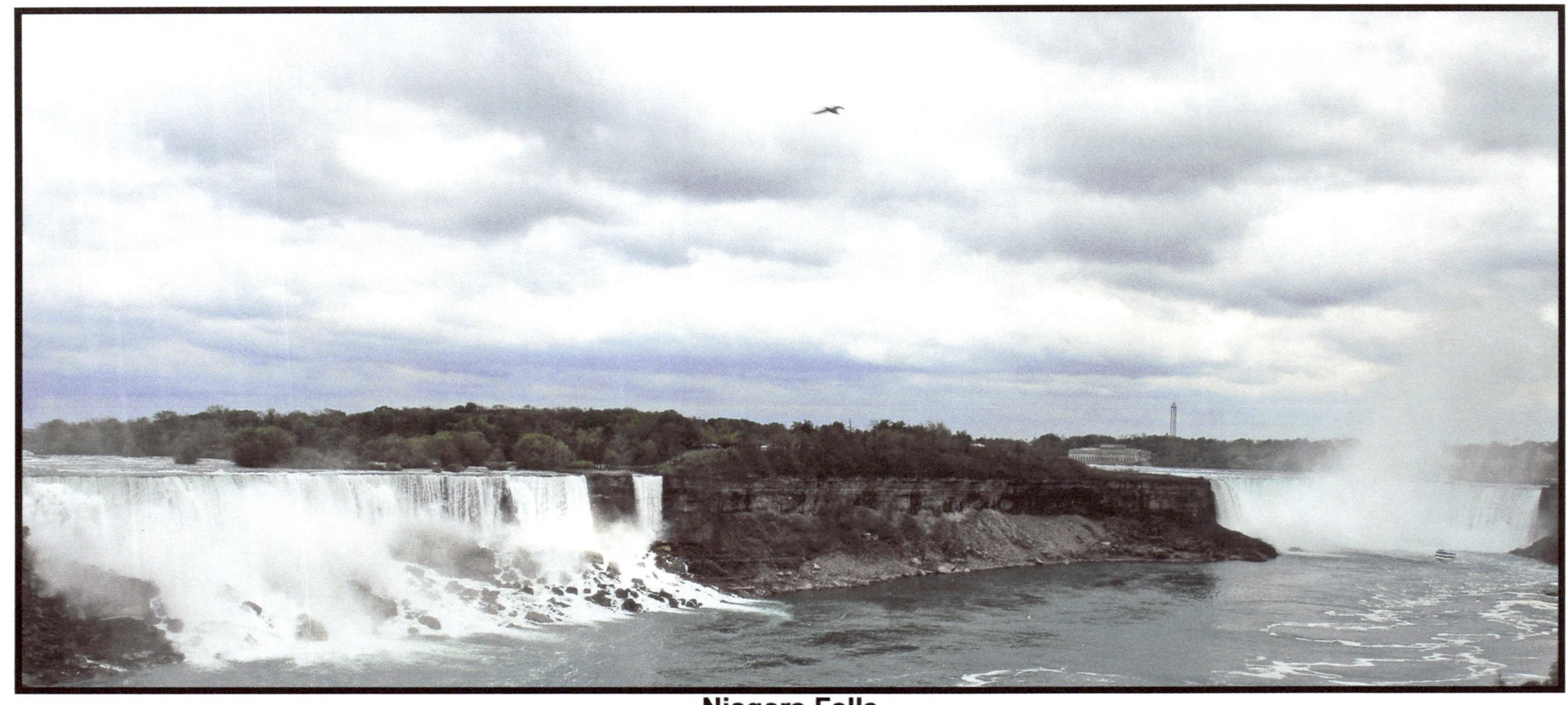

Niagara Falls

A famous honeymoon destination for couples. I was able to include both falls, the U.S. and Canadian sides. The feeling and sight was magnificent – it touched my heart! The grandeur of it all: two main falls, one on the Canadian side and the other closer up on the U.S. side. The rushing water with deafening sound and spraying on my camera, oh no. The sky had a layer of clouds and there was a single bird flying above, seemingly without fear. Of course we have heard many stories about the great falls, a man trying to walk on a tight rope across them, people who went over the falls in a barrel, endless stories.

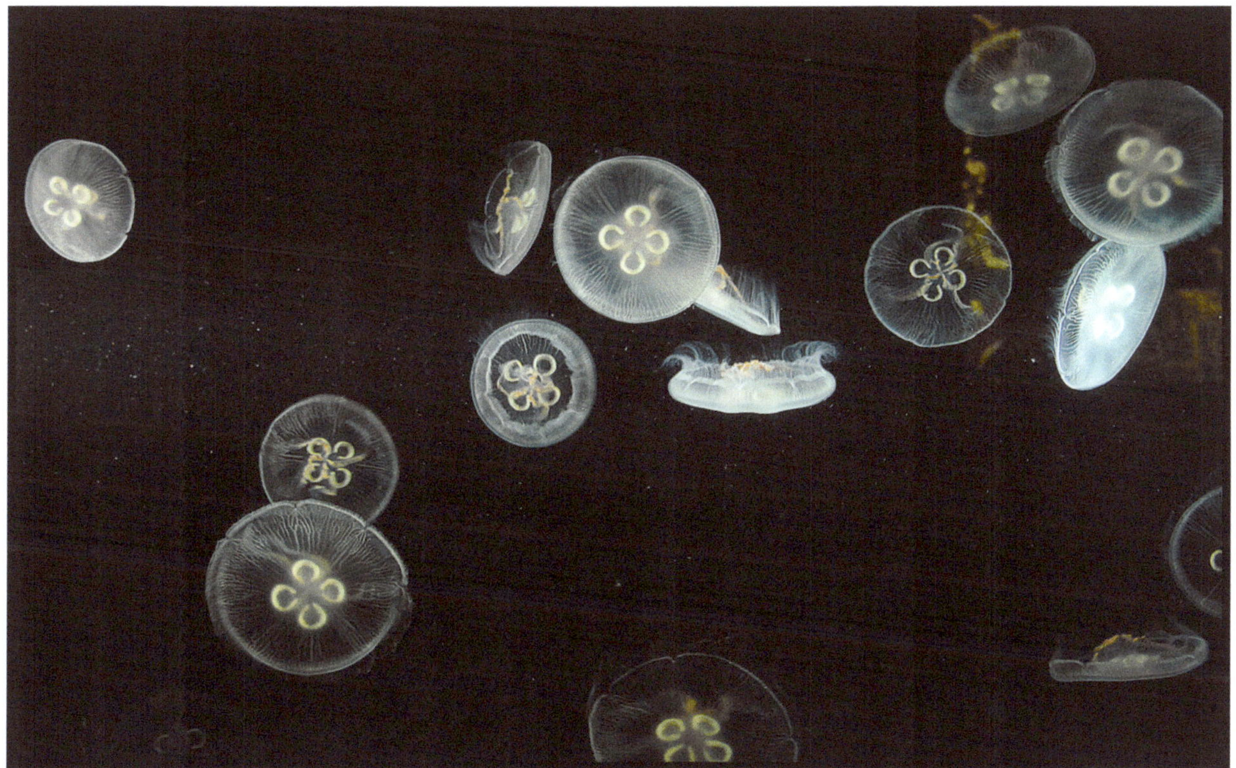

Notes in Nature

Notes in Nature are jellyfish arranged musically. The translucence, with the outlines given by the back light, reveals the delicacy of the jellyfish and the positioning creates movement in silence.

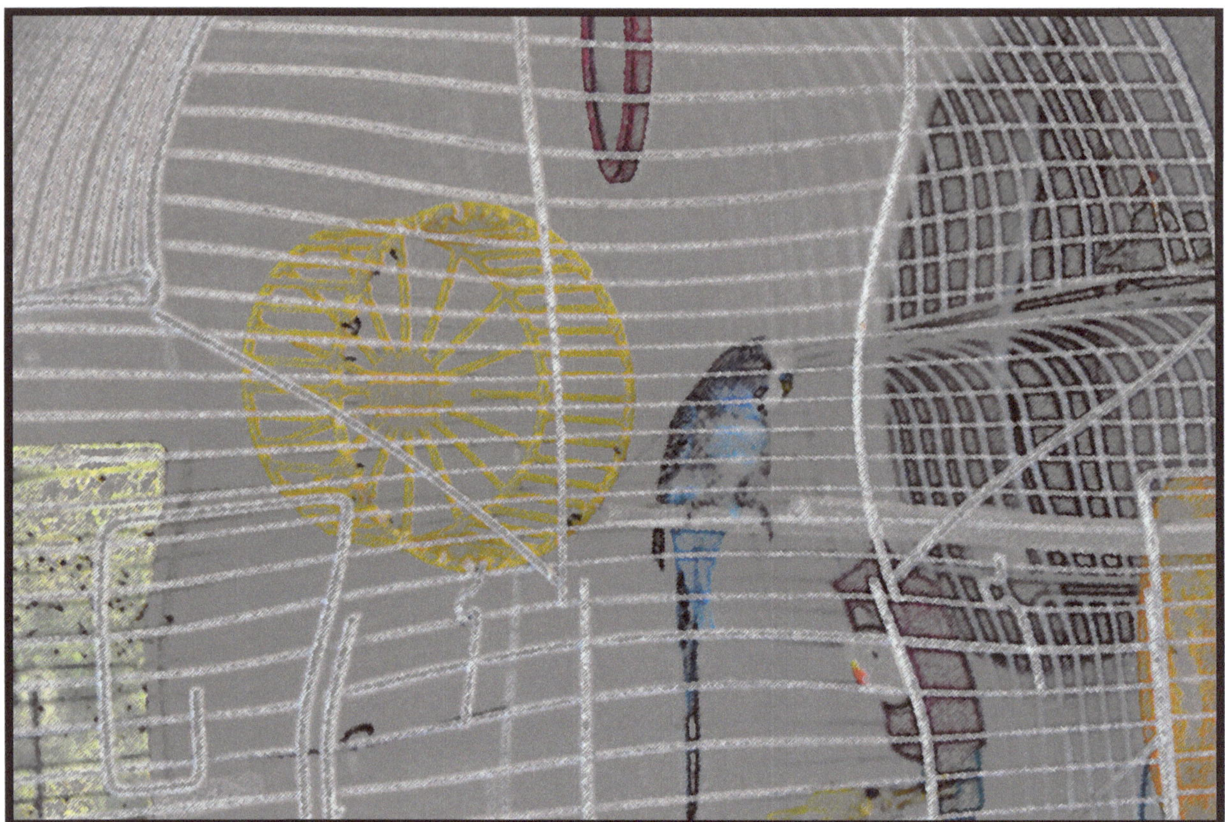

Only a Memory

Only a memory – it was once a bird in a cage. I like freedom for all, and birds as well. I was walking and heard a loud screech; as I looked up, a crow had taken a baby robin from its nest and the mother was trying to free it. Nature can be cruel in our eyes but that IS life in the wild.

This bird was kept in a cage, fed and looked after very well. I asked myself: what is more cruel, nature or this bird in its cage? I am not able to judge. I value the privilege I had to photograph the bird in its lifetime. Now it is preserved as a treasure of art in the owner's home. It was loved in its time and a memory in the photograph for my client. The feeling with embellishment – with colour that is unique unto itself. I like the impression that it made, the truth, an art piece in the process. I used Photoshop to make the photo a pastel impression.

Praise received:

"I did not understand why you would have a bird in a cage, and this is one of the few times words from you were needed. I still do not like birds in cages, but it did get me thinking and that's all that's really important. A colourful, thoughtful work!"

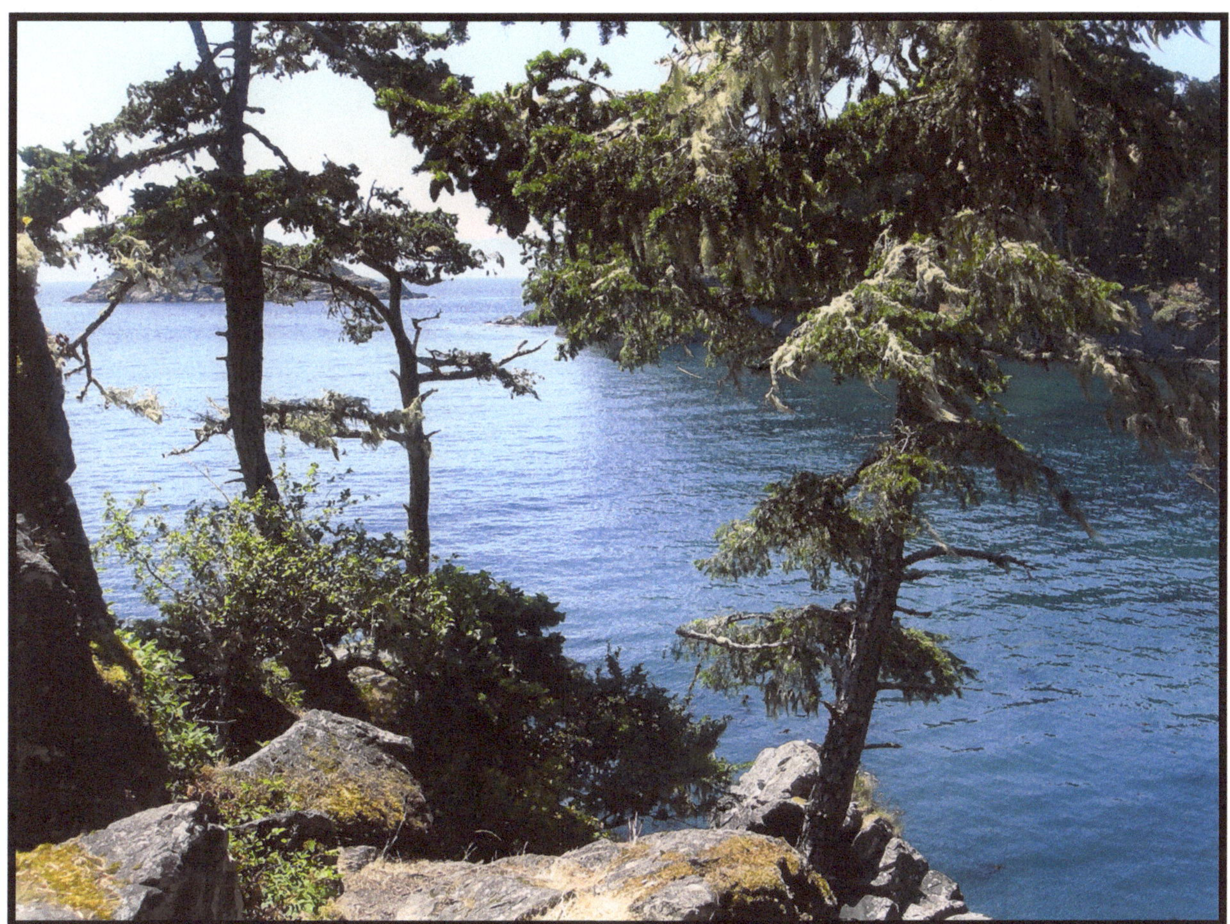

Pike Beach

The Group of Seven, sometimes known as the Algonquin school, was a group of Canadian landscape painters from 1920-1933 who always interested me. I love looking at their work, and their influence can be seen in this image. I like artists who influence my vision and touch my heart. The feeling in this image was just that. I had in mind not just the depth of colour, but also the reminder of the influence.

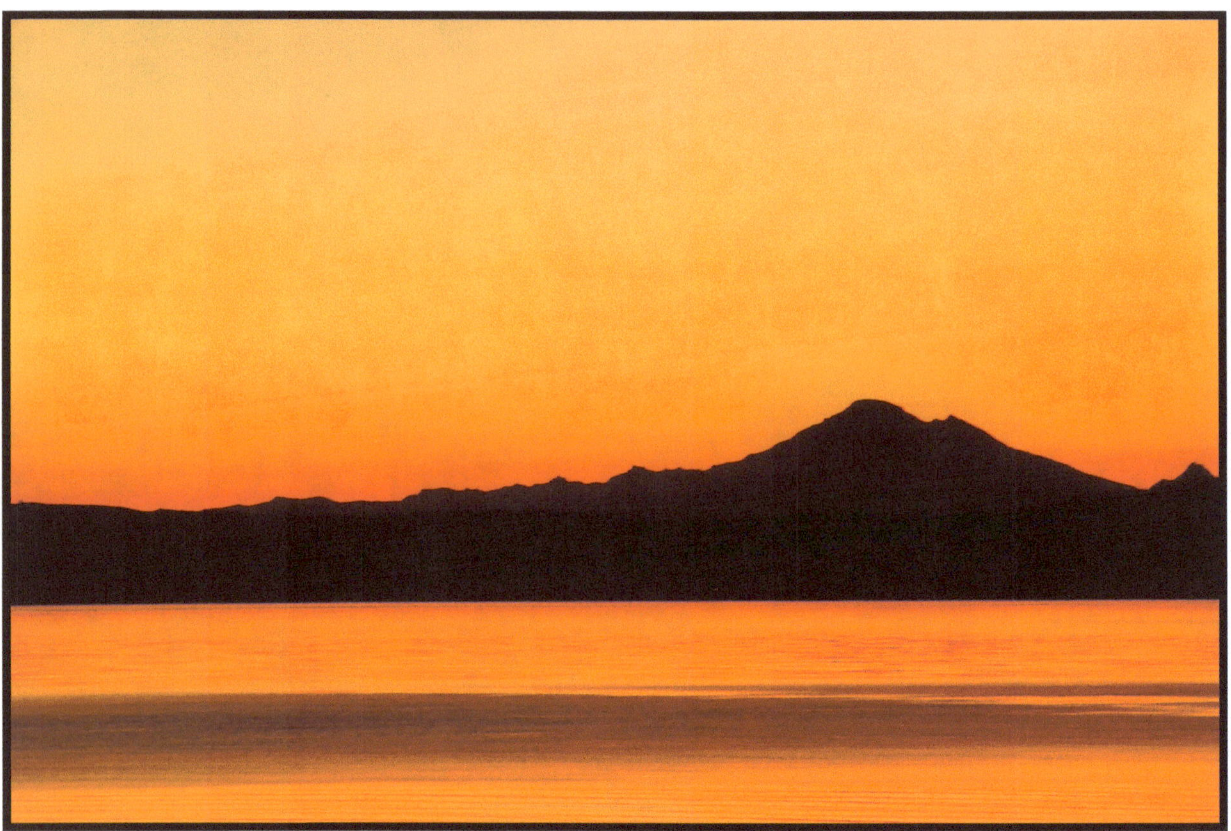

Red Sky in the Morning

As I awoke at my sister's home, I looked out at 5:45 am. Breathtaking view from Victoria, B.C. looking across to the United States. The image says more than I can express in words.

<u>*Praise received*</u>:
"Look into the horizon...
and let your soul drift into a haze full of HAPPINESS!
Bravo, Klaus."

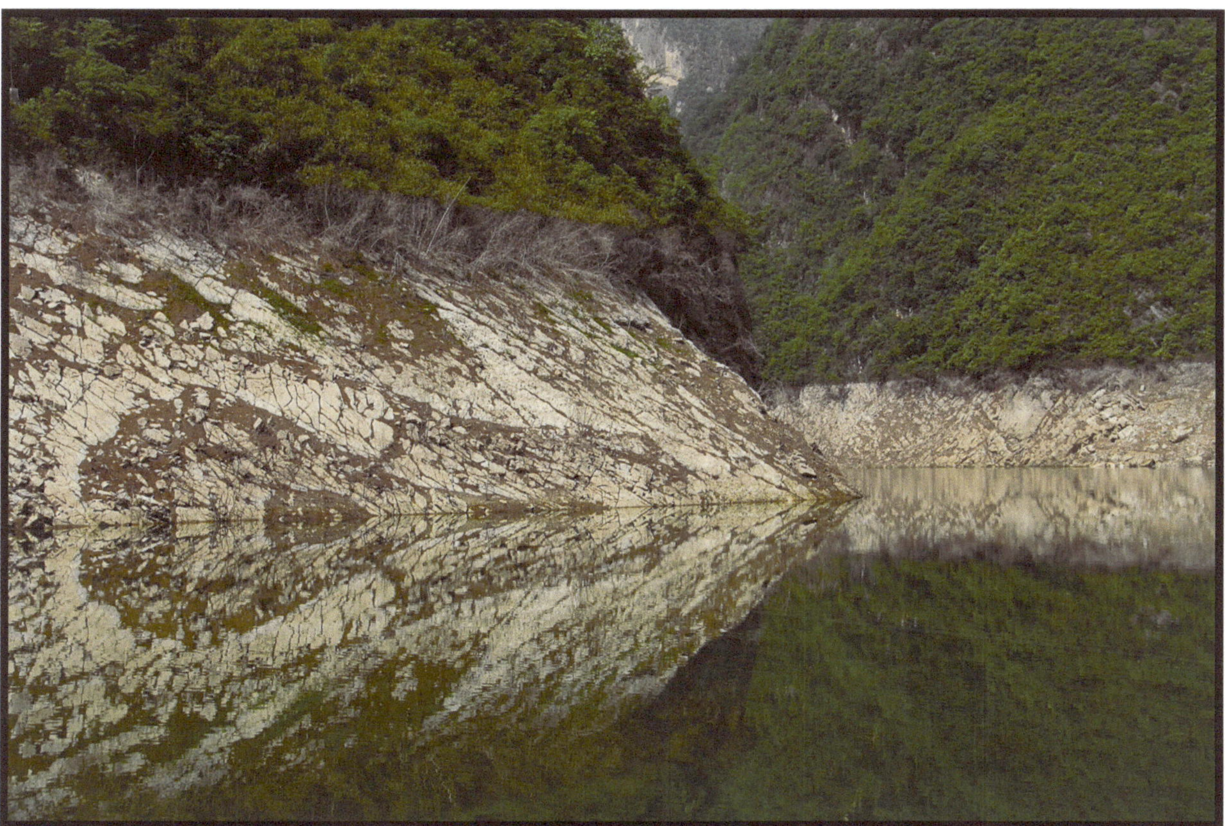

Reflection

This photograph was taken on a river canyon in China. Its reflection is so perfect that it gives one an illusion of what is up and what is down. In reality we feel somewhat deceived in being able to tell – if it weren't for the fact that the sharper part of the image is at the top.

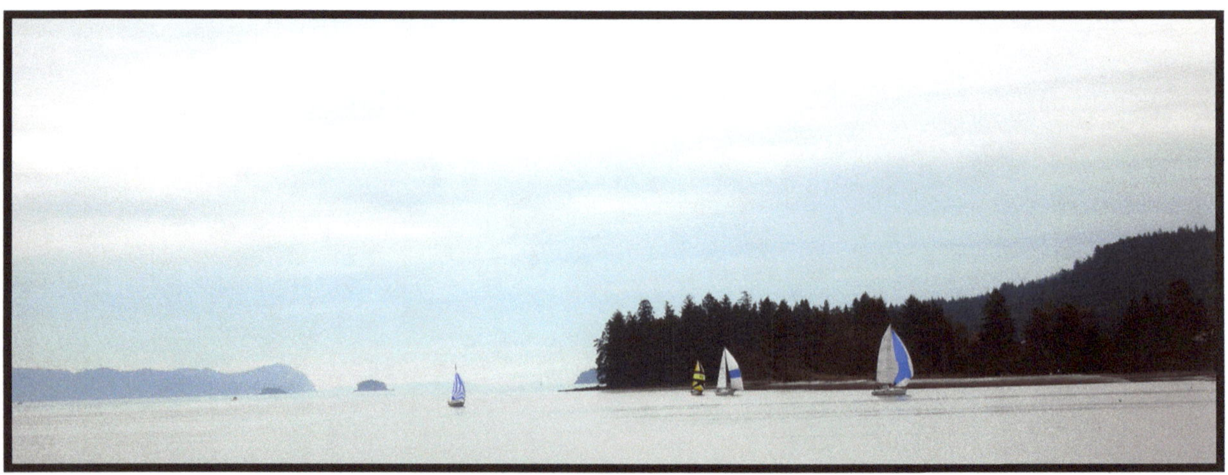

Salt Spring Island

Salt Spring Island is a very interesting place to experience.
Lots of calm yet exciting, wonderful, experiences happening. Many emotions!

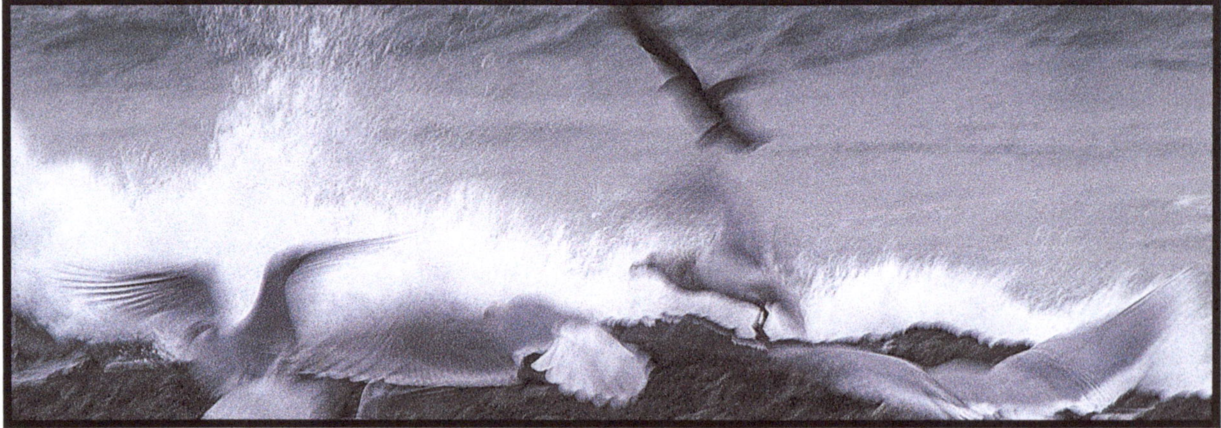

Sound of Music

Just to listen and feel the spray of the ocean
is locked in my mind to this day.

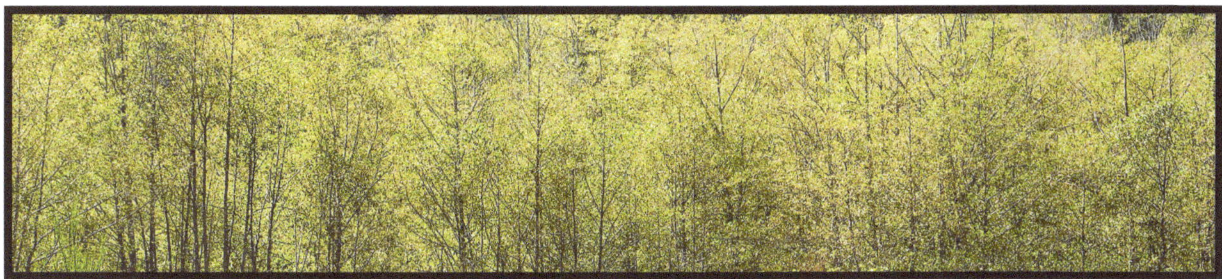

Trees in a Row

I was on a field trip with my photography students,
and I made this photograph for the art gallery that is showing my images.

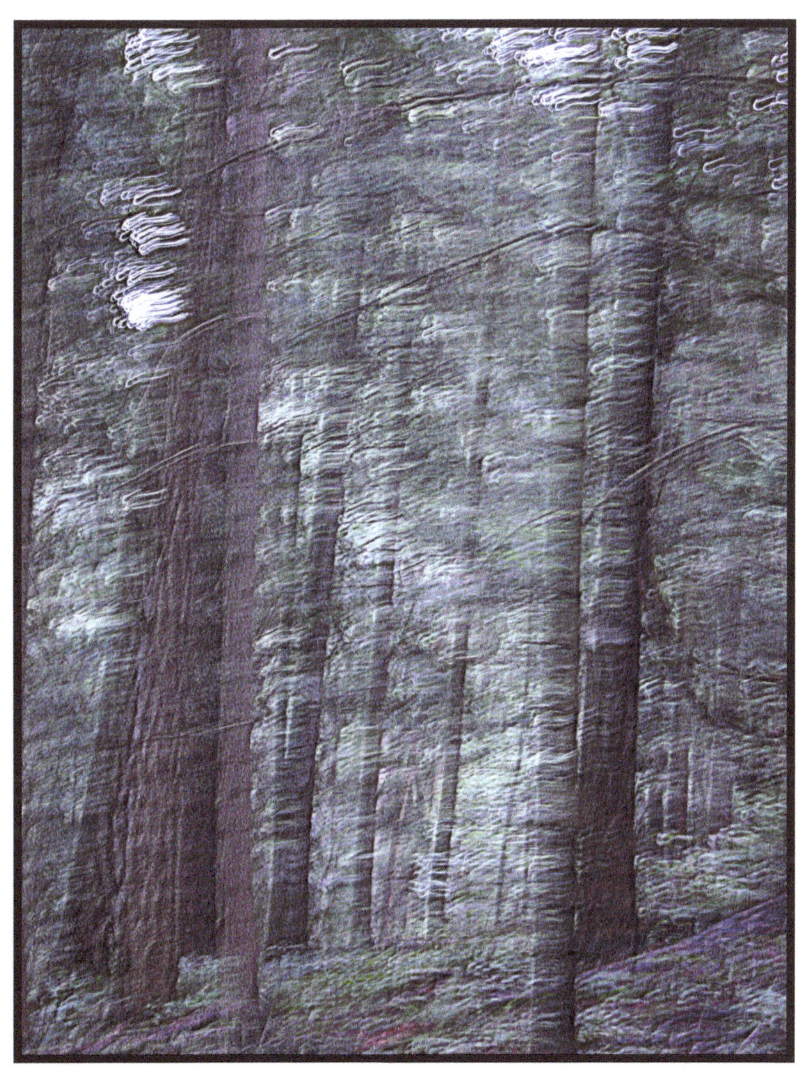

Trees in Motion

I was running and accidently pushed the button on my camera. When I looked at the image I was so excited by what I captured. I don't believe in accidents – there is an influence upon the artist within each of us that is unexplainable, but exists nevertheless. An image of illusion maybe, but it has a reality of its own. The little wisps of light on top of the tree are like spirits moving with trees. It appears to me like I am stationary but the trees are moving – revealing another world which we ignore or are unconscious of its existence.

To discover the impossible can be made possible when we allow it to happen without reservation – the alpha level within us. Between the conscious and subconscious mind…

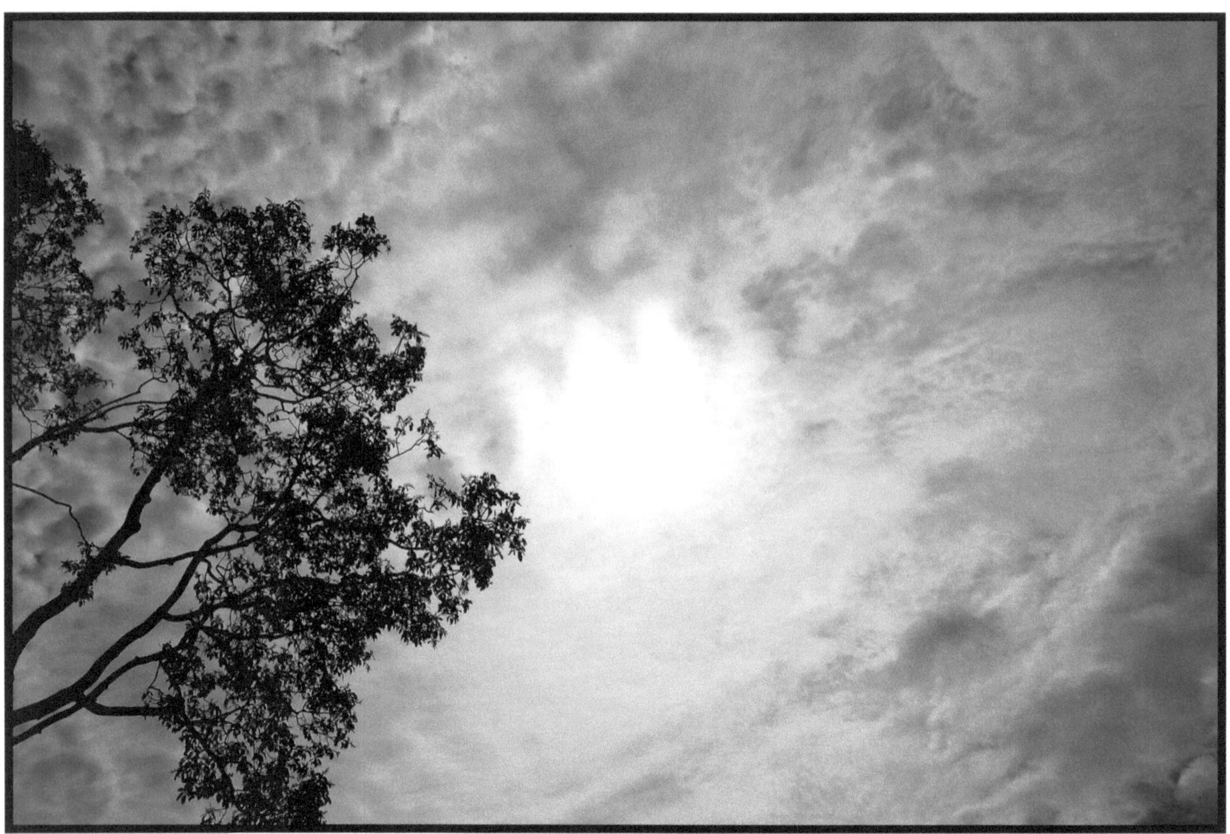

Walking Together

I looked up and saw this image – so real, no changes, just took what I saw.
Stunning, yes, like two people walking in the heavens above.
Illusions to our imagination, yes,
and yet the camera captured what there was.

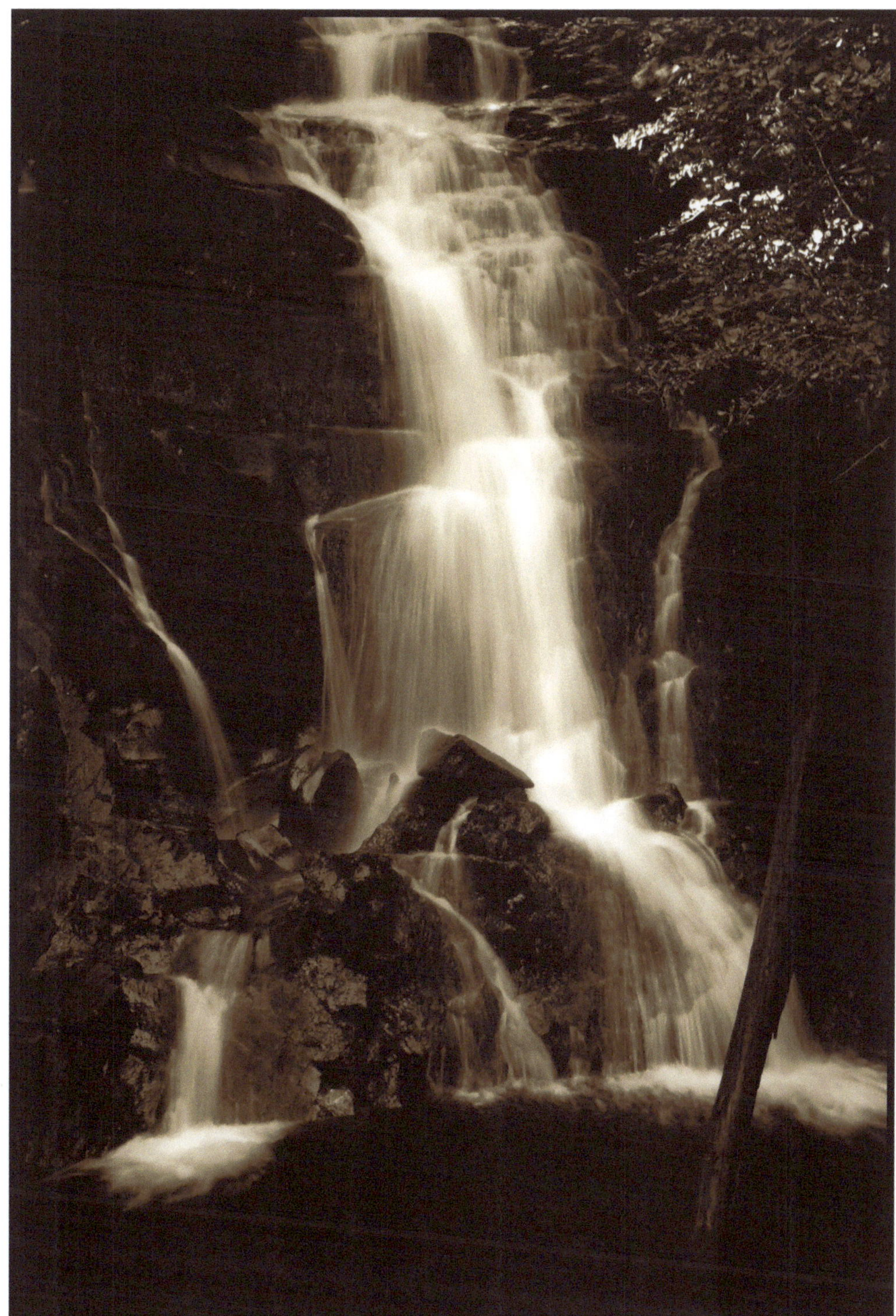

Warm Sound

Alaskan waterfall – just listen to its warm sound. I tried colour and black and white, but then I turned the photograph into warm brown... and it spoke to me.

<u>Praise received</u>:
"Great shot, I admire the clean simplicity of it!"

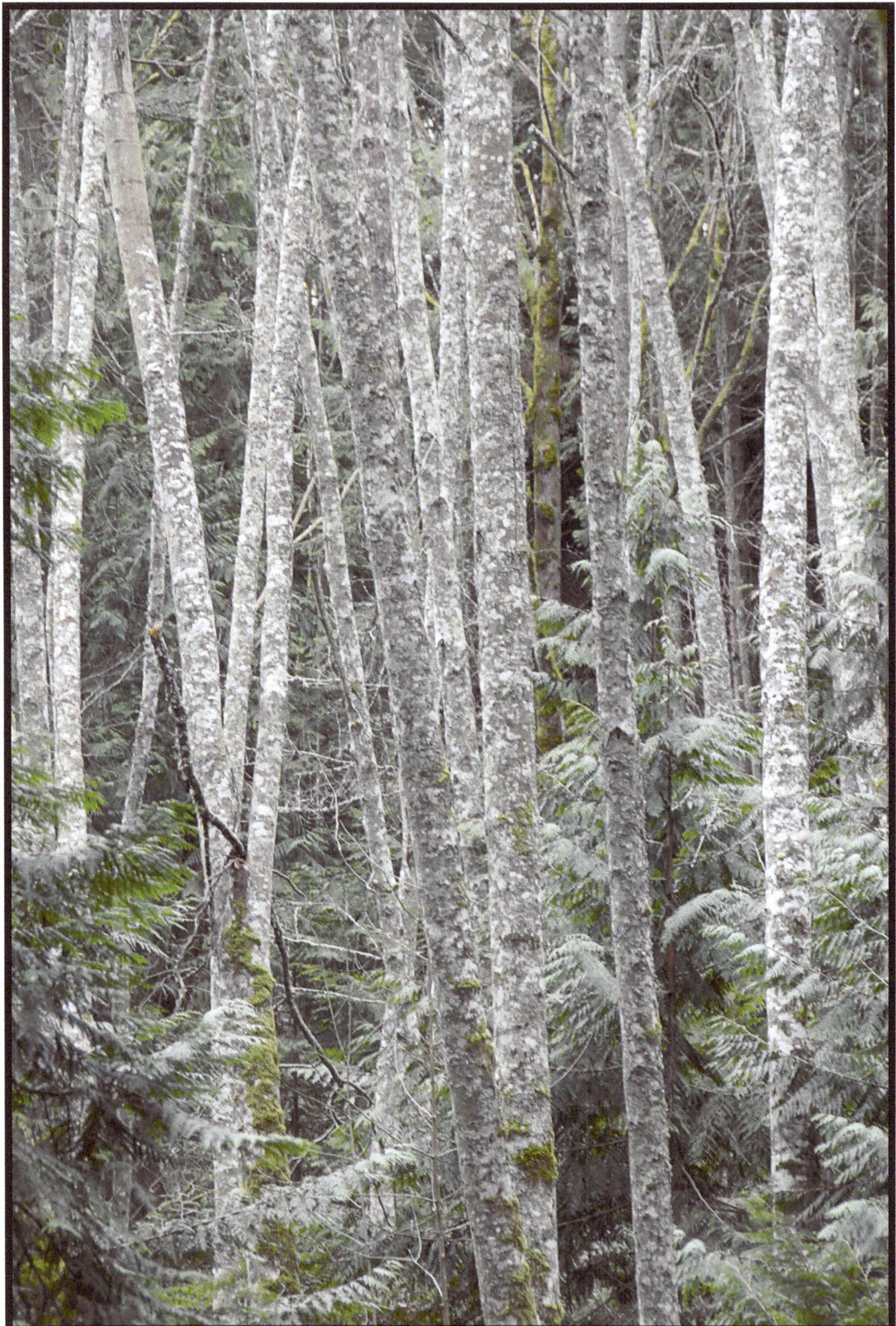

Whispering Trees

This is one of the favourite photographs that I have taken for myself! I used a filter and my shutter was slow enough to show a little movement in the leaves. As I was walking, I felt as though the trees were whispering to me. I walk among these trees often, and it is one of my favourite paths to walk. I made a print for my wall... it speaks to me and gives me goose bumps when glance at the photograph. I made a giclee print of it for quality and longevity.

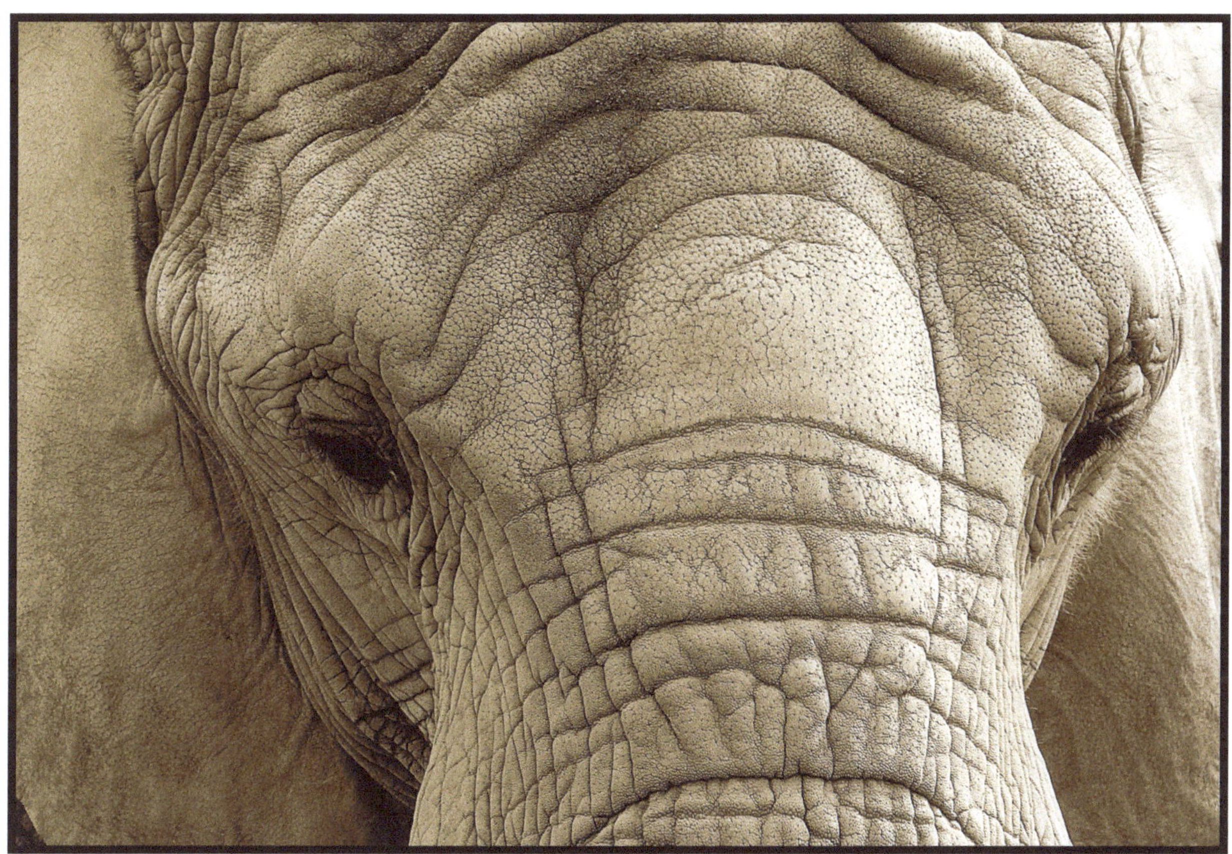

Wisdom

Wisdom of an elephant – to look his age... and how he should look in his skin – deep wrinkles and all. My feeling was more of a close-up – somewhat sad eyes. He was kept in a large confined space with other elephants. I could feel the loss of freedom in his eyes. No matter where we are, or an animal is, there can be wisdom in spite of the environment. True freedom is in our mind!

Inspirational Concepts

One day I was helping out at Coast Collective where I sometimes teach photography courses. This young lady was trying to put together her web site and wondered what she should call her product which she had a name for, but wanted to know how to express it more clearly. I suggested that she needs a brand. The brand is not what the product is, but rather what you as an artist have within yourself: your personality, your talent or your skill, if you will.

I shared with her my discovery many years ago about my slogan. Back then they were referred to more as slogans than brands, but my slogan never changed and it became my brand. All this began when I started to teach professional photography. I was asked, badgered even, to come up with a name for my course and one night as I fell into my alpha level I got up and wrote (I always have pen and paper by my bedside): *feeling more deeply about photography*; that is the core of my message. Since then this has become my brand, and it never changed. It is not a mission statement – they are always too long – I like it short and to the heart of the matter.

The young lady liked the word Inspiration. She used that word for her product but wanted it to be more specific, more about the product. I encouraged her to name the products as she liked, but to also create a brand. On my way home that evening the thought flooded into my mind "Inspirational Concepts" – that is what she is all about, creating new art pieces. Although she had only one product at the time, with this brand it can branch out to as many products as she's able to create in the future. I also offered the idea to use other words that could work with this brand such as creative, talented, imaginative and so on. The two word brand was my favourite and I also ran the idea by others including my son, whose input I always value, and there was a general consensus in the simple form of just *Inspirational Concepts*.

What makes us the person we are, and how can we express this in very few words? I spent a few hours with her and felt her spirit and ability to be creative in her life, and with her art!

Simplicity is the key to everything – even if it looks complicated to others. We must learn to break it down to the lowest common denominator. Creativity is complex but it needs to be expressed in some art form.

I like to teach photography – it is more than the camera, or paper, or the automatic digital equipment that makes it seem so easy. It is inspiration, it is creativity, it is our past learning, and it is who we are and how we express our ART!

People

A Self-Made Impression

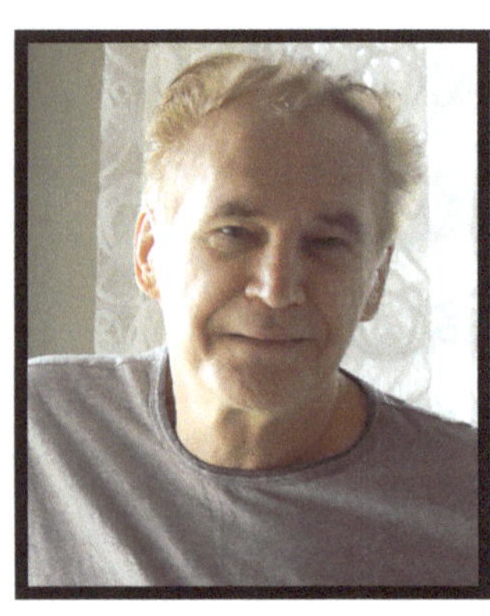

Every year on my birthday I take a self portrait and I have encouraged my students and other photographers to do the same. It is a challenge to come up with a new and hopefully creative look. Art is not reality or even a pretty impression, but rather a desire to express a moment in time with the illusion of permanence in no other way but with art that lives on beyond our time!

A portrait is not just about the face, or what is unique, or some distinct features we possess as an individual, but rather our individual concept, whatever that may be. It's an outline of life, an impression of the world we live in, our relationship therein, with or without detail.

The suggestion of a self portrait has to do with the self, not with what we have been indoctrinated into believing, what this concept should or should not be. To stretch our imagination, to go in a new direction, the saying "To go where no man has gone before," the inner world is still less explored than we may think.

Who are we, just a figment of our imagination embodied in skin, or the illusion of reality that we have learned to believe in? What is right for one person is boring to another, so let us explore the simple to the sublime because we are all this and more, much more than we can conceptualize in this life.

The image that I made of myself is not a passport or a so-called normal photograph that would fit into our respective traditions and costumes in our society – we have reached the 21st century don't you know! We believe we are thinking outside the box but guess what, there is a bigger box we are in now and another box outside that box, and so on and so on. What would truly enable me to not see any box? Looking up frees us from earthly limitations; look up to a new way of thinking. Not the way it has always been, but maybe a new, yet undiscovered path. Keep looking not at others, their work, their influence, but rather keep looking up to new inexperienced possibilities.

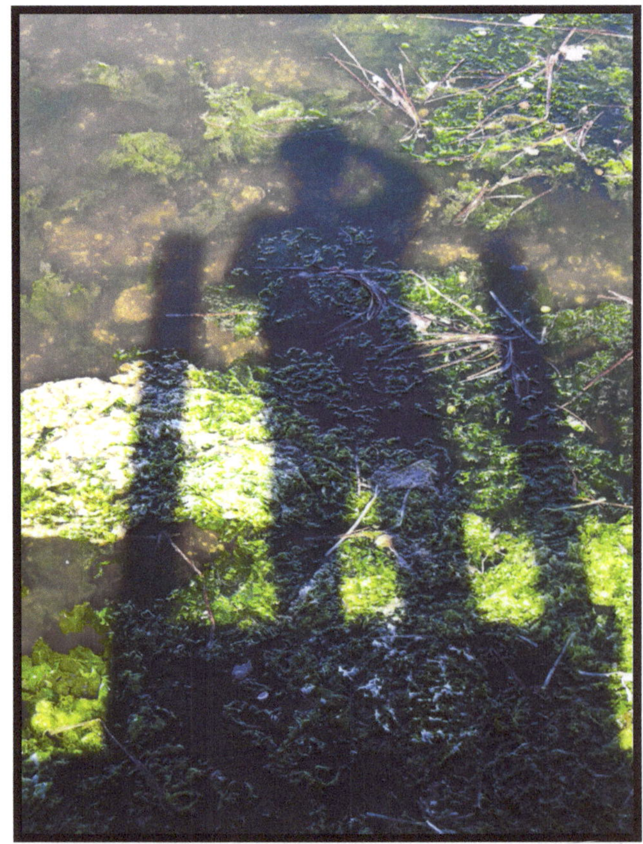

Let's explore this self image just for arguments sake. Begin with the foreground. What is under the earth that can't be seen in our logical mind, the underworld that has fascinated so many writers? In this image it suggests a place of rocks, hardness, solid support, stone upon stone, and layer upon layer. Let's look up a wee bit, a platform, a place where we can find solid footing and yet it is only a shadow of reality, the shadow of humankind. Who is there is of no consequence for it is just an impression, an outline. Look up and what do we see; Earth swirling at a dizzying speed, but is it reality? Look up and we see heavenly dazzling colours, meshed, or is it only my world?

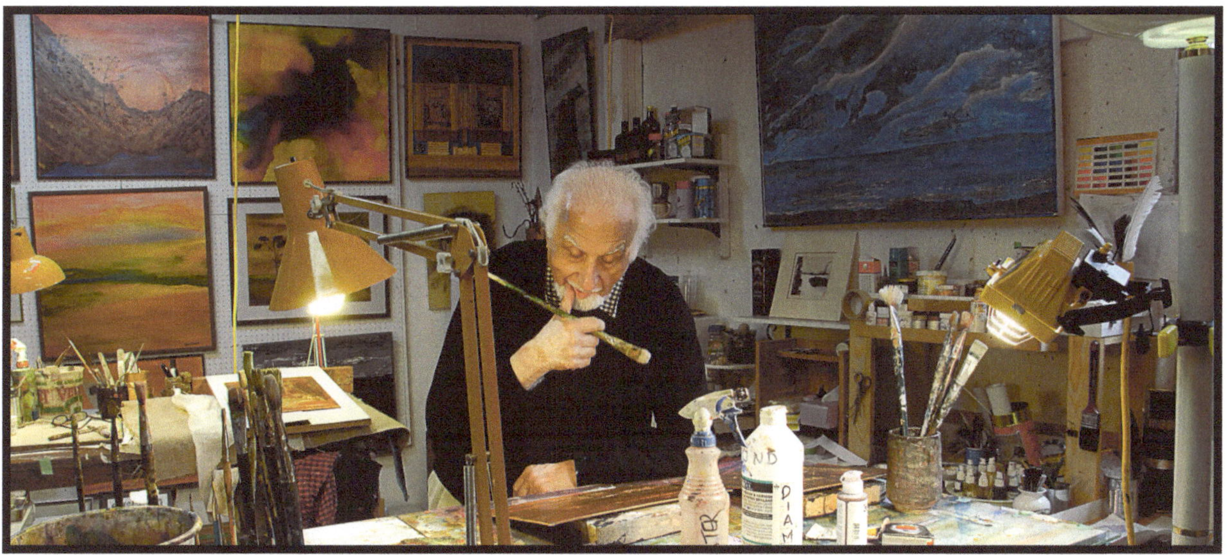

An Artist

The artist shown above taught me something I knew but didn't practice until now. I said to him, "I'll show you some of the images I took and you can pick the one you like best." He said to me, "Do you think you are an artist?" I didn't say anything. He responded with, "I only paint one painting of a person's portrait, I don't paint five. So why would you show me more than one photo? Show me the one you are the most happy with, and that will be the one!" Only one, the one the artist wants to finish because we are the artist, the image is in our hands, our vision, our creation…

I was so impressed with this man's work; it shook me to my core. Over the years his work kept changing and renewing itself. My great surprise was that I photographed him on his 85th birthday and shared his cake. I originally met him in a group of artists; I asked if I could photograph him and he was delighted. I wanted to record his personality, which as you can see in the photograph, is interesting. Likewise, so is his life story. One photo just doesn't do him justice; I took 100 but here is one more that touched me among the many. It was my privilege to get to know this man even now, towards the end of his illustrious life and art. I can only say one word about his art (speechless)...

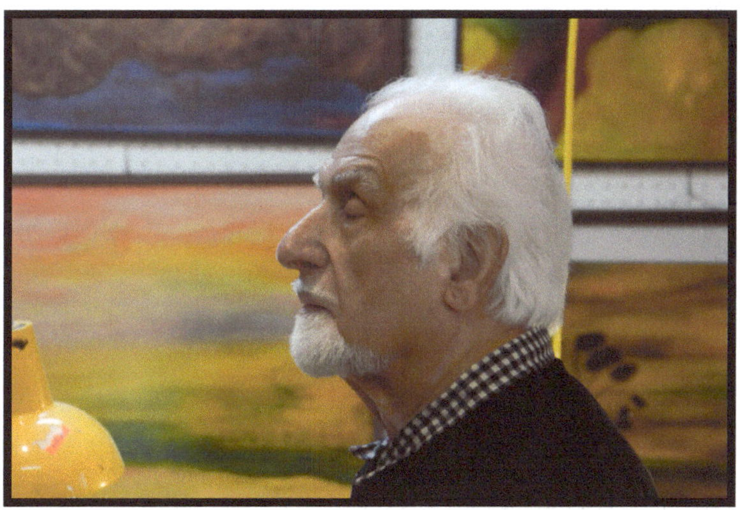

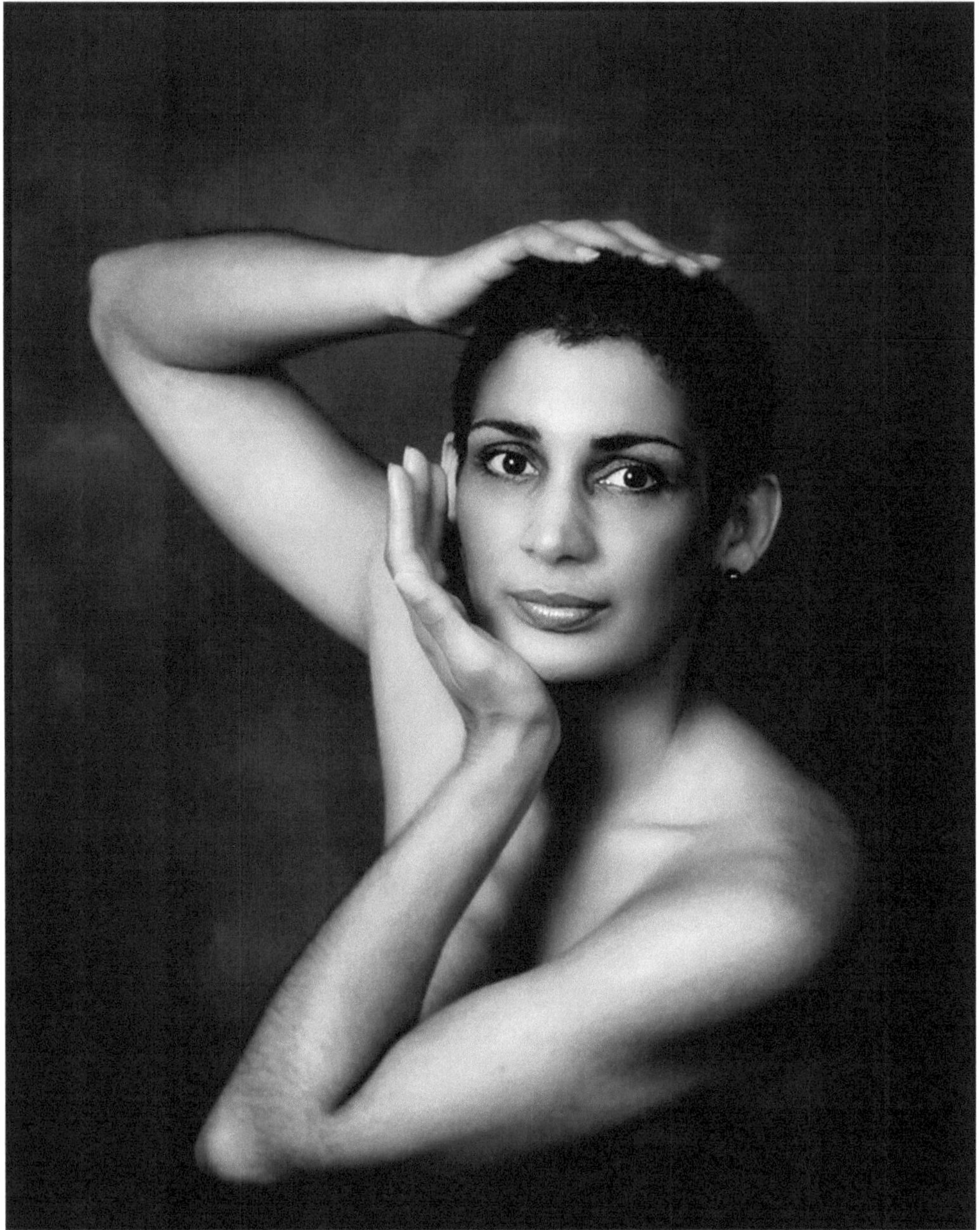

Beauty in Shape

When my client came in she had another shape for her body in mind, and she purchased a different design. I loved this one more though, with its own beauty and feeling. The chocolate tones seem to work for this image. I used my digital camera and Photoshop to change the colour and background.

Praise received:

"Klaus, the tones, everything in this speaks to me… lovely all around. So well done, and her eyes… the light in them... wow. I love your care with her."

Joseph: "Nice creativity. I like how you had her frame herself. I have just now become familiar with your work, but you have a creative talent for capturing women's inner essence along with their beauty. They are absolutely stunning."

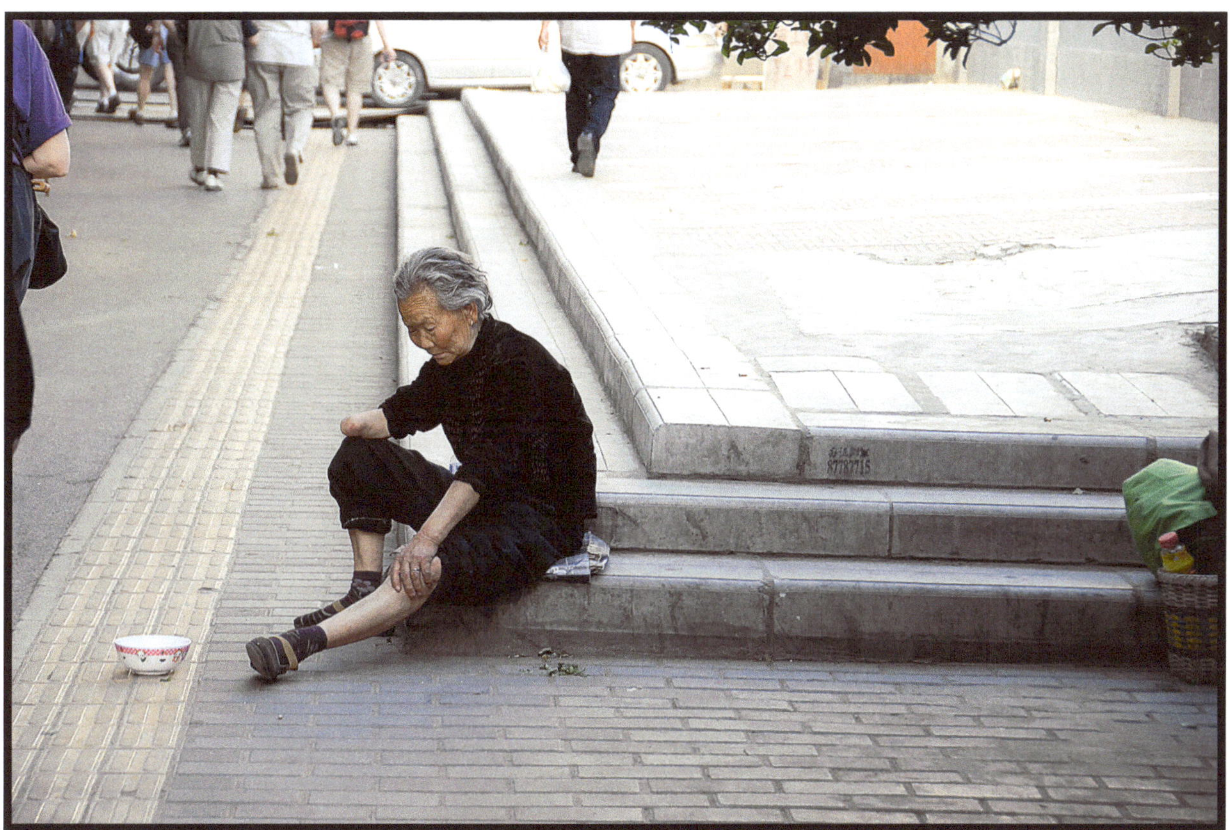

Beggar Woman

She seems to be just so far from reality in her own world of thought. I wondered what she was thinking and then realized I could never enter inside. The feelings overwhelmed me as I took the photograph. All we can see are legs walking by her…

<u>*Praise received*</u>*:*

Karen: "I can see how you were overwhelmed by feelings. What an amazing peek into someone's world… a world, as you said, we will never be entirely privy to. Truly a wonderful capture of a small, yet huge, moment in time. It just drew me in. Wonderful work."

Shaheen: "I'm speechless! Unfortunately this is the reality for many people in this world – as I work for them I know their world, but yet it's so true that it's difficult to get a true understanding of her world."

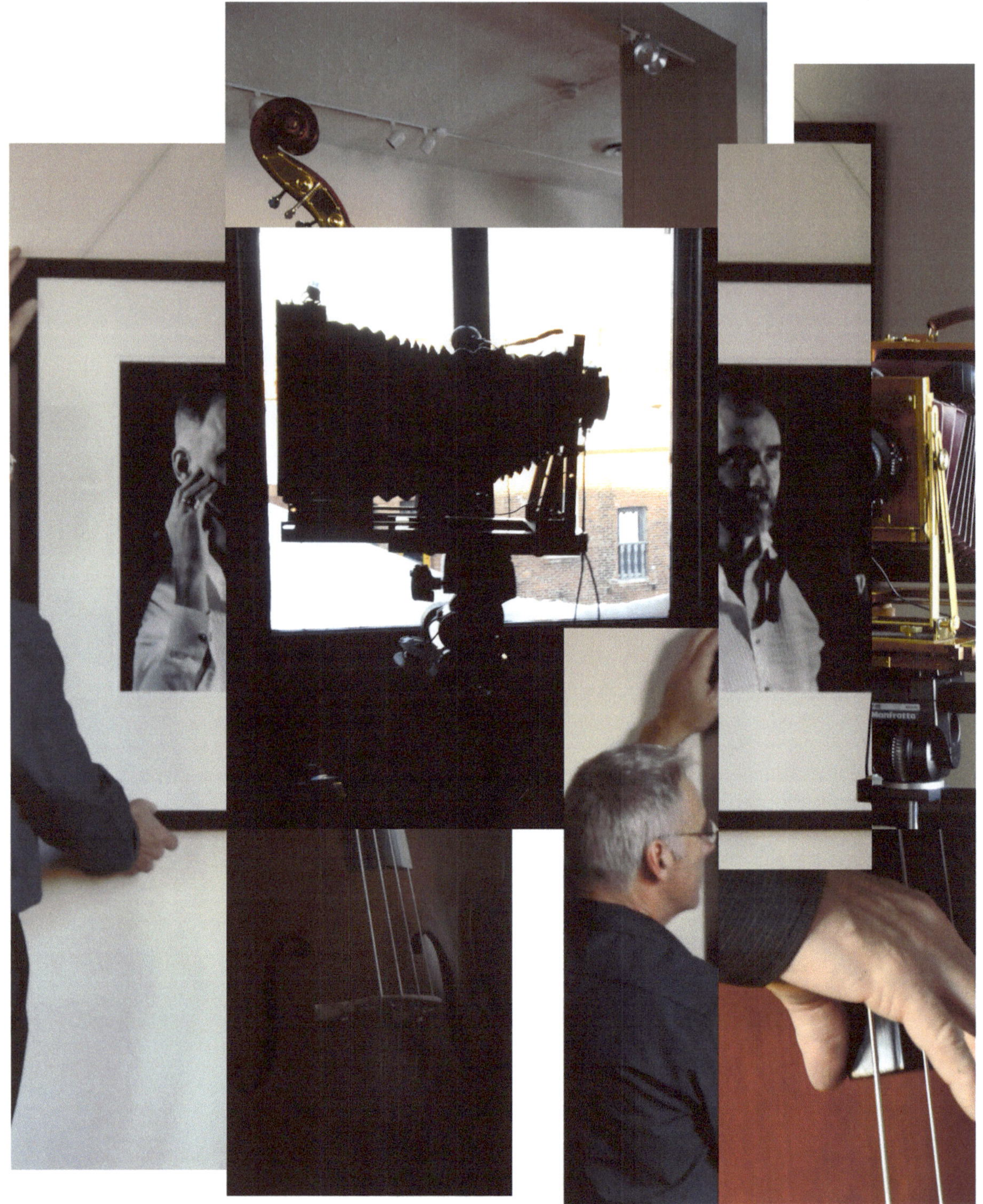

Bits and Pieces

He's a photographer who I went to photography school with; many years later he came into my studio and asked me to photograph him. I was thrilled to do so. I saw him as a photographer and a musician, so I composed this montage for him. Bits and pieces as I saw him, and felt it represented my view.

Client's comments: "I like the white space and the paper... the space makes it very readable. Can't think of anything I don't like, and that is odd."

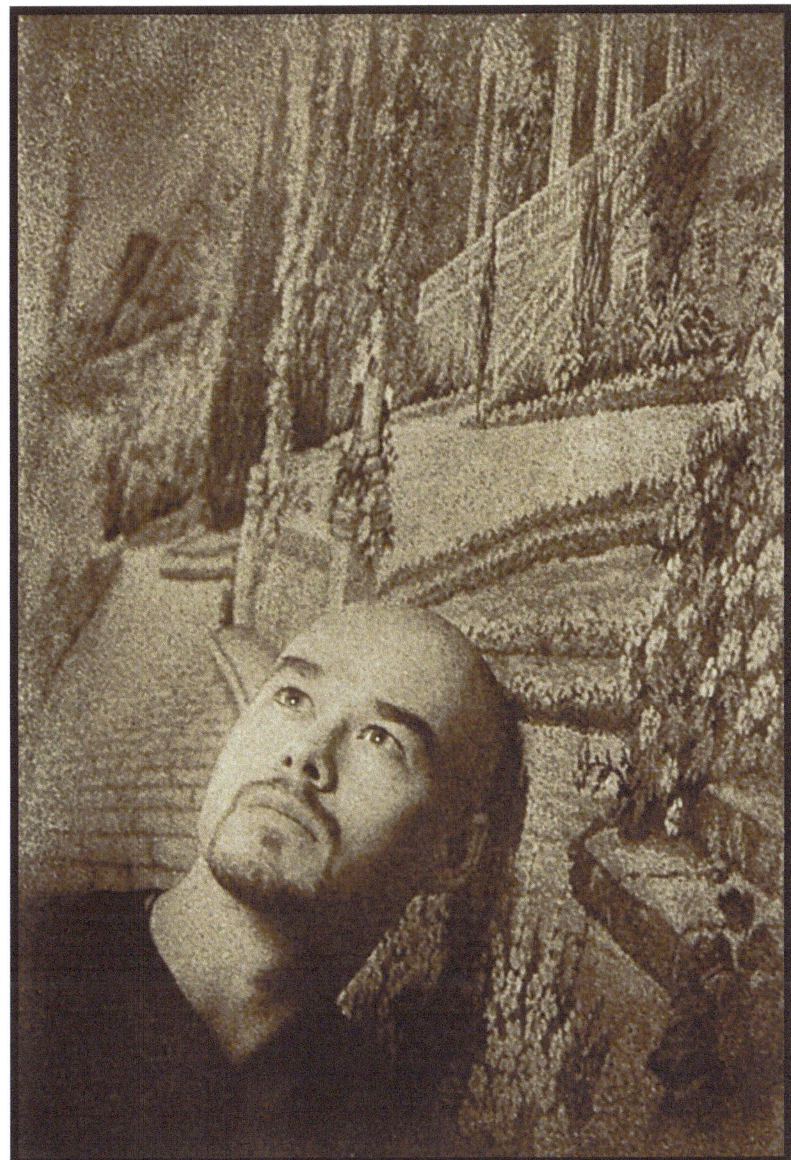

Bromoil

My drive has always been to learn alternative processes. When I heard about the bromoil print process in 1994 I became quite intrigued. World renowned photographer David W. Lewis set up a class for two of us and we flew out to spend a few days with David in Ontario. It is one of the most difficult processes, but it has a rich reward in learning to master the process.

We began by making our own paper, while I believe David used paper that he had purchased from France. The steps we learned took my breath away. The chemistry, inks, oil, brushes from England, putty knives, paper, chammy, and so much more.

We were then instructed on how to expose the paper 25%, 50%, 100%, 150%, 200%, over or under, depending on the negative contrast density. Once we had this dialed in then the matrix had to dry until the next day. The next step was to super heat the matrix and start to ink the paper. This is the most difficult part, layer after layer, and the more layers the more beautiful the image becomes.

The process is quite complex, but suffice it to say that as you can imagine there is so much more to the bromoil process than is discussed here. I love the art of it, the longevity of it, the difficulty of it, and the beauty of it. It produces an image that could not be produced in any other way. The photographers of old truly were craftsmen and dedicated their lives to their craft without sufficient compensation, yet had the drive to do so.

David W. Lewis is still teaching bromoil classes. More information may be obtained at David's web site: **www.bromoil.com**. I would highly recommend these classes if you want to stretch your own personal learning curve.

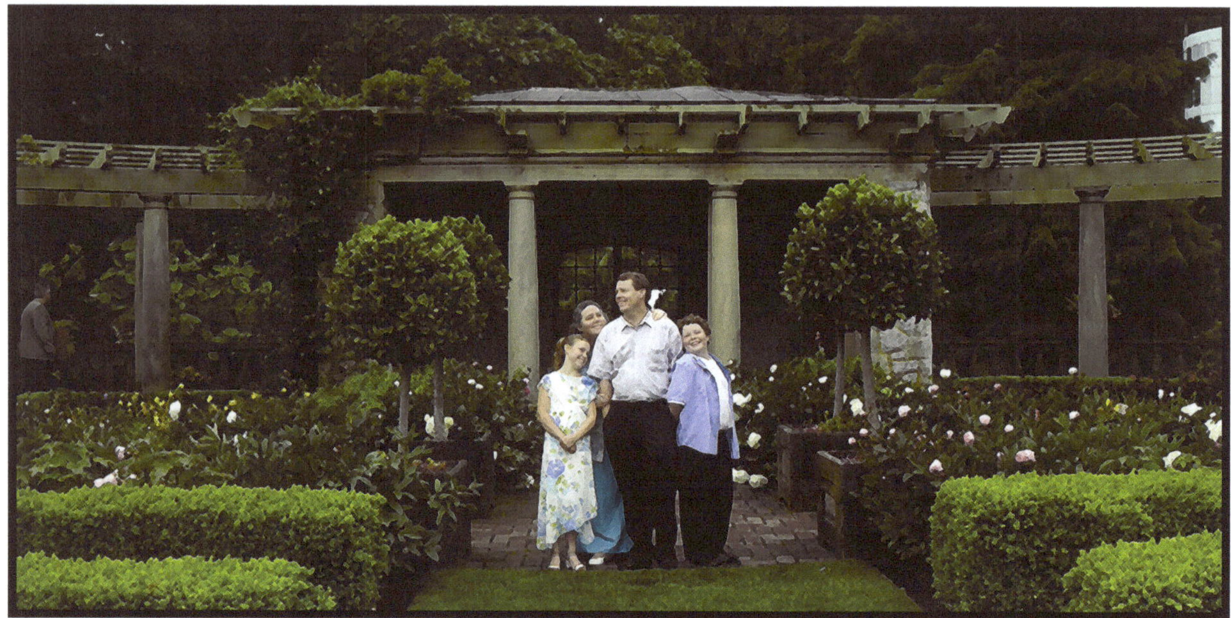

Close Family

The photograph was taken at Royal Roads. I was asked to make a wall-sized photograph that would represent the family's closeness. On Vancouver Island there are many totem poles so to represent the closeness of the land we live in though our family, and art pieces, illustrates the past and present of our country. The design of the family interwoven as one may be seen in totem poles, wrapped around as it were, the strength and love of the centre.

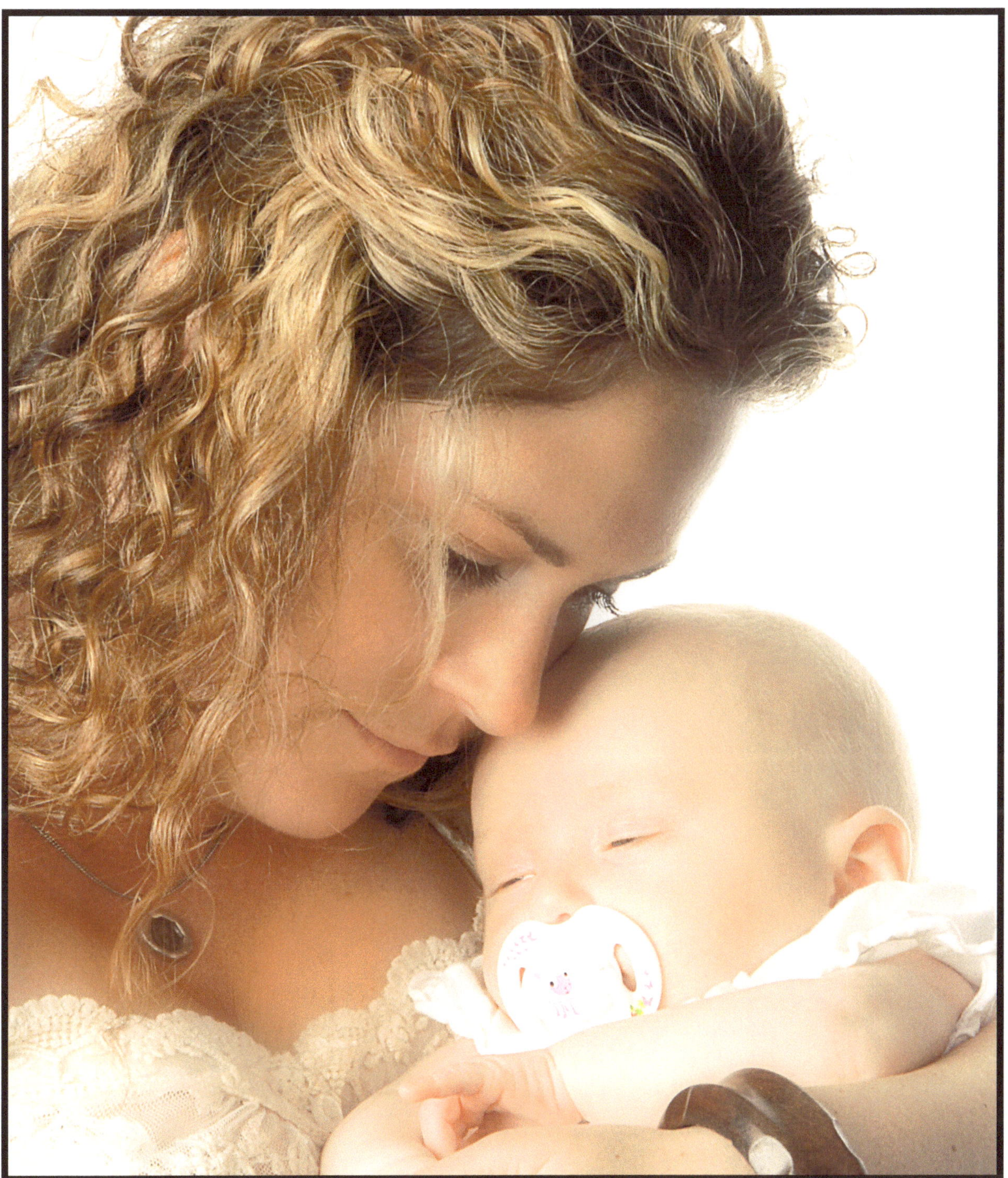

Close to Mother's Heart

Edgar Degas, a French artist famous for his work in painting, sculpture, printmaking and drawing once said, "Art is not what you see, but what you make others see." My sincerest hope is that my art makes the viewer think and see.

<u>*Praise received*</u>*:*
Shanina: "How beautiful! Lovely soft tones and such a gorgeous capture, they both look so blissful"

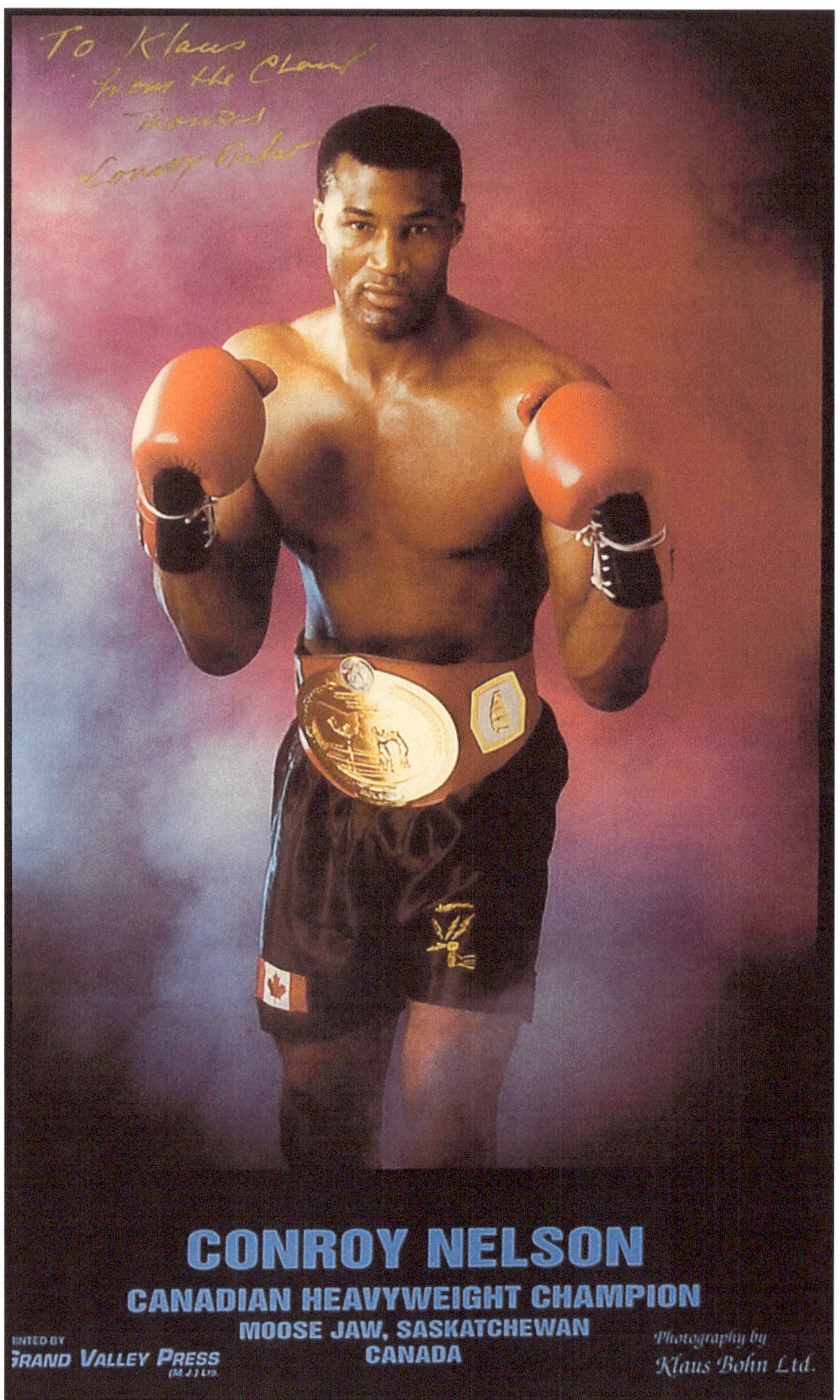

Conroy Nelson

Canadian champion boxer! I had the privilege to photograph him for the poster and at ringside. It was a great opportunity to be right on the edge of the ring, and even had blood splatter over me – it was a new adventure!

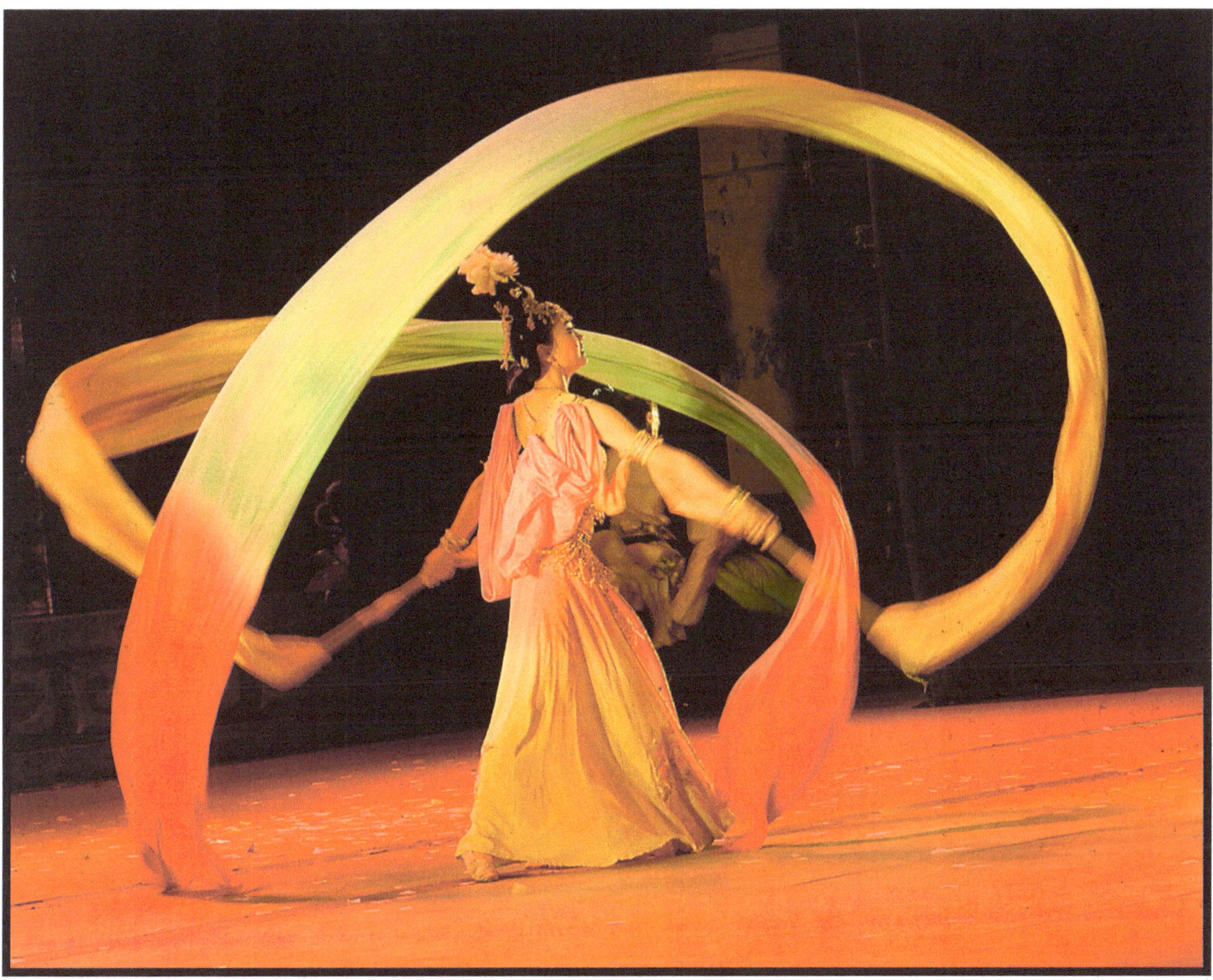

Dancer

Pure magic as she danced with the long ribbons flowing so perfectly and with such ease. It felt like an illusion to my senses, but the camera captured the reality. Most beautiful!

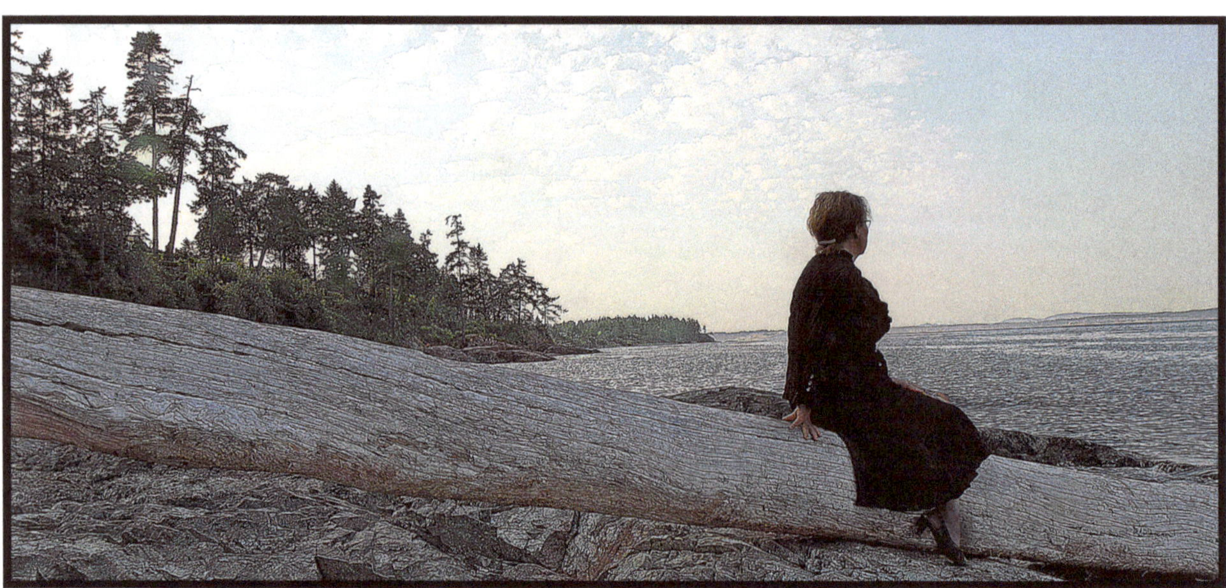

Distance View

Creative, illusionary, peaceful, textured, thought provoking, feminine – all are characteristics used by viewers of the "old master paintings". For someone who dislikes having her photo taken, enticement to have the "painting" done resulted in rewards. Another chapter of my journey was beginning, and the artwork reminds me of that step.

Client comments: "Trusting Klaus at the sitting was so easy following our earlier discussions of what I might want. My husband watched Klaus work his magic. Peaceful thoughts flowed through me as I gazed into the ripples and waves. The horizon reminded me of the possibilities ahead; the trees were my buffer representing the strength gained through my past experiences. The experience from the planning stage to the framed item on the wall was timely and full of positive sensations for me, and for that I am so thankful to Klaus – a true master!"

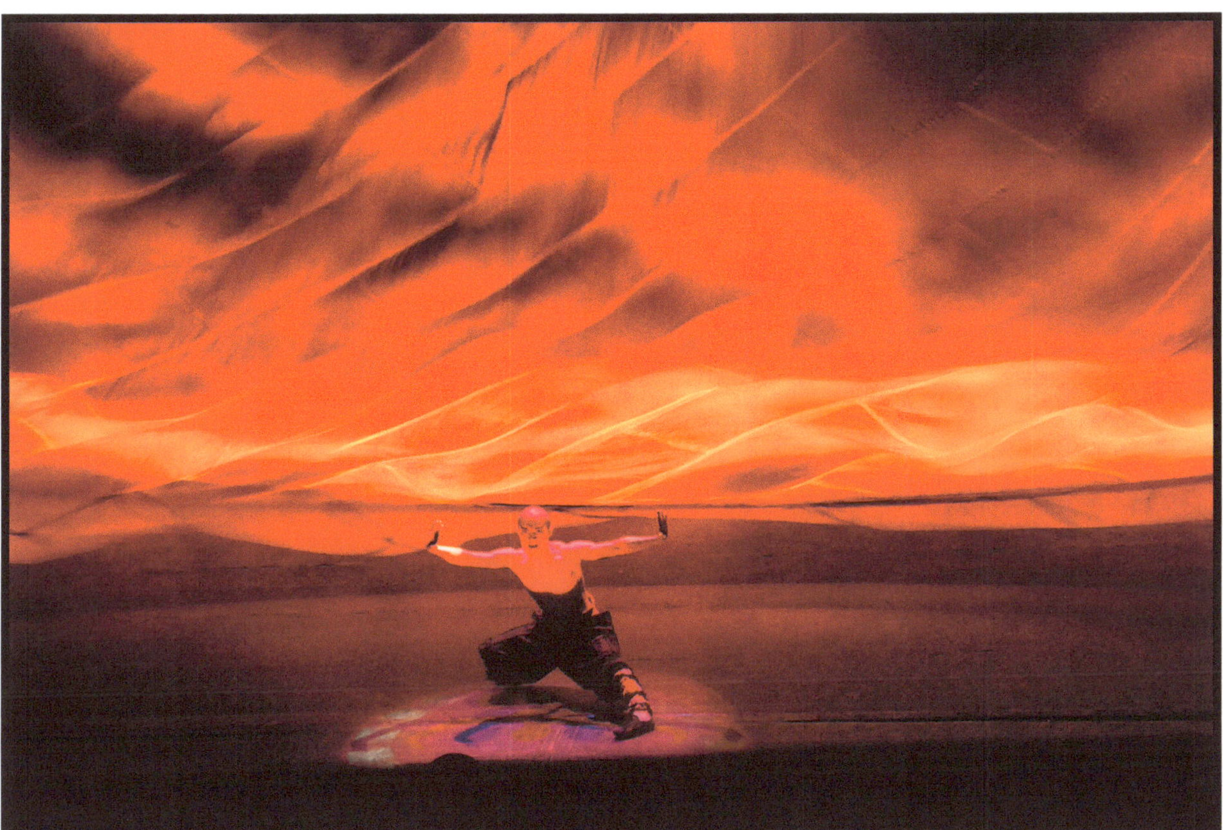

Dramatic Fighter

I sat at this great performance watching, spellbound, and was able to quickly make this image. The drama was so intoxicating that I sat on the edge of my seat – the emotion and feelings were so real. I was given permission to photograph during the performance.

Praise received:
Diane: "You caught a very exciting moment – you can actually feel the energy. Good job!"

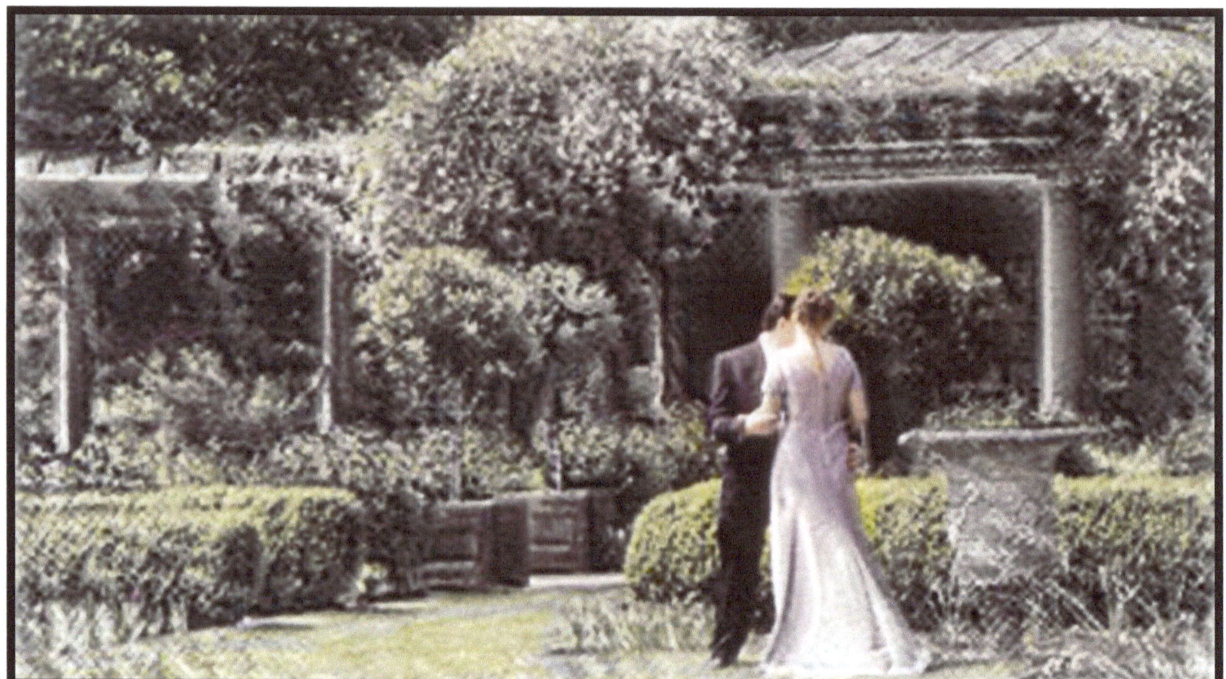

Dream Wedding

I was hired to photograph her sister's wedding, and they asked me if I would photograph them as well. They got dressed up as if it was their wedding. I said I do that often, referring to it as a post bridal wedding. They asked for more of an art piece, to make it look more painterly, and purchased the image on a 40-inch canvas.

I do like the feeling in this image; it was not about the faces, but instead the place and what it generated in their emotions towards each other. I believe they had their wedding in this same place, Royal Roads in Victoria, British Columbia, a famous place where movies have been made.

Praise received:

Karen: "Stunning! Wonderful work! Such a responsibility too… and I know because we had our three girls all get married within two years of each other, and a good photographer is well worth the money!"

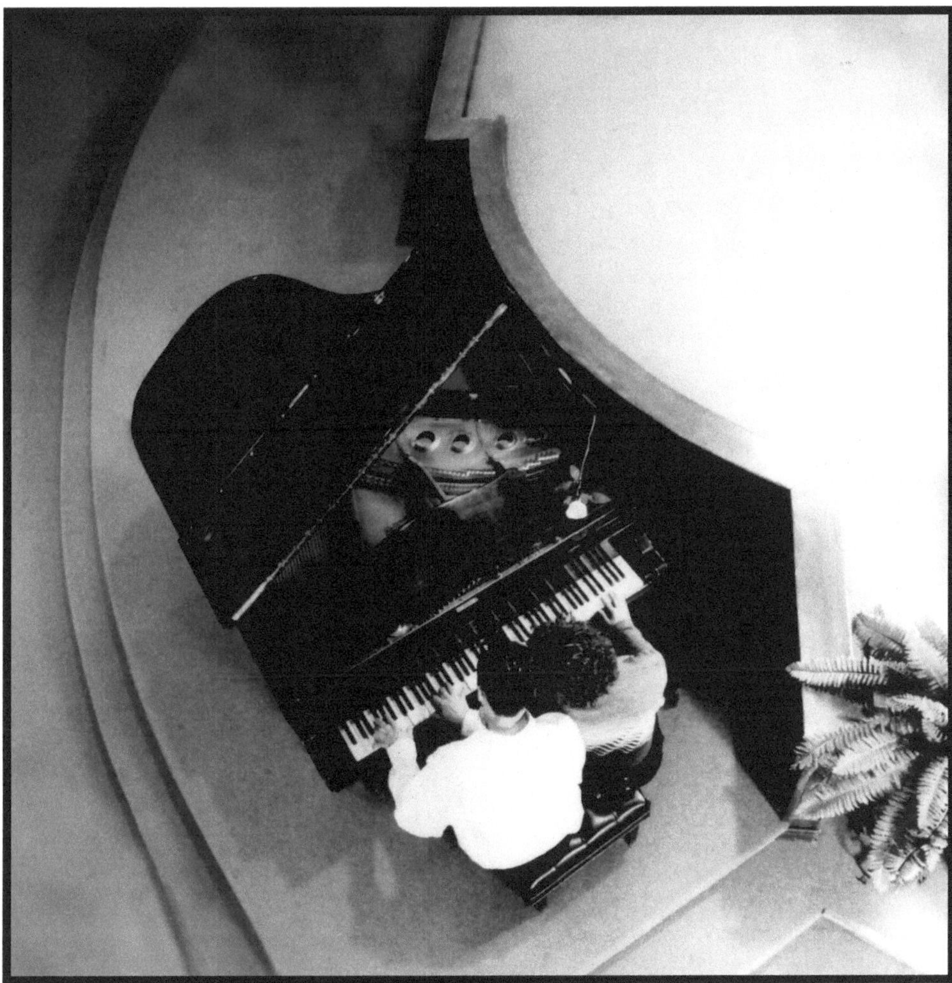

Engaged

I had previously photographed their high school graduation photos. They came in for a consultation, asking what I could do that would be different for their engagement photograph. Because they both play the piano we agreed on a piano concept. This piano is in a church so I was able to photograph them from a higher angle which provided a very good overview. The idea was their relationship – engaged in playing the piano, and this was to represent their engagement as well. I did some other photos for the family where the faces were showing. This is the one they liked – it shows true feeling and passion for each other. Life needs a comment, a bridge, to connect two lives shared in so many ways. I am happy they purchased a giclee and it is hanging on their wall. I hand painted the rose and the green plant to add to the photo, a touch of my own hand.

Praise received:

"Such a wonderfully inspired image Klaus, has a very Bogart feel to me. Black and white is the perfect medium. As always, your work is exceptional!

John: "Fantastic composition and interaction of the couple!"

Joseph: "I love this shot for many reasons. The angle is incredible. Being shot in black and white gives a softness to the couple and of course the grand piano, the most perfect instrument there is. I am not objective, however, given I play one. Superb shot."

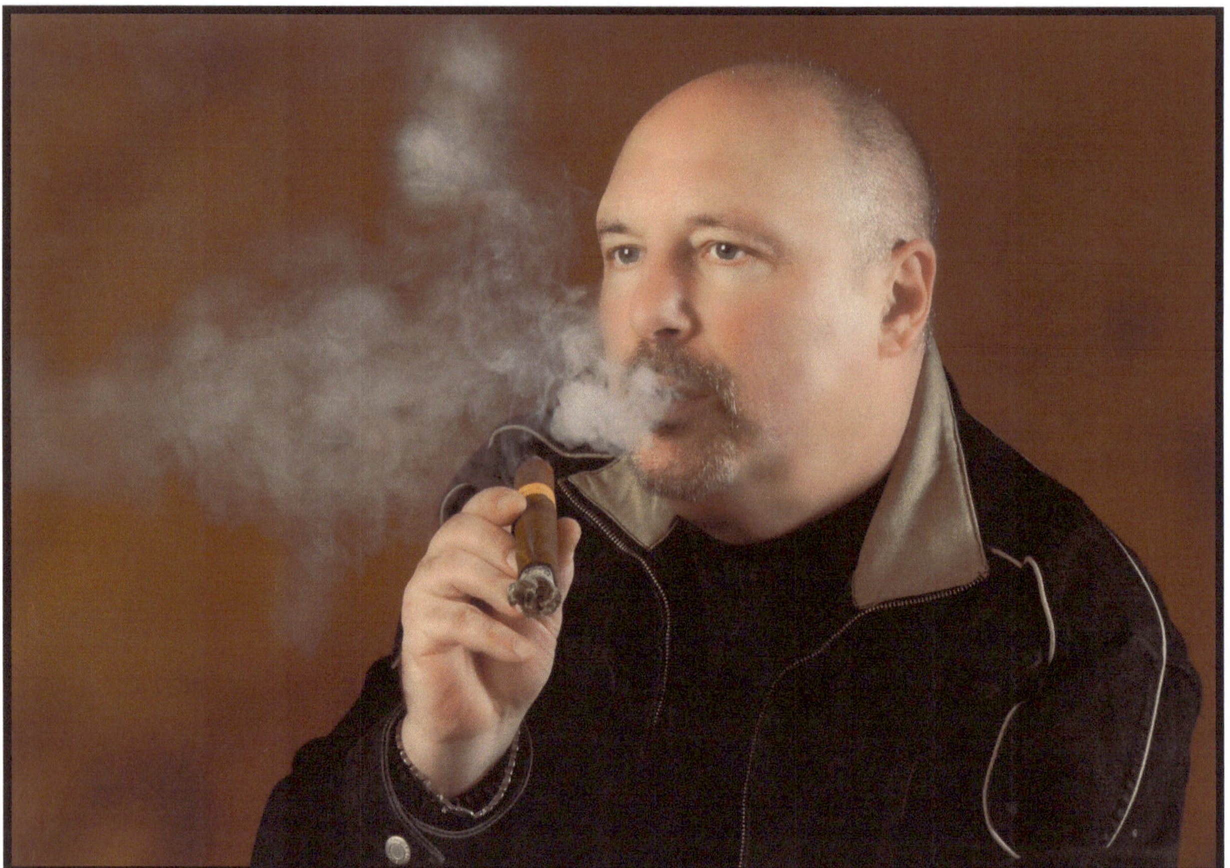

Exhaling

The client requested an image of himself smoking his favourite brand of cigar. I believe I managed to capture the right moment, with his expression and the smoke just so.

Praise received:

"You captured a very special moment… superbly photographed indeed… but that's the norm for your photography."

"What a wonderful capture and pose. I love the effect of the smoke from his cigar, and the tones and background all come together nicely. I am sure he will love this photo. It's great in its entirety. I love your photography!"

"A fantastic and unusual portrait! You did a great work on light and expression. Unique!"

Carol: "Fantastic portrait, Klaus… I love the tones, the set up, the cigar, and especially how you've captured that beautiful expression and the smoke… I reckon this rates among your very best portraits."

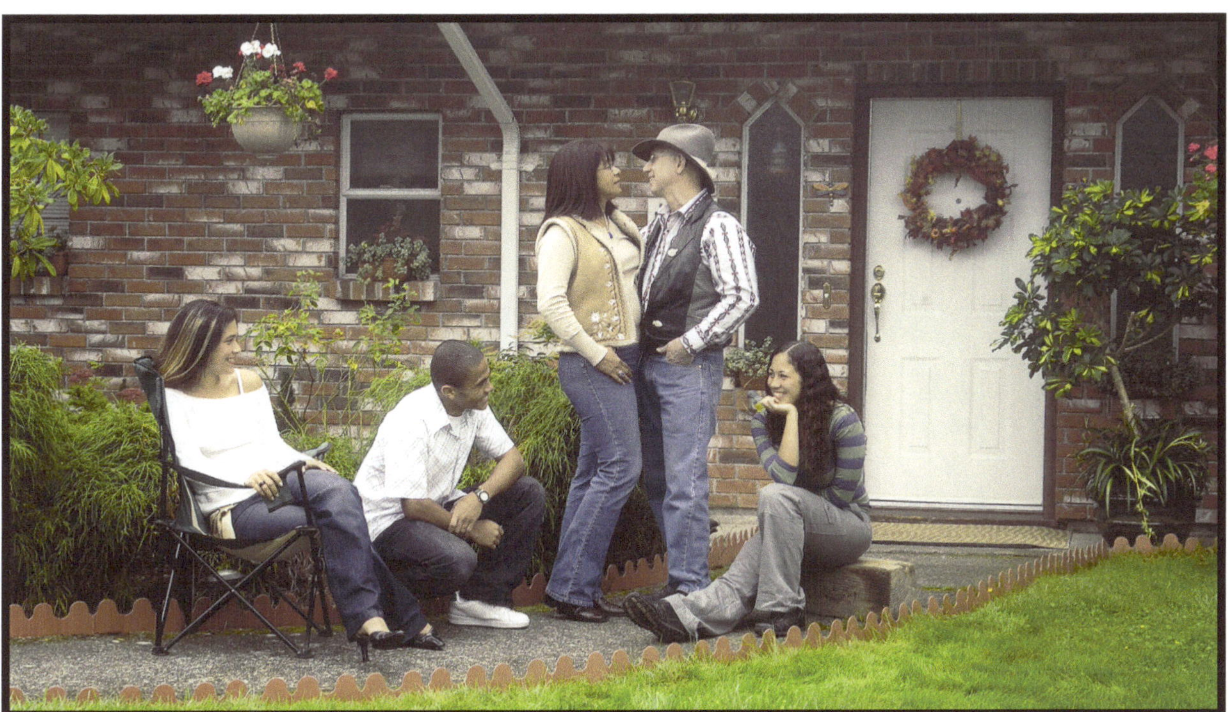

Faces Never Lie

The consultation went very well. The mother and her grown children were so happy to have the photograph taken – the father was flying back home the week we scheduled the session. He worked outside Canada. The premise was to show their happiness as a family, united. The concept fell into place quite easily, but showing the closeness of the children and yet revealing the closeness and intimacy of the couple – separately – was the thought. My intuition kicks in when I am under pressure, which I work from most of the time. To show the relationship between the children was rather easily attained. The challenge was the couple – to keep them separate so to speak, yet involved with each other. I like the smiles, so real and natural. The feeling of the photograph is important, with a composition worthy of its design. If I may say, the photograph hanging in their living room finishes the warmth of their home.

Praise received:

Sinisa: "Great image, love the title!"

John: "So candid and yet formal at the same time! I love the interaction between the groups."

Rick & Deb: "A very nice family portrait... it's nice to see the different slant on a family portrait where you took the image outside. Everyone seems so relaxed, as if it is just the five of them gathering together as they usually do... all so very natural. A fabulous portrait, we can just imagine how great it looks hanging in their home!"

Joseph: "The photograph jumped out at me. You certainly captured the emotional connectedness of the entire family. Very nice."

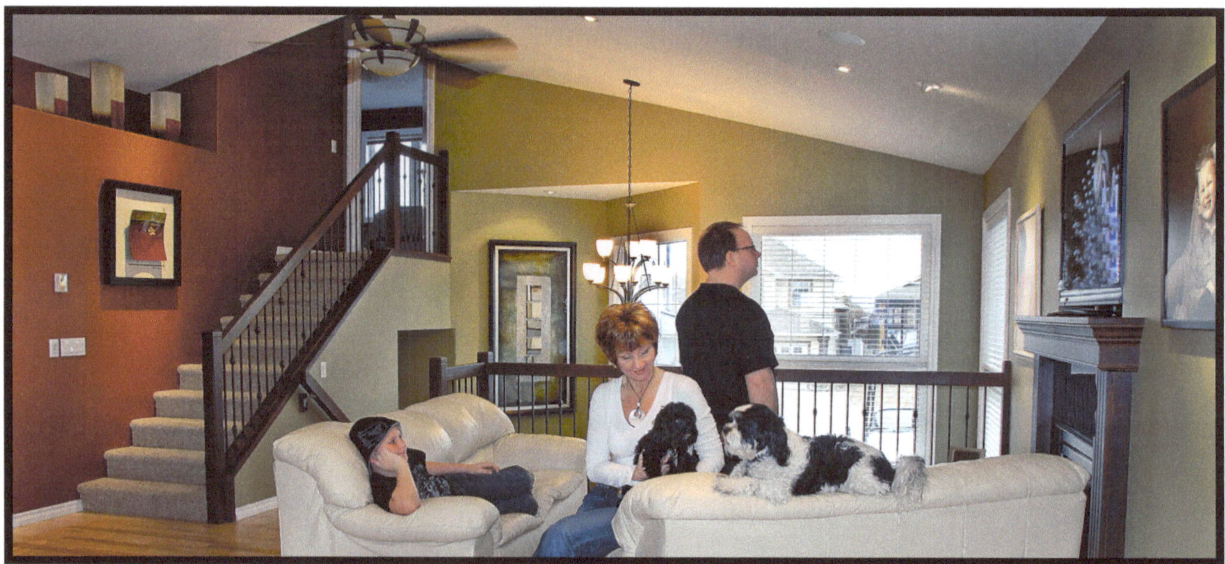

Family Environment

I was invited to photograph this family and flew out to Regina, Saskatchewan for the session. Since I've known Shawn, a fellow photographer and friend for many years, he didn't provide any guidelines. I felt a need to express their individuality, and yet still be connected by design. The concept of "individuality in a family environment" was my goal. I showed the technical side of Shawn by having him look at his flat screen television, while I liked the way is wife was playing with the dogs. Their son shows a sense of boredom, but unites them in composition and freedom. I was happy they felt the image represented who they are. A 40-inch giclee hangs on their wall beside the television.

<u>*Praise received:*</u>

"It's a beautiful shot and says so much. What struck me at first was how isolated they were, each in their own world and it felt lonely… that was my fist impression. They have a great home so it makes a very stylish portrait. Great job!"

Carol: "Terrific work… a great reflection of the dynamics within a family and individually… wonderful format too."

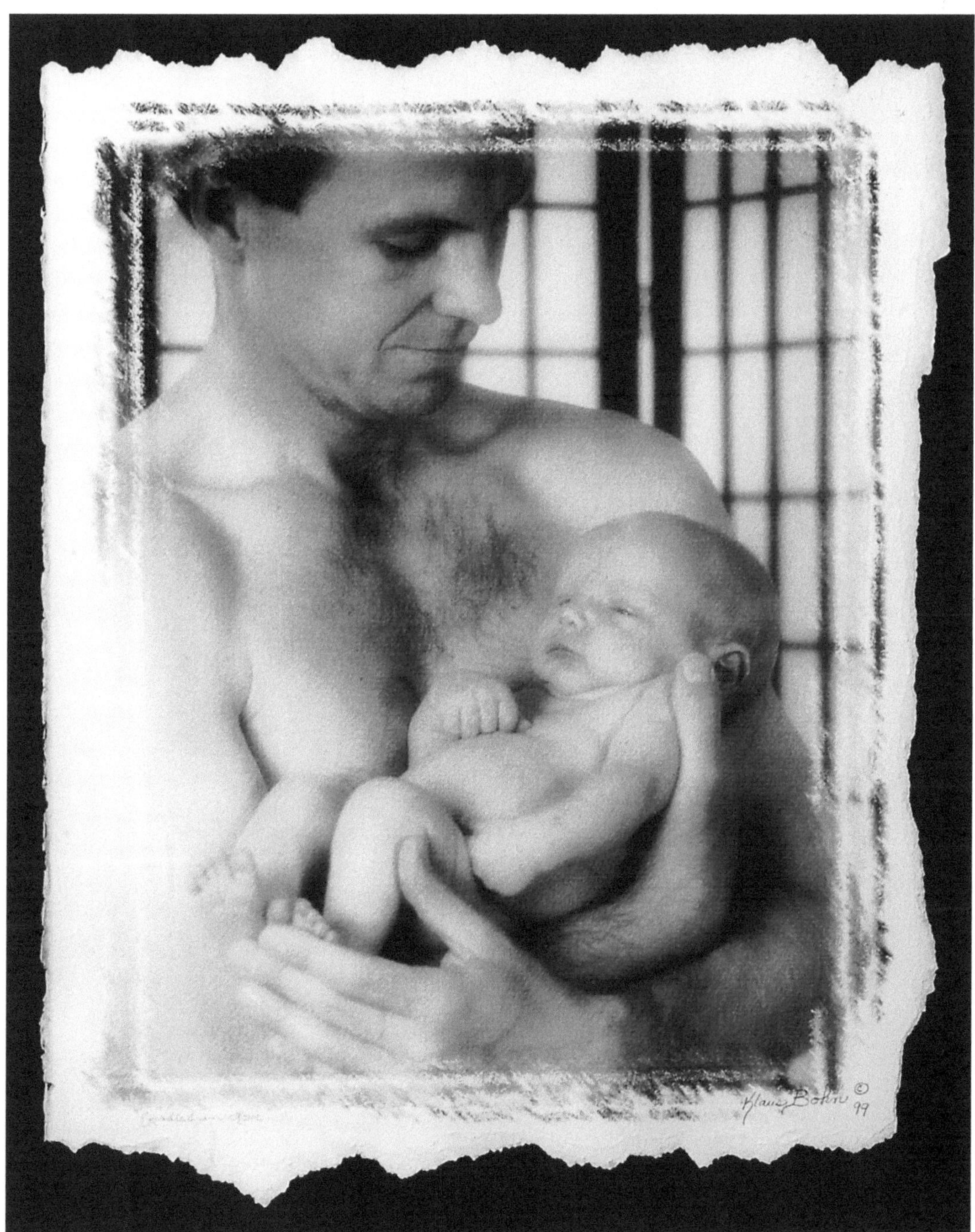

Father's Joy

I had photographed his wife with their, baby girl; I called it a Madonna session. When they had a baby boy, he wanted the same type of art piece with his son. With admiration the father looks with pride. I used the background for a more manly design, depth and texture to match the subject. It was in my mind to capture his masculinity since he works on a pipeline.

<u>*Praise received*</u>*:*

"In my mind, Klaus, there's nothing more precious than a father's love. Your photo speaks without saying a word. A beautiful and very endearing image."

"Lovely feel to this one, Klaus. I love that he is at once strong and yet tender. Well done."

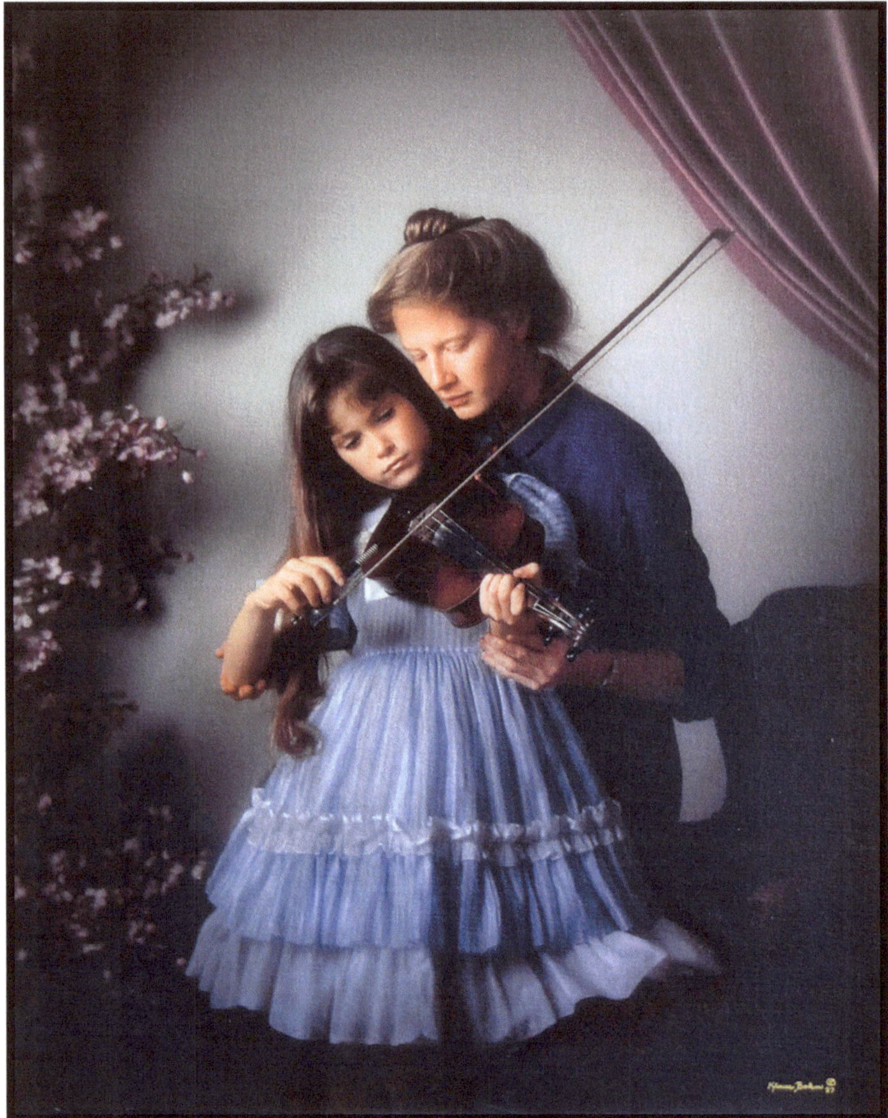

First Music Lesson

This was her first music lesson and I wanted to record this moment in time to preserve the special, first-time experience. I could see how my little girl, my daughter Tammy, was trying so hard to focus and look professional. The feelings in both faces touched my heart. The set was created in my studio. My feelings and emotion of a proud father – I think came across in this portrait. Now she is grown but I love this image and will treasure it forever.

Praise received:

"Truly beautiful. I love the expressions on their faces. You certainly are skilled at capturing a moment, Klaus. This has a very classic, vintage feeling to it with the lovely hues and colours, just perfect, not to take away from the focus of your daughter."

"Klaus, it's as if you've resurrected the art of classic portraiture. Everything about your composition, framing, lighting and colours come straight from the timeless work of the grand masters. Through all the re-inventions of the art over the years, it's actually a treat to see a modern work which adheres to the original definitions of fine art. Right down to the perfectly positioned diagonal of the bow. Awesome work!"

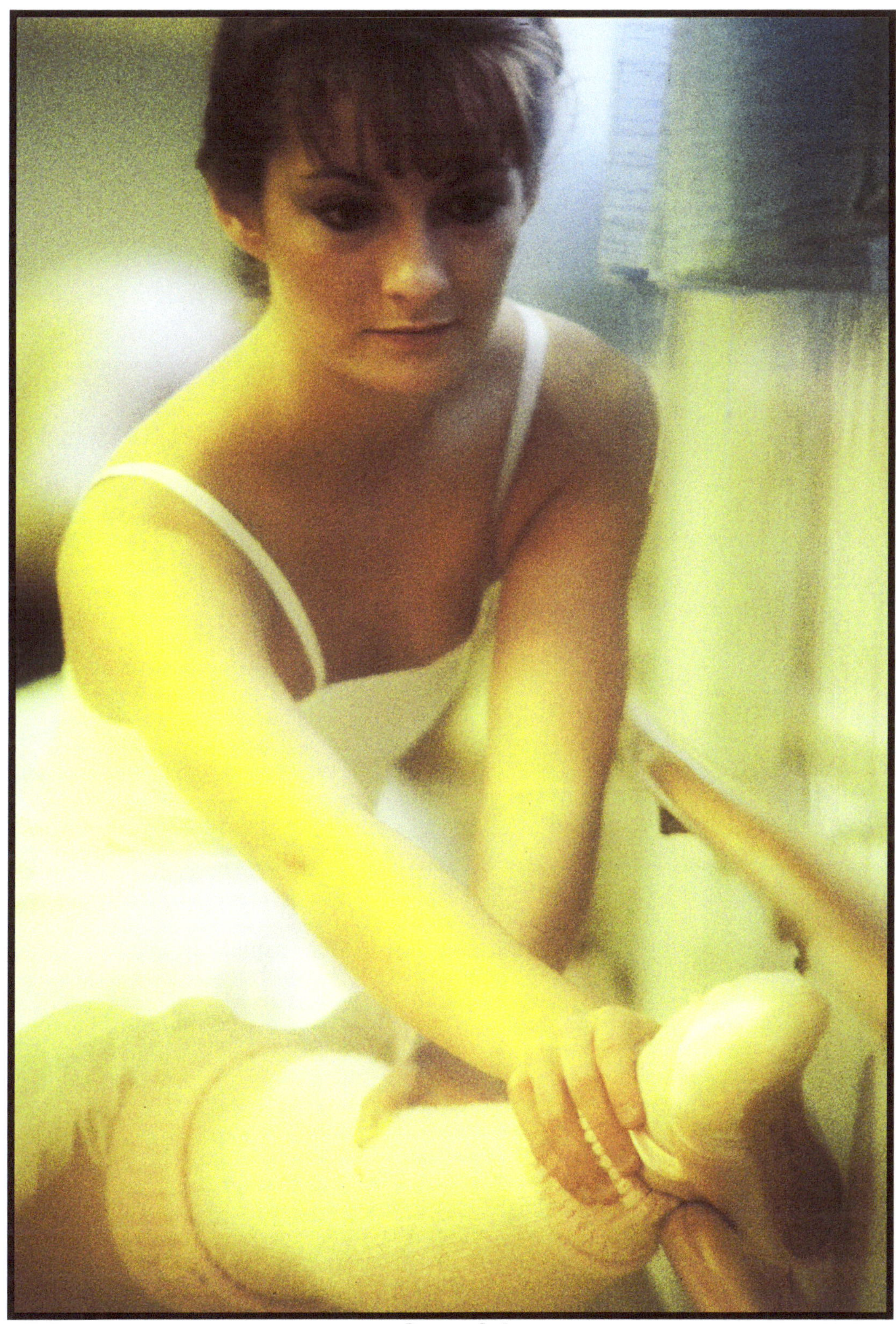

Graceful

She was so graceful in posing, a delight to work with. I used slide film on my RB camera and a black chiffon scarf netting with some holes in it placed over the lens to give this look. I made an interneg. – 4x5 inch.

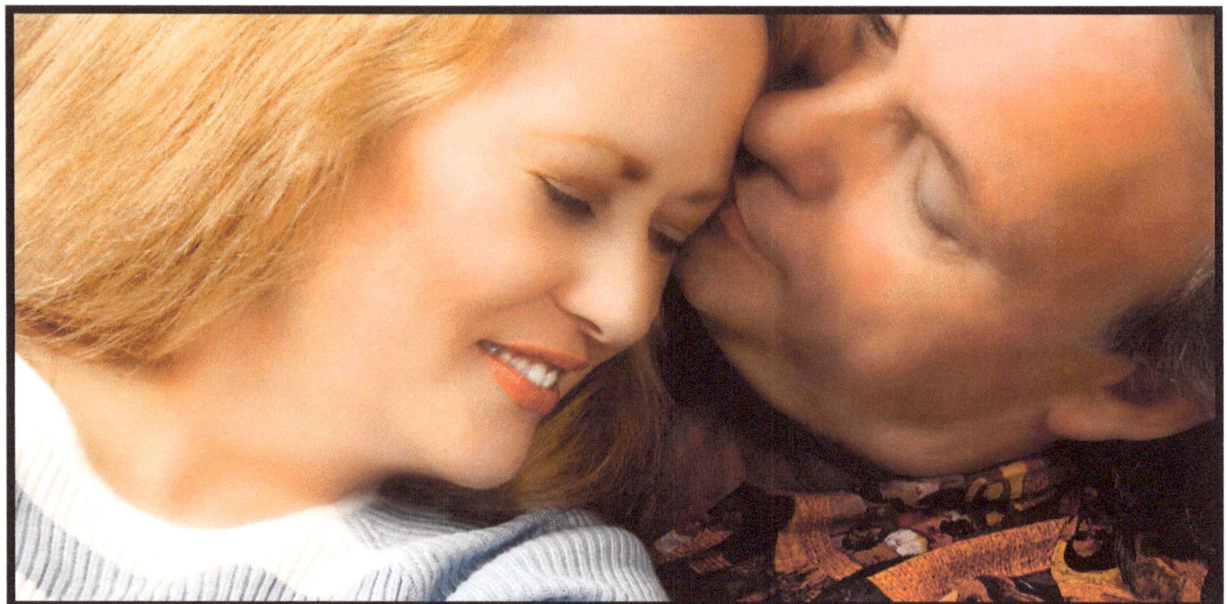

High School Reunion

They met again after twenty years and rekindled their love. I think the photograph tells the story.

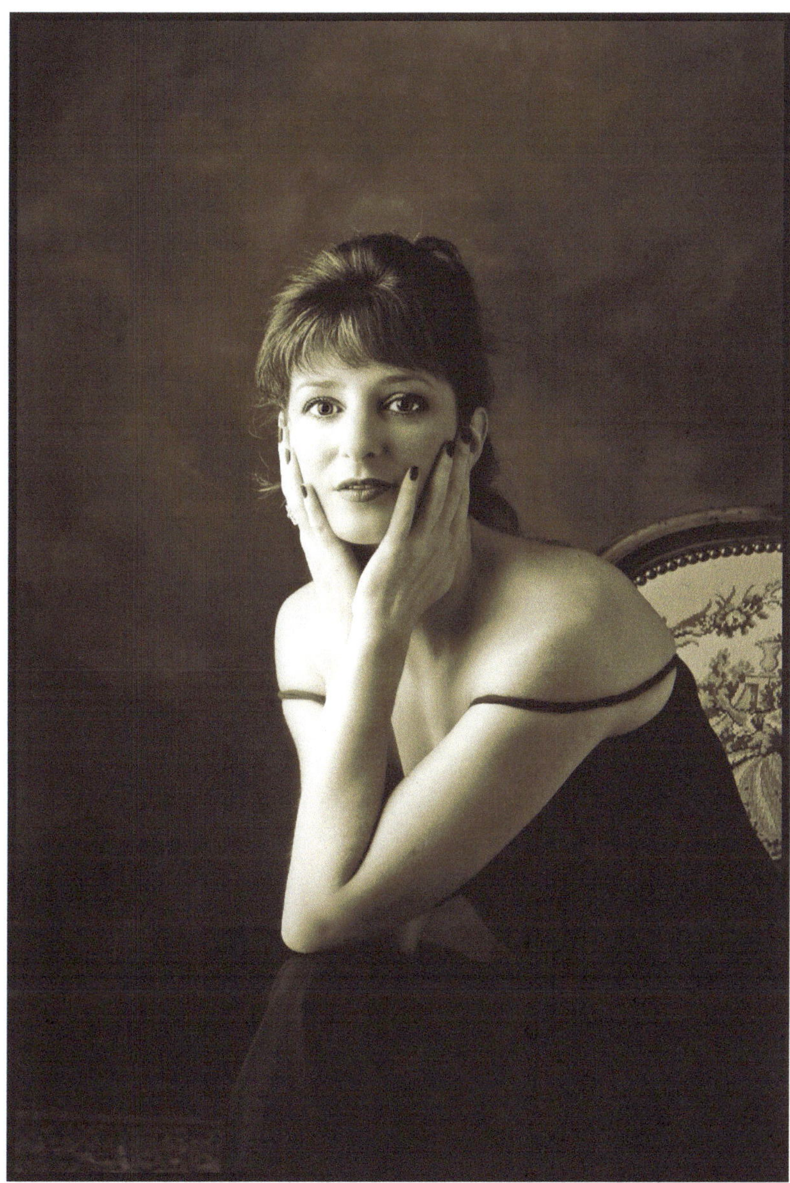

In Sync

I had photographed her sister's wedding, so she came in to ask if I could photograph her as a mature model. She lives in South Africa and wanted a large image and some smaller ones for her portfolio. Immediately there was a connection as I read her body language – to show her in a classic way, being a beautiful and mature woman. It is this feeling that I wanted to portray with expression and body, as well as darker brown tones. She looked at me and I spoke with her in a way so she would mirror my expression – that would match her eyes with her mouth, both in tune, and her hands added to the look.

Praise received:

Graham: "Very classical Klaus. Lighting, pose and treatment are gorgeous. I'm sure both photographer and model were very happy with this classy outcome. Well done."

Joseph: "This was so well thought out. From the classy black dress with the straps positioned around her upper arms to the fingernail polish. You have a great ability to enhance her natural beauty with tones and soft lighting that caresses her face. In this portrait the relationship between you and model is very close – you two were a team on the same page. I have noticed this quality (with other models) even though I have only recently discovered your work. You create very beautiful portraits."

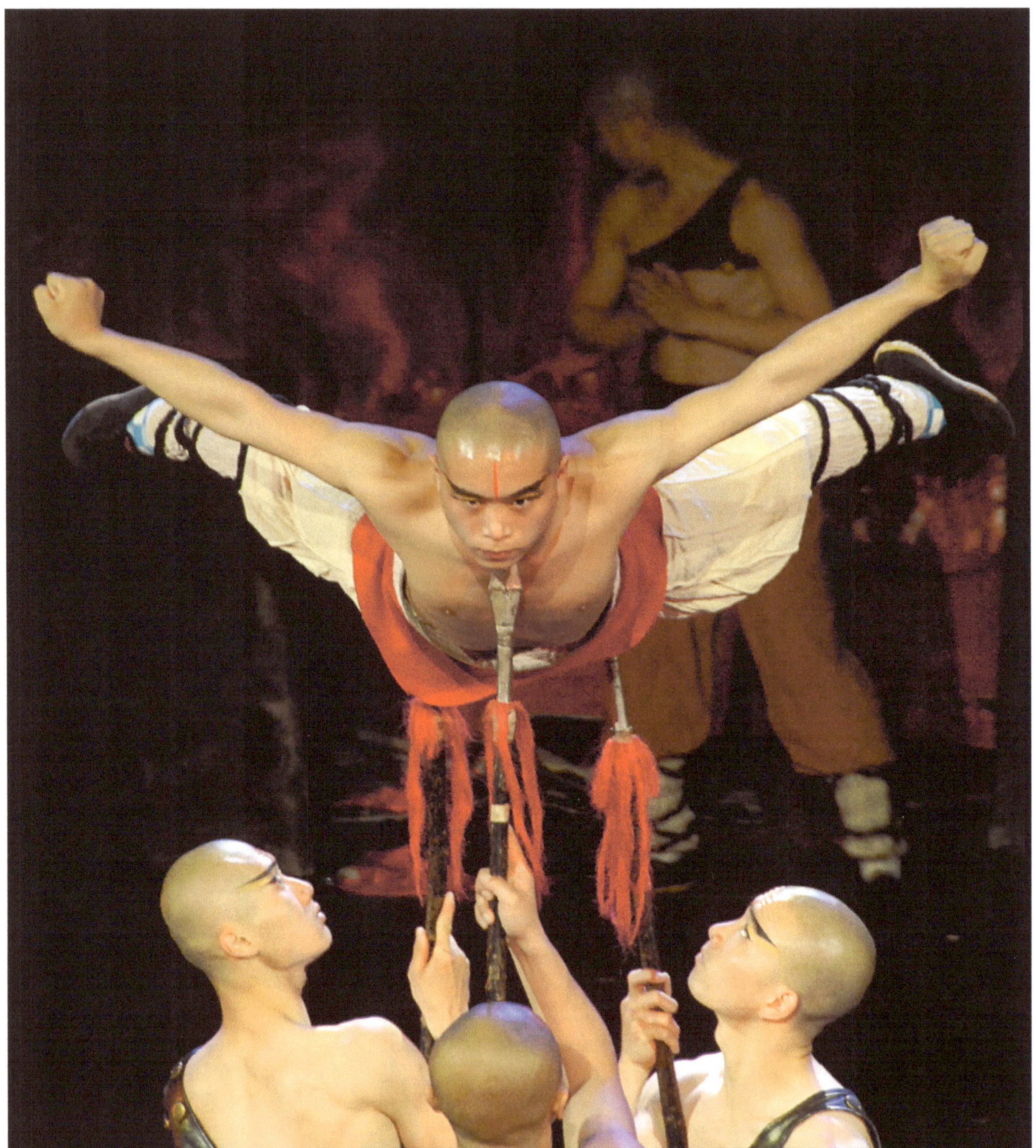

Karate Dancers

I was given the privilege to photograph this performance. The sign said no photos allowed, but I was given permission because I am a professional photographer. I guess they thought I would benefit when showing my work, and that at the same time it would promote their school of karate dancers and China.

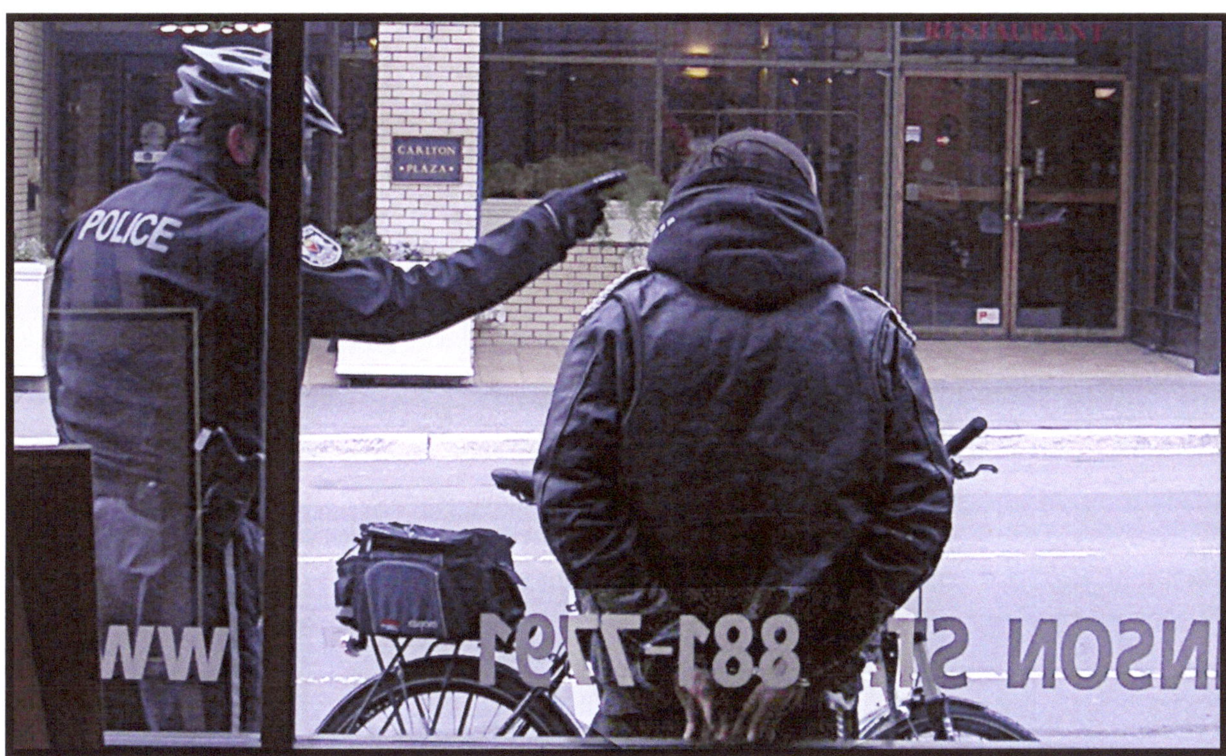

Last Shot

I enjoy taking candid photographs because it is the anticipation that thrills me. This was taken in my studio as I was packing up and moving to another location. As I was leaving, I saw this scene in my window. The man was handcuffed and the policeman was pointing his finger at him, like a gun. This was the last shot in my studio, and seemed so ironic that it was being played out at that moment in time – when I was leaving this place for the last time. I felt emotional because I was leaving, but I also felt emotions from both the policeman and the handcuffed man. I think these feelings entered into the photo from me, and I am sure from the two men as well.

Praise received:
Submitted and approved in the
Inspired Art Group on RedBubble.

Tori: "Great shot. Funny that this should happen
as you leave your studio for the last time."

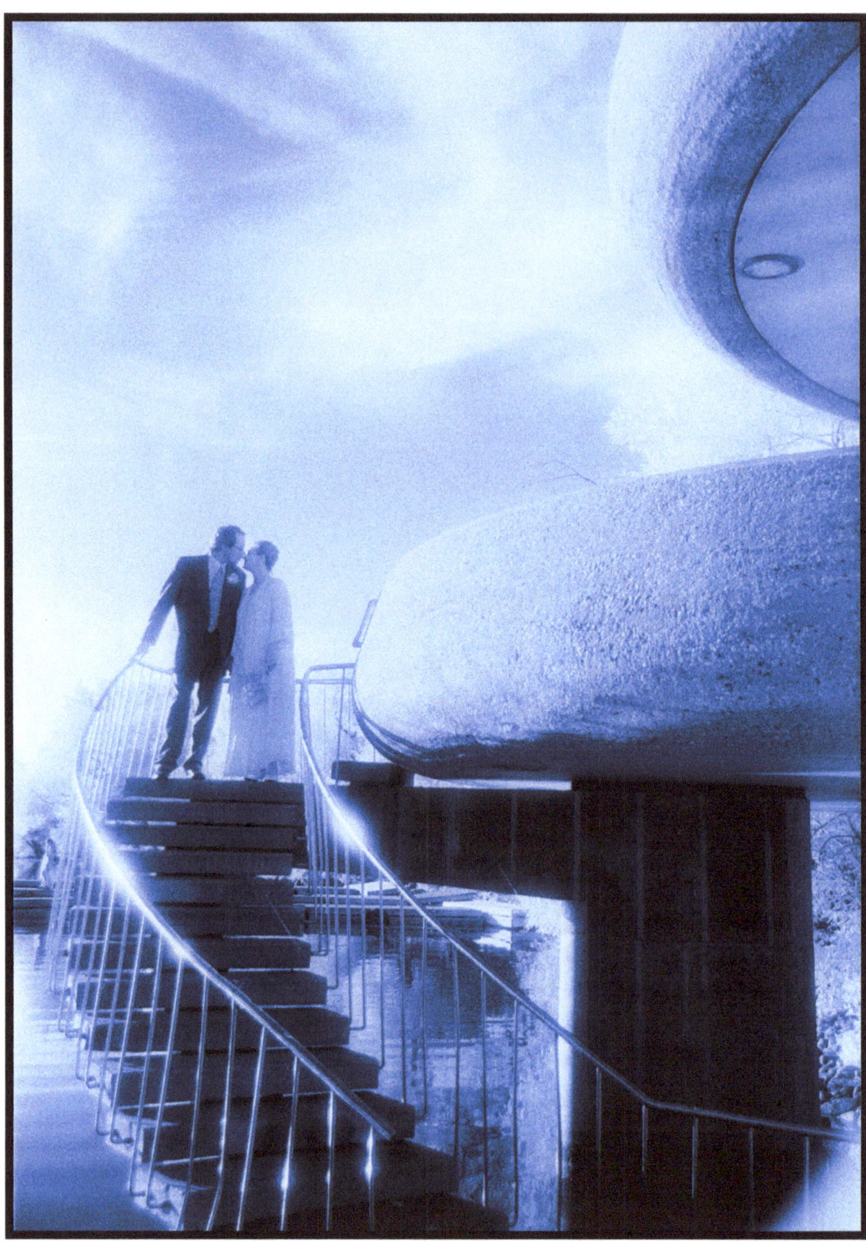

Love Has No Time Limit

I was asked by my good friend and photographer to do one part of his wedding. My part was to come up with an art image of their wedding that they could hang on their wall, and it ended up being the only one that is still hanging in their home. It was my great privilege to have this honour.

My desire was to create an image that was unique to me, and of course to the bride, groom and other photographers. Infrared film seemed to be new in our area at the time – no one had been photographing with infrared film for one reason: it is so sensitive to light. I found a design that expressed the feeling I wanted to convey. The texture and design of the structure with two shapes representing the couple. On the left was reality – the stairs of life – as they descend to live life as husband and wife, with both feet on the ground. There is a sense of make-believe that we feel with infrared film, the glow, the contrast, the texture, and yet a feeling of enlightenment and permanence. I'm glad that this lovely couple is still together after so many years.

Comment from groom: "Our wedding portrait still hangs proudly in our home. It's one of my favourite images!"

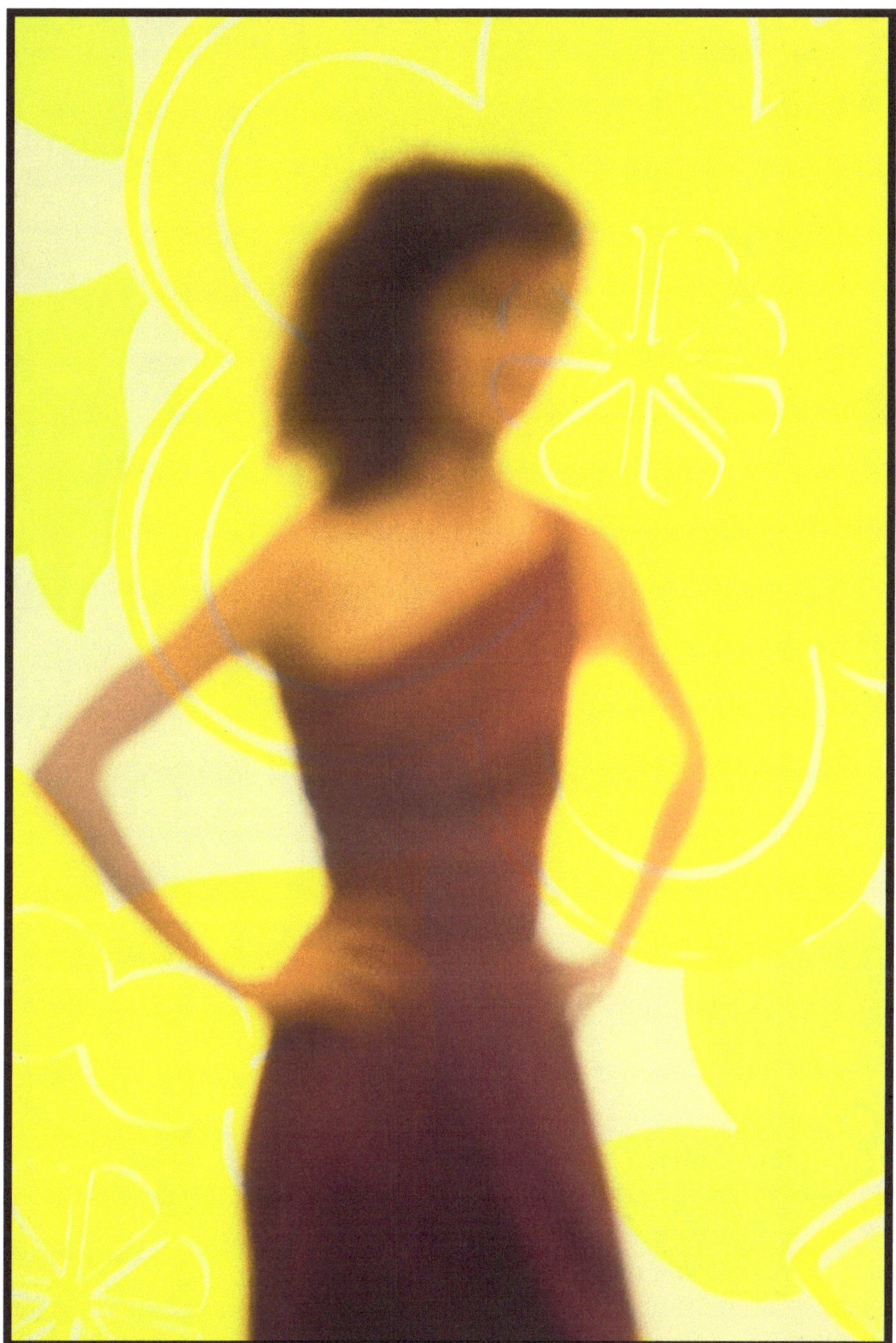

Make-Believe World

I first photographed the girl out of focus on slide film. I then photographed a shower curtain and sandwiched the two slides together… Make-Believe World. The influence came from Robin Peary who taught classes on putting slides together to create a new artistic look, long before Photoshop. I felt it was creative when I took the class, and it has influenced me in my work.

Praise received:

Peter: "This one is especially wondrous, the dual planes, the fancifulness, the eeriness-cum-cheeriness, the in-your-face colour palette along with the blurry restraint in the depiction of the woman. Fascinating."

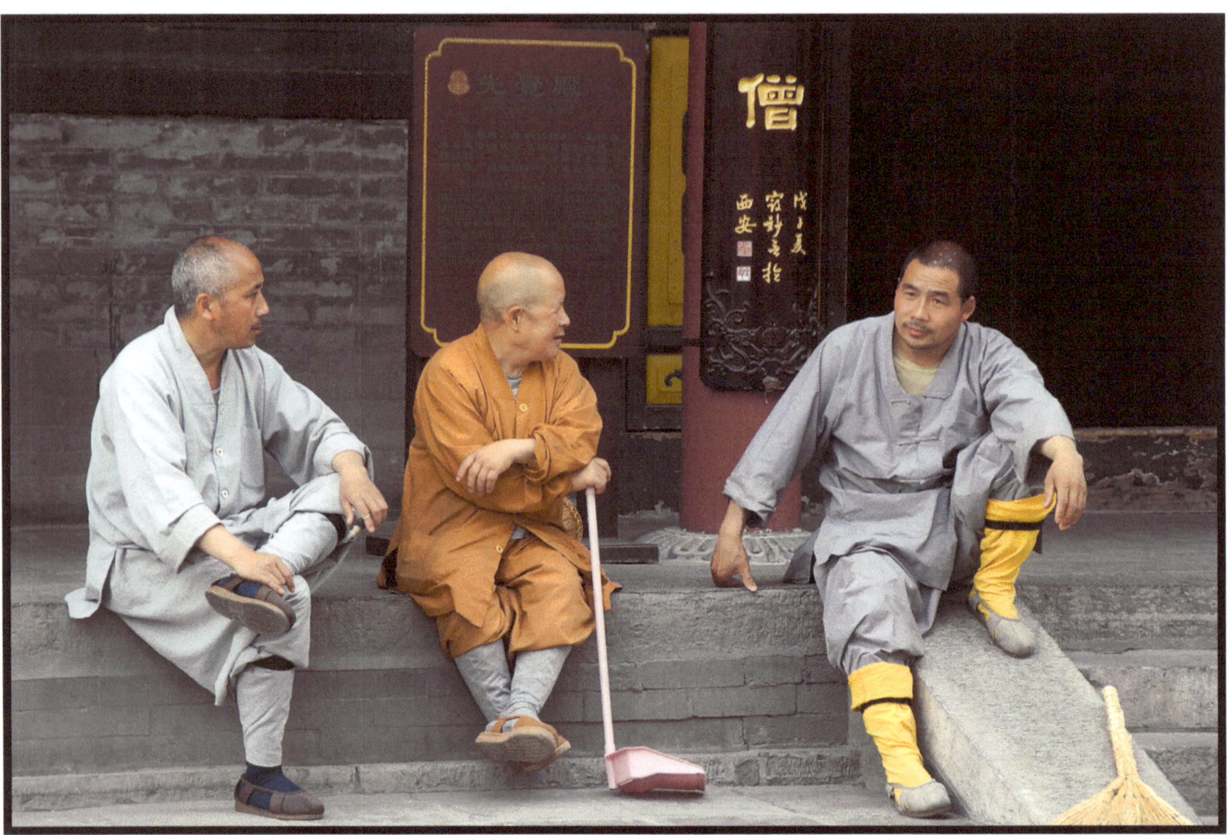

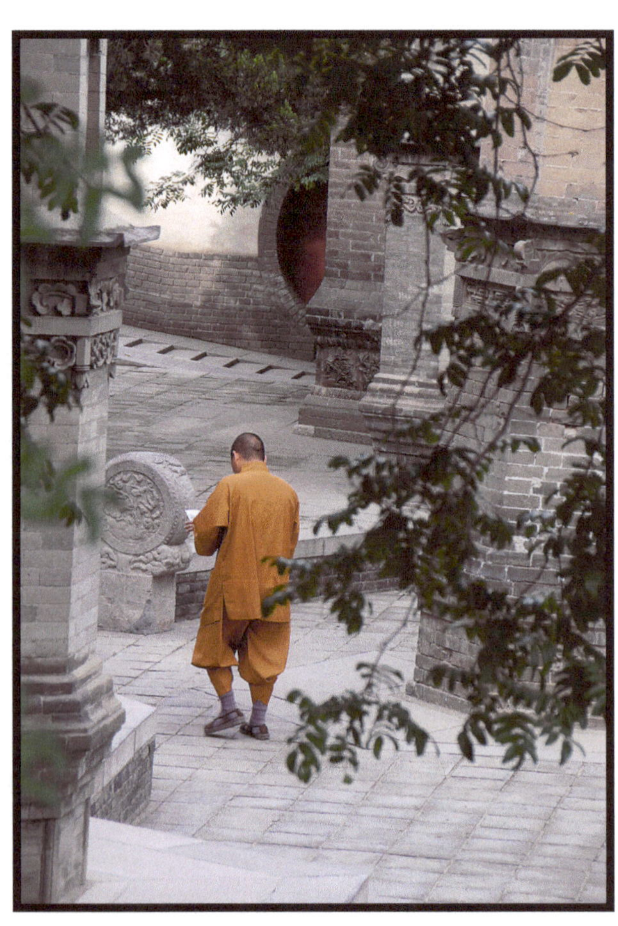

Monks in China

It was a thrill to be in the presence of the monks at their temple. It gave me quietness as I photographed a number of them in silence, never interrupting their meditations. I like the feeling I captured, so natural.

<u>*Praise received*</u>:
"This must have been a wonderful time for you. I long to do this... far from the gaze of people, you have captured a sense of solidarity. Beautiful."

Constance: "There is an ineffable sense of peace and tranquility that you have captured so well, bravo!"

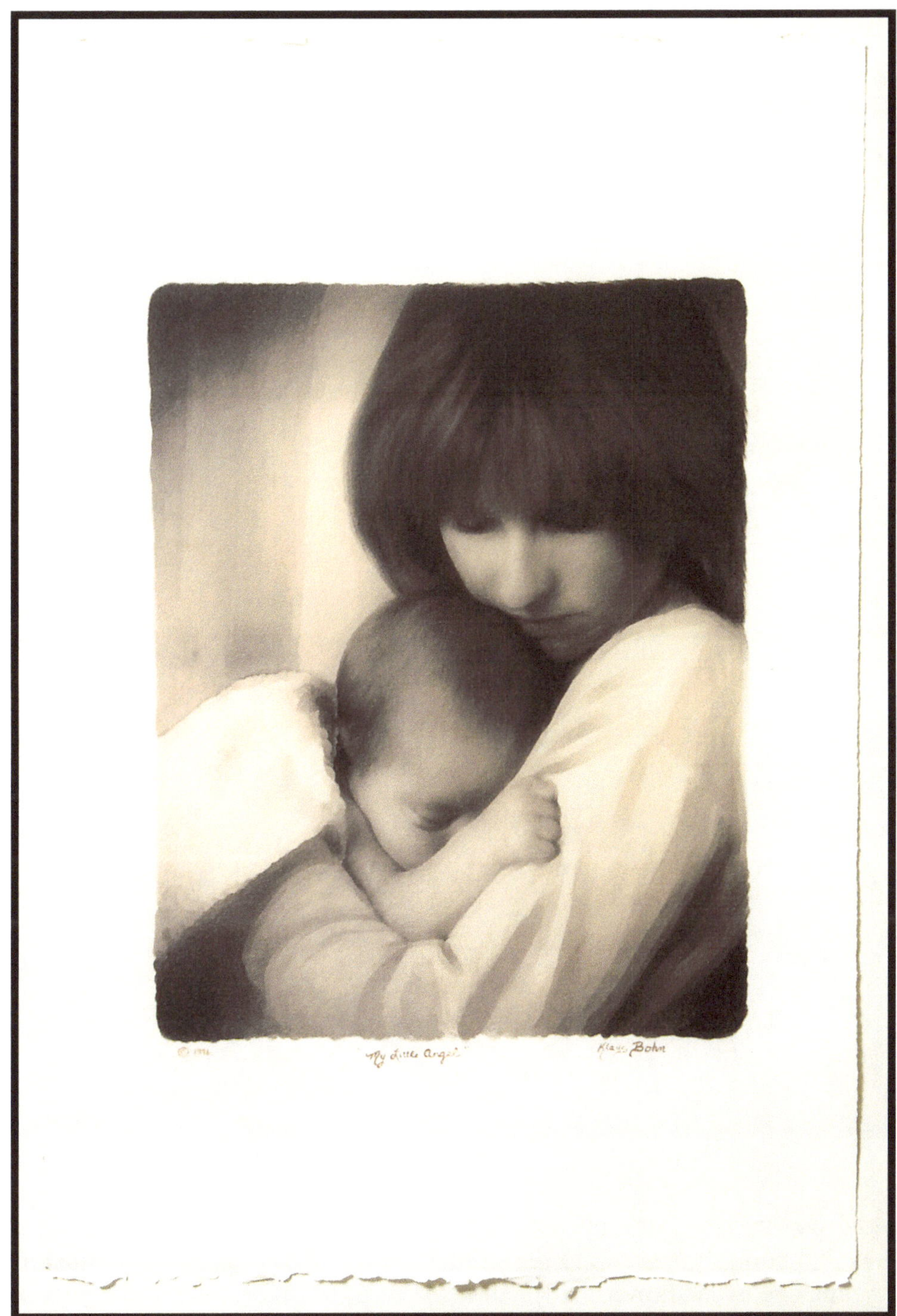

My Little Angel

When this new mother came in for her consultation she was already familiar with my procedure because I had photographed her once before. She shared a funny yet true story with me. Being a nurse in Los Angeles her friends and co-workers asked, “Why are you going to Canada? For a vacation?” “No,” she said, “I’m going to see my photographer.” Stunned, they asked, “Why go all the way to Canada?” She replied, “Wait until you see the art piece, you will be green with envy.” I don’t know if it was so but I do know that both of us cherished the feeling of love we got from looking at the finished piece.

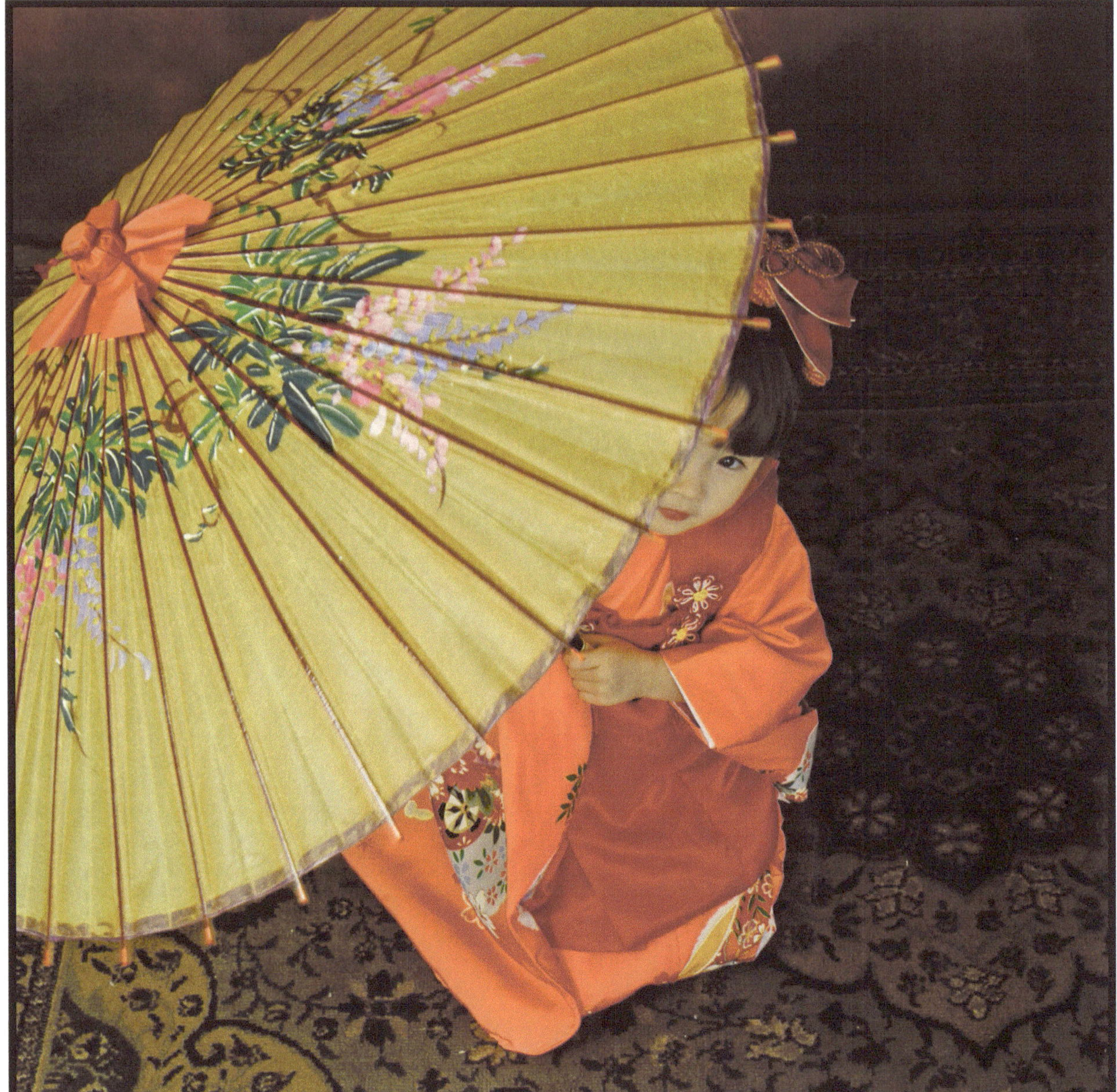

Peek

This little girl was so shy that I needed to play with her as she hid behind the umbrella. I coaxed her with a book she wanted to see. Little by little she peeked around the umbrella and after a long time she even showed her face. Peek was my favorite look – it tells the story of our experience together – the feeling is so real. I did some Photoshop work on this image.

Praise received:

Kathy: "Wow Klaus, this is a really superb photo. Her shyness is apparent but I also see a bit of curiosity in her expression too. Really wonderful. So glad you could share this work with us. Well done."

Rick & Deb: "Oh, this is so sweet… an image that tells a story without words. Simply a precious portrait capture."

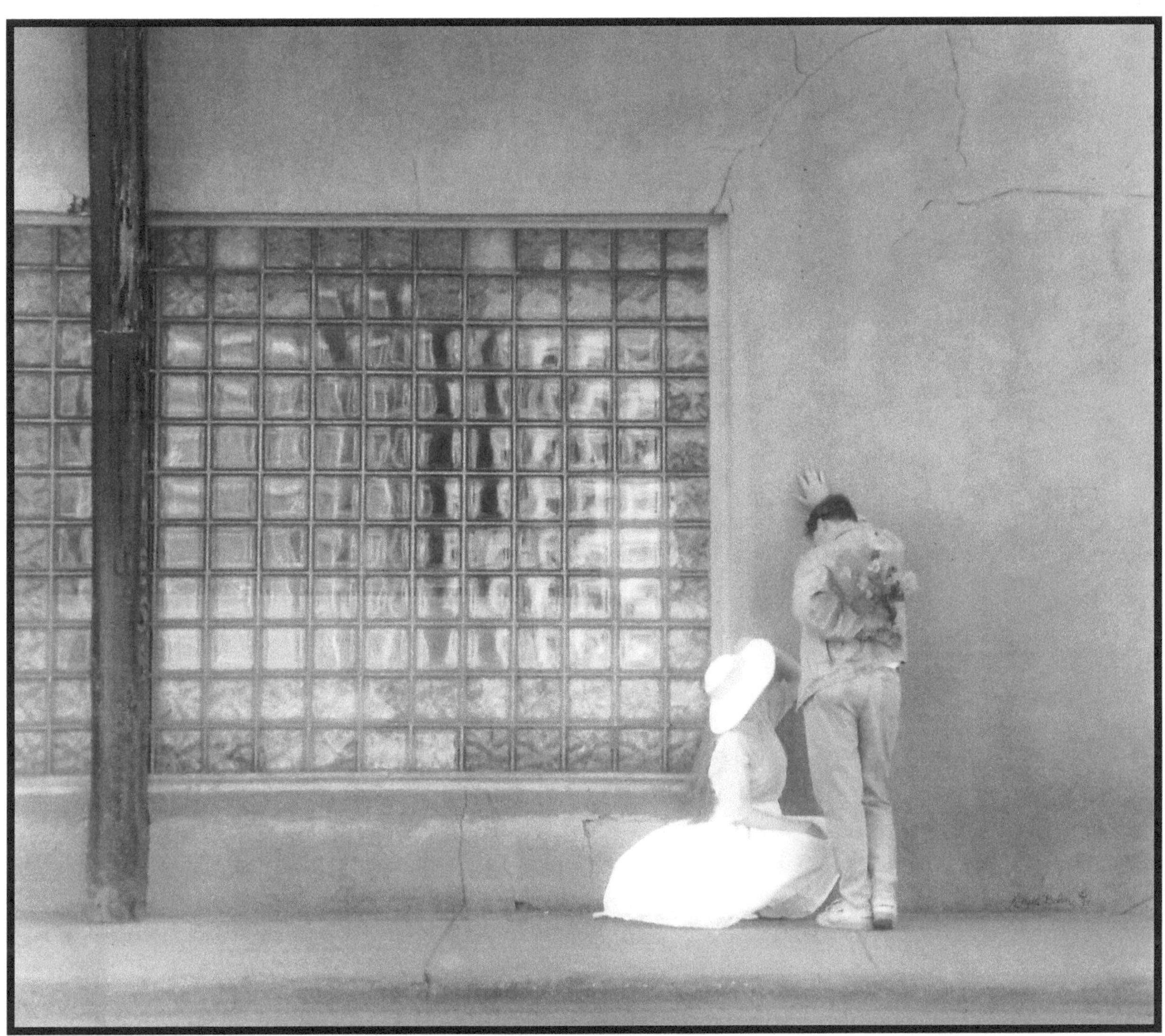

Private Time

One year after their wedding, I was asked to photograph them in a most unique way. This was made in the 1980's, the first time I photographed people and didn't show their faces – a milestone for me. I was asked to make a photograph of my choice and print and frame it so they could, sight unseen, unveil the image at their anniversary party. I was nervous, thinking the family may not be too excited about my choices. I was right about the family, but the couple were very happy – and we are still friends to this day.

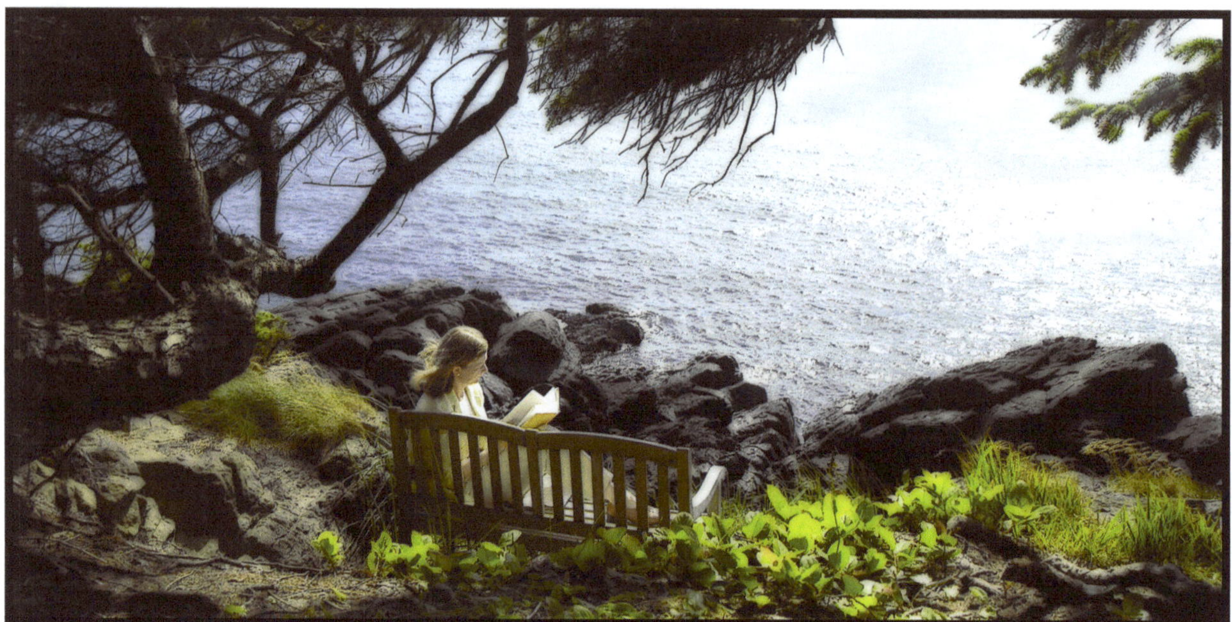

Reader

I had the privilege to photograph her on a very special birthday. The subject felt shy about close-up photographs, so I asked her what she liked to do and her response was 'read'. "Where do you enjoy reading?" I asked. Her favourite place can be seen in the photo. When I went to their oceanfront home about one hour outside of Victoria, it was indeed a perfect place to live and enjoy the breeze and soothing sounds from the ocean, with some protection afforded by the nearby trees. I was so thrilled to have had this wonderful experience. She was pleased with the final image and purchased a giclee for their wall. I love the feeling and the story it told.

<u>Praise received</u>:

"I love this, Klaus, such a beautiful work. It reminds me of my favourite place and a cherished personal shot. I love the way you worked with her to overcome the shyness and produce this work that really tells us so much about her spirit. It is sweet and tells a whole story without even knowing her name."

Constance: "Your photographs are wonderful, Klaus, but what makes them exceptional is that they tell a story. This is really beautiful, it tells a story of time that should be enjoyed."

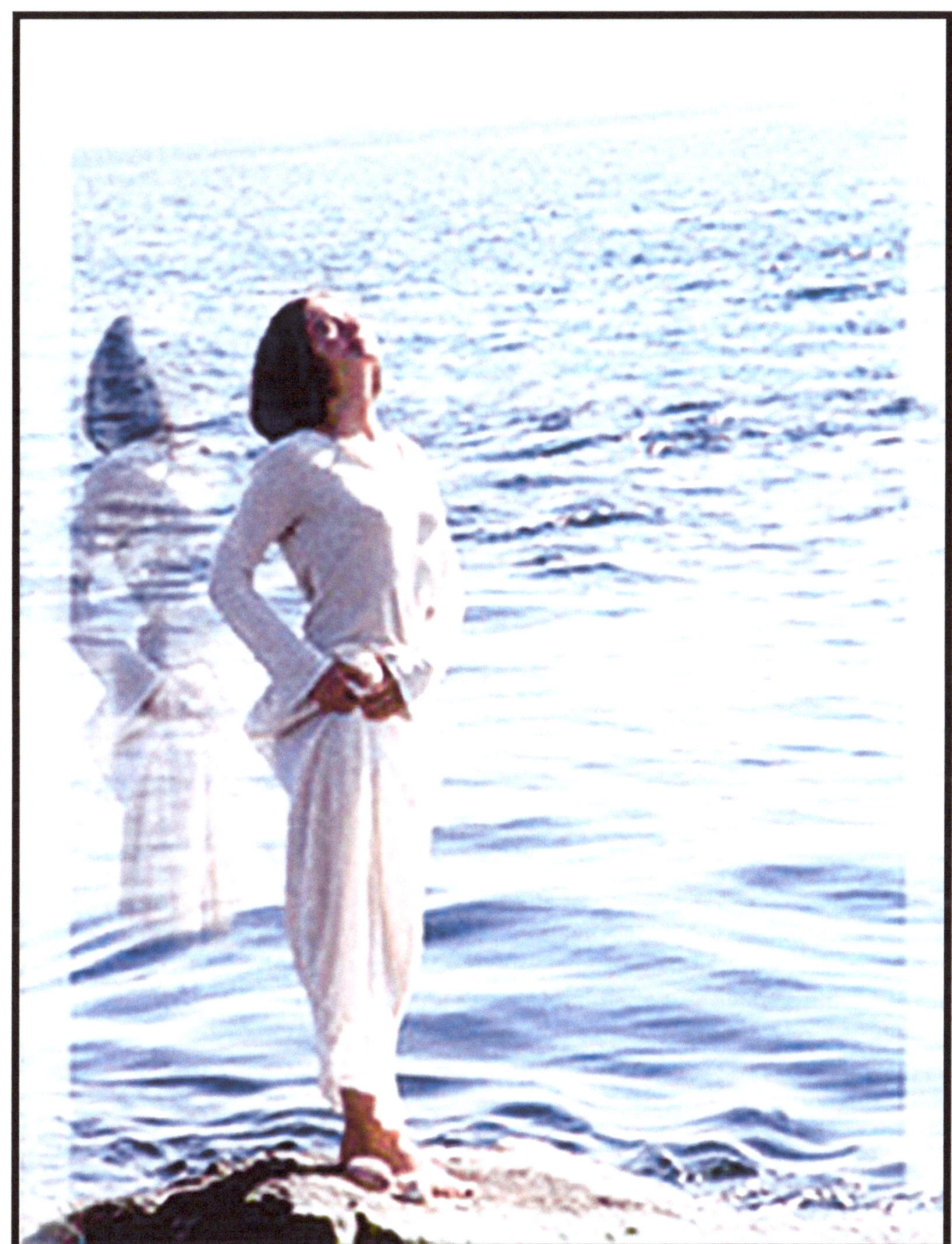

Reflections

When given the task to photograph an art piece of this woman to hang on her wall – I took it as a challenge. She's an artist and she worked in an art gallery – experiencing so many art pieces with an eye for unique art. As we spoke, I could see reflections in her personality as a young person so driven with the desire of what she may become – her lifelong dream. The finish is fantasia, maybe even a little unearthly. I studied David Hamilton and liked his work for its simplicity and imagination beyond reality. Not that my work measures up or I compare my work to his, just that he had an influence even in this piece!

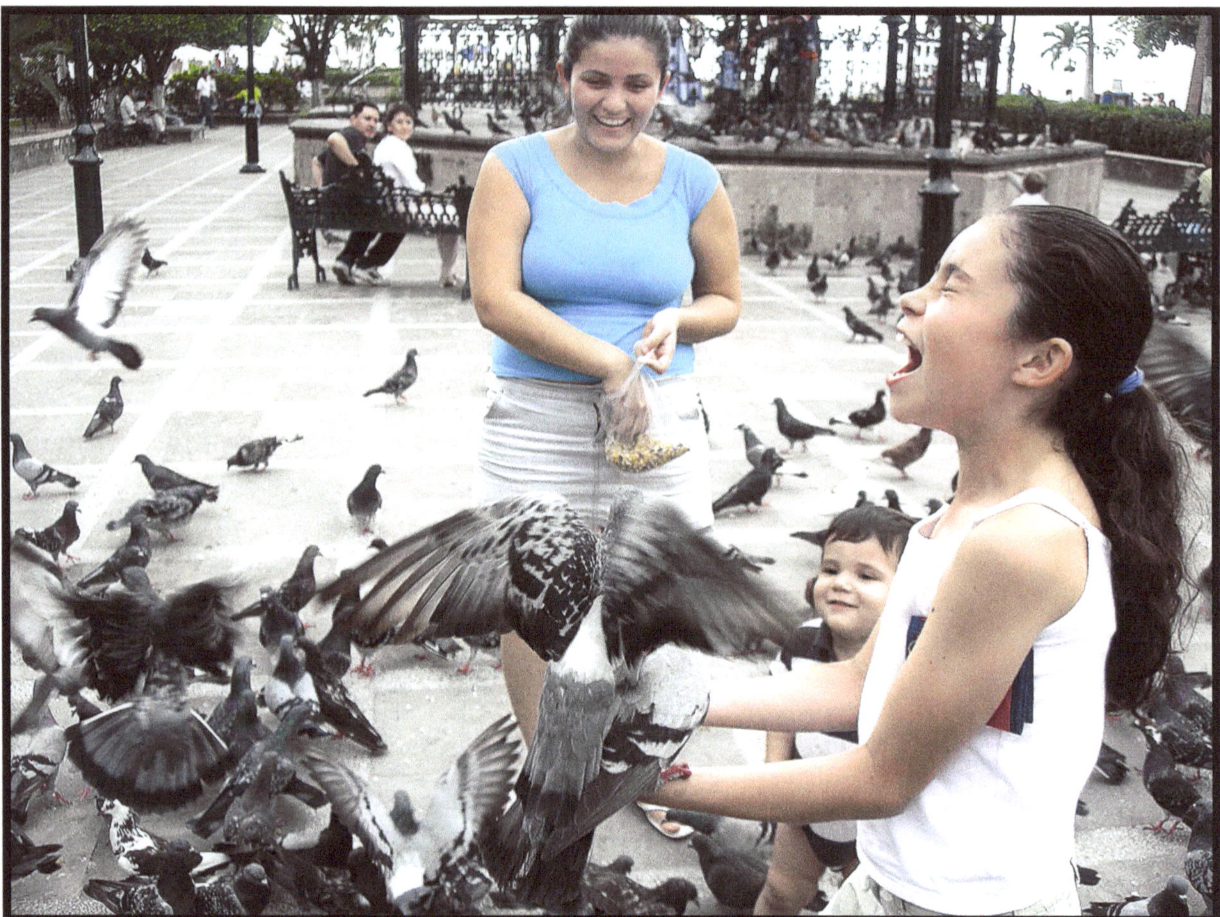

Scream

Scream was taken in Mexico while on a holiday trip. I saw this mother and daughter feeding the pigeons. I ran towards them as I knew the pigeons would get scared and fly – as you can see in this photo. My feeling was to add drama and action to the scene. Take a look at not only the daughter and mother, but also the son. Look past them and see the people looking in the background – what impact. I love doing candid photography and the feeling one gets from the timing and impact even a still photo can give.

Praise received:

"Alfred Hitchcock's 'The Birds' springs to mind here! Great capture, so natural and vibrant, well done. It's awesome!"

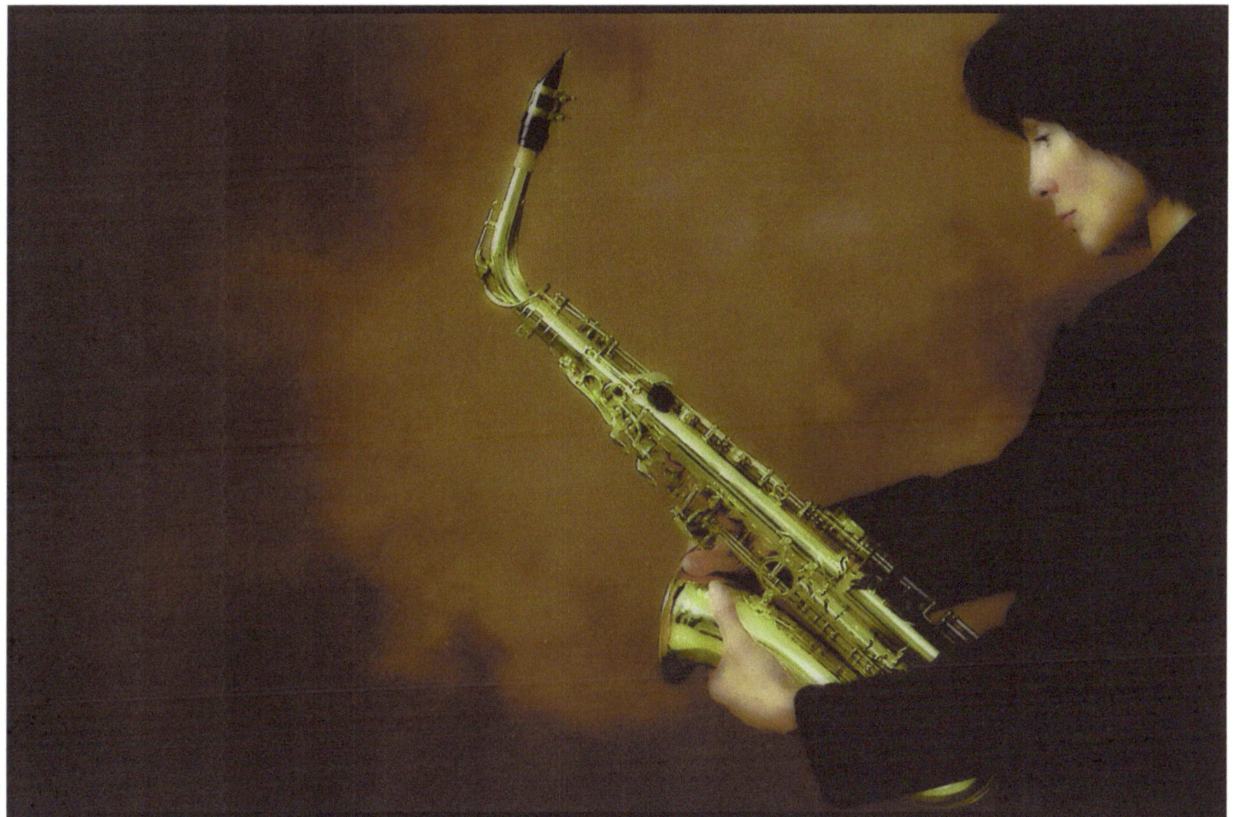

Space

If space is infinite, why are we as photographers so shy in expressing it? Do we have to play the instrument in order to hear the music? Many such questions are on the tip of our tongues but never asked.

Let us explore space for a moment. Why do we feel the need to crowd every image, make the viewer feel claustrophobic and unrealistically squish the subject into a tight space out of proportion? Can we value an image that is too small? We can house small photos easier and then they become record keepers which is valuable in that sense so as to recall the event.

To produce an art piece we need to explore the space we have to work with, the size of the paper, canvas, wood, etc. and the subject matter. All these things must be taken into consideration as well as the artists' own impression and that which they want to leave behind.

Sound is something we can hear through our ears or just feel the music and hear it in our mind. There is also the sound of silence. Just seeing an instrument can change our mood and affect our heart in a musical way that need not be heard by the outer ear. Most of us have heard the philosophical argument: if a tree falls in a forest and there is no one to hear it, does the falling tree make a sound? I'm not trying to bend our minds but to simply accept other outcomes or be open to different approaches to each and every subject.

In the image of the woman and the saxophone, she has been given much space in front to lead the viewer into the photograph. Take time to gently observe the statement. Here is a person with an instrument, holding it carefully, clutching it almost as if she was a novice, not playing, not yet but she is in deep thought, mesmerized by the possibility of playing. It's like the camera is panning towards her and has not yet fully discovered the musician. She isn't fully occupying the space that exists which allows our imagination to fill in what is missing: the rest of her body, her playing the sax, the music and the sound are all left to our imagination, the infinite scenarios. May our photographs reach this stage of wonderment, of art.

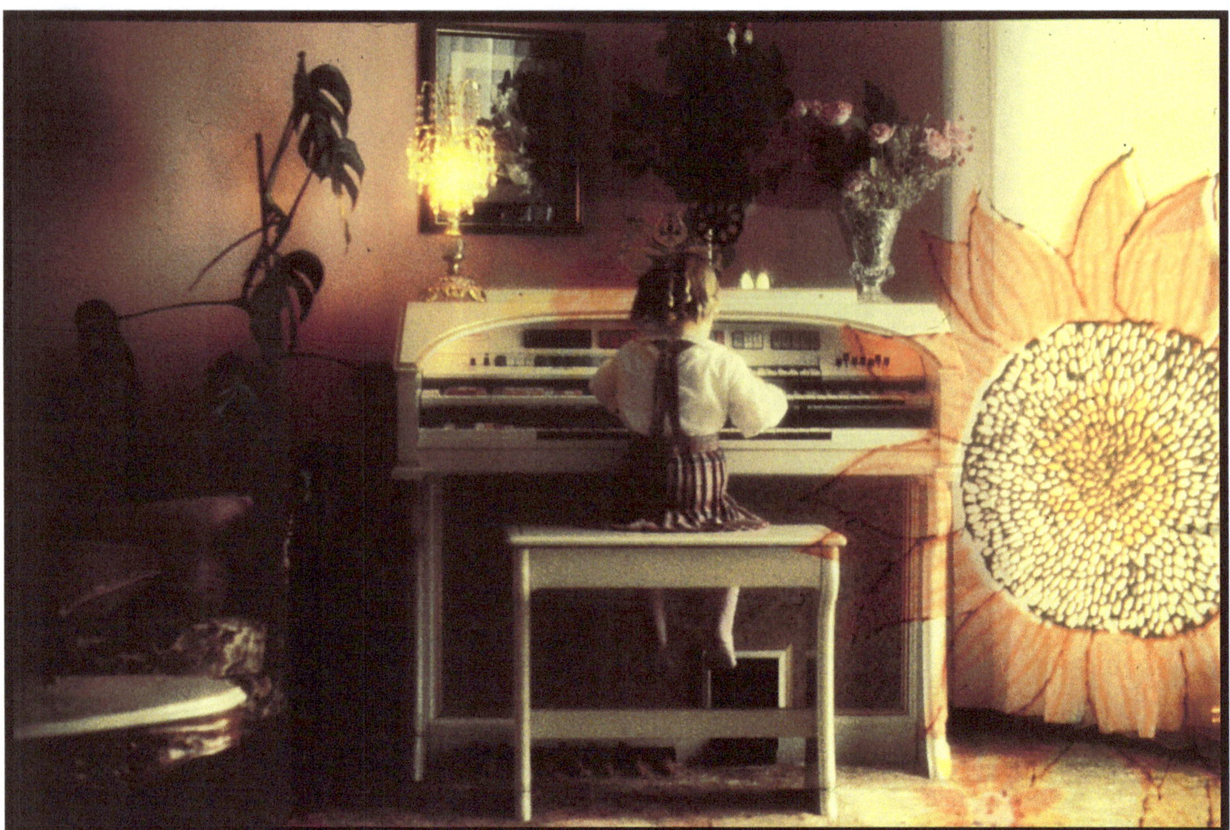

Tammy-Organ-Flower

This seemed to speak of a little girl's imagination and wishful thinking; trying to learn to play the organ on her own with colours of design by her imagination. The flower speaks to her wanting to go out and play in the bright sunshine – a sunflower reflecting her heart and wishes. The texture and colours happened by using two slides sandwiched together – long before Photoshop.

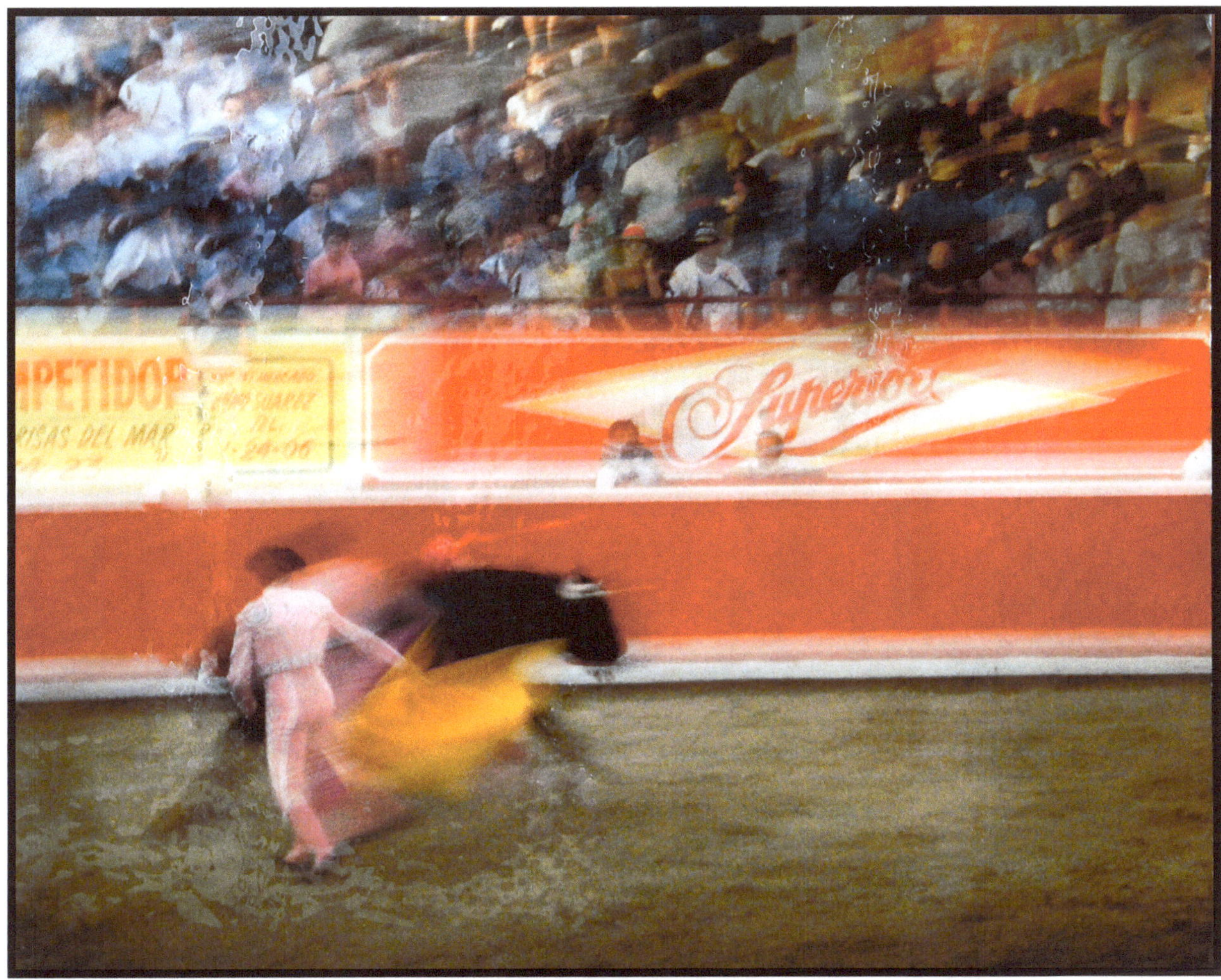

The Bull Fight

I had the opportunity to watch a bull fight in Mexico. A number of Canadians were there with me, but most left halfway through. I wanted a photograph that showed how I felt – the art of bull fighting. To me it was not something I condoned or condemned, since each country has its own sport. In Canada we love hockey but it has become so rough, and many players have been injured for life – how am I to judge a sport. If I don't like it I won't promote it. I am not promoting the sport of bull fighting but love the image I was able to capture, the feeling of movement and artistry in the making of this image.

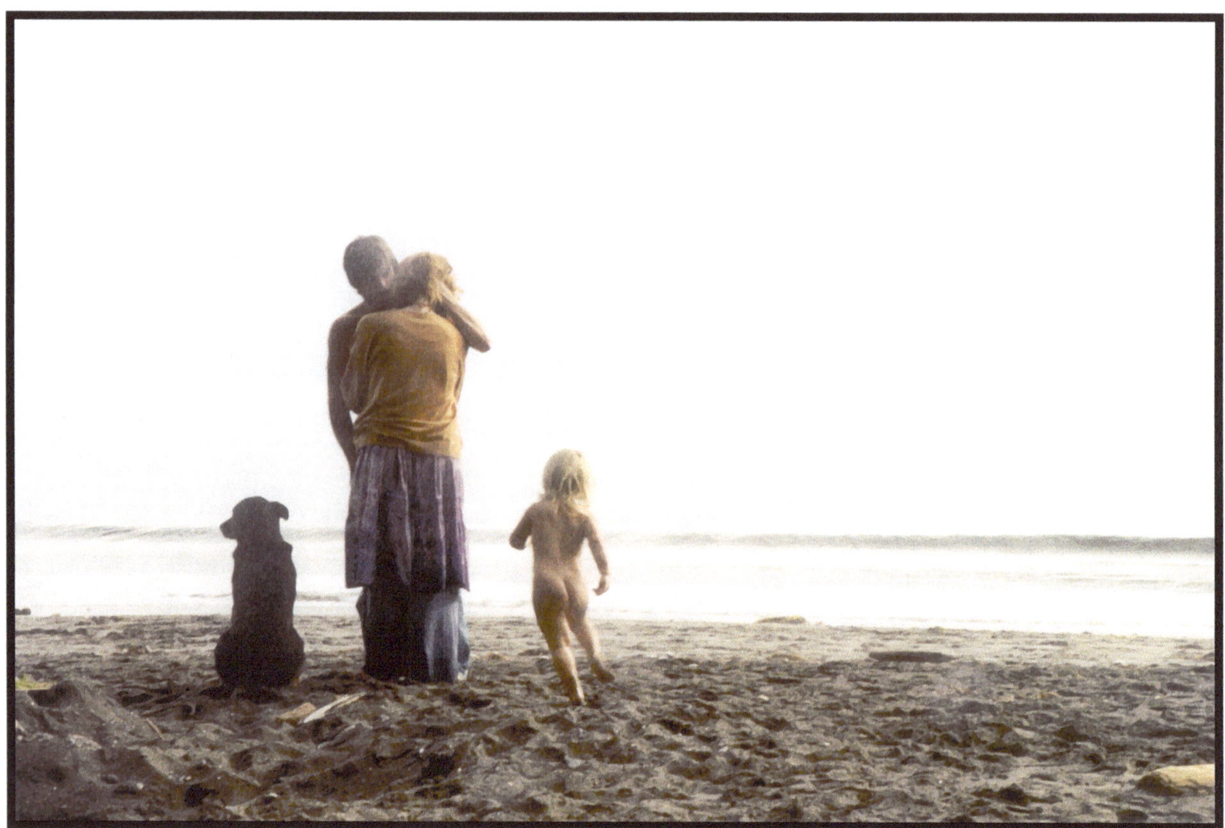

The Decisive Moment

I believe Henri Cartier-Bresson coined this phrase. When I encountered this difficult situation I knew I had only one shot, maybe two. This family by the ocean was a challenge to create, an image that was most spontaneous. They were a hippie family as you can see. I watched with anticipation but provided very little coaching. Then the couple hug and the dog walked up, sat and looked off into the distance. I was waiting for the right moment as the little girl, their daughter who didn't like to wear clothes, ran into the composition – one chance, my decisive moment. In my portraits I always want to include feelings and relationships that are beyond the norm, but at the same time real.

Praise received:
"Lovely, a child's innocence, a faithful dog and two people on a beach affectionately sharing… terrific."

"A wonderfully heartfelt and evocative portrait. You've captured the love and joy of 'family' so incredibly well with this shot. Beautifully done!"

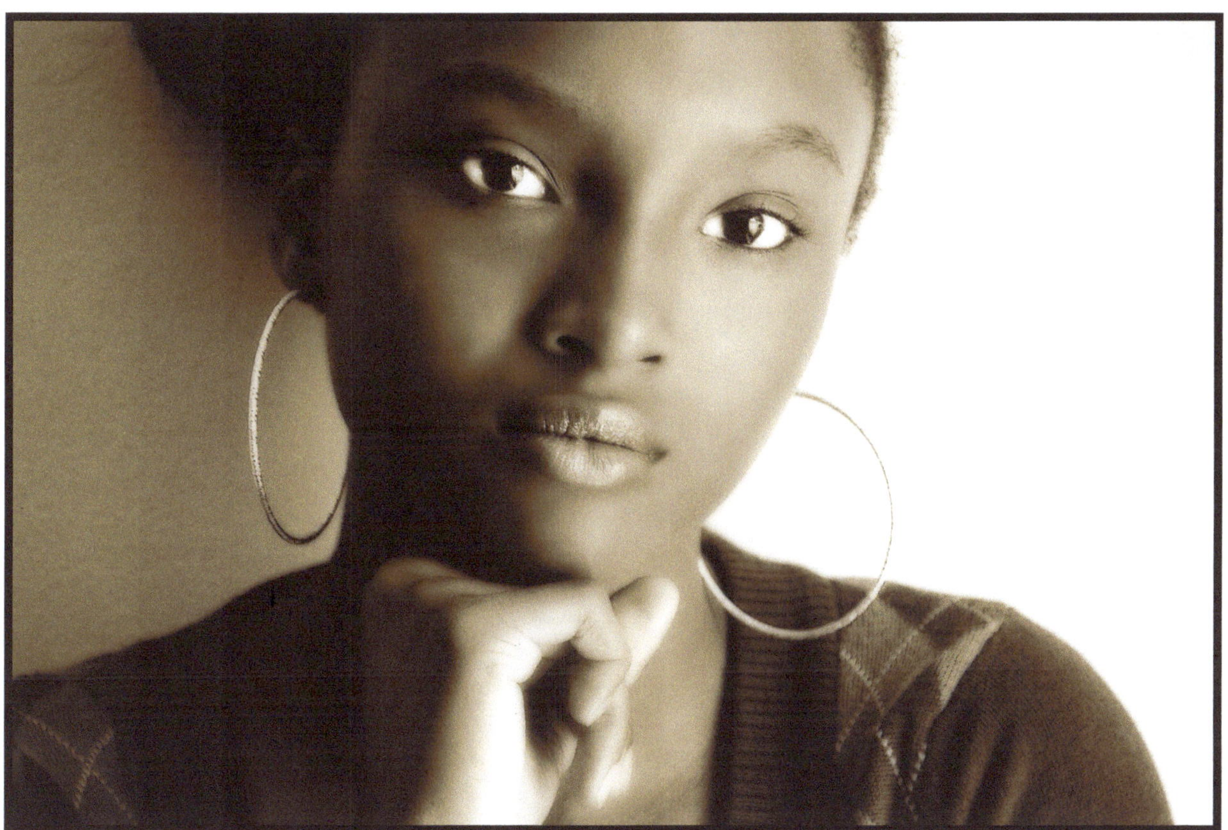

The Model

Star is an up-and-coming model from Toronto, Ontario, Canada. I had the privilege to photograph her, and she showed a natural response to me. It was a delight to work with her. I used window light only – not even a reflector in this shot. The photographs were in colour and I changed them to black and white and then to darker brown – which is my favourite. I felt a connection and it shows in her images. I wanted to express what touched me, the mood and spirit in her, as I photographed. An expression that we could read into – not a big smile that I feel has been over done with models, but instead a hidden reality. I used a digital camera, no filter. I used Photoshop to do the rest.

Praise received:

"There was only one moment in history that you could capture that look, that skin tone and those bright eyes... it's so beautiful in every way. It really is a moment captured in time! Masterful, by both you and the model!"

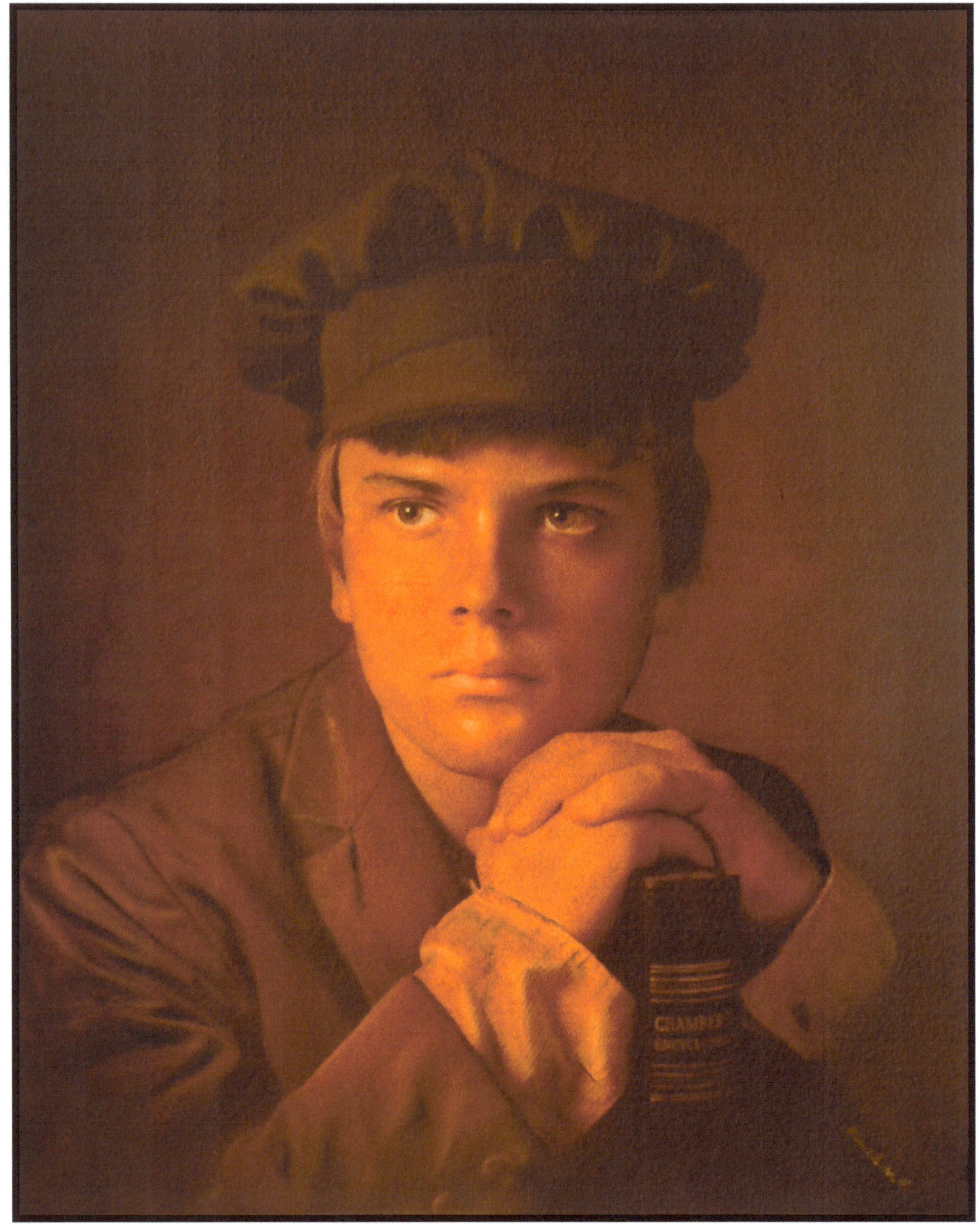

The Young Immigrant

This boy was in a school play and he was featured as the young immigrant... long before photography was invented. As a result I endeavoured to make the image feel like a simple painting. Paint was added to the image, smearing it a little to give a feeling of thought, as an old image from the past – burnt umber was in fashion with artists of that time. Smiling would have been unheard of and his intense look is in keeping with what he was going through and portraying in this well known play.

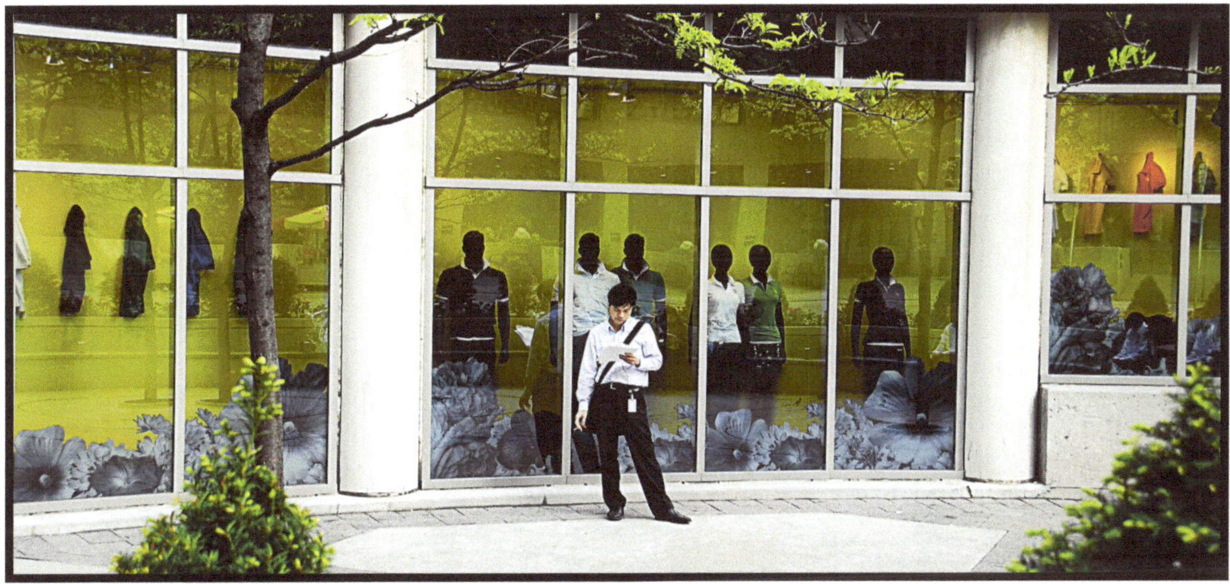

Waiting

Not wasting time while waiting – he's reading and smoking. Ambidextrous too! The dummies behind him just wait and can't do anything because they are not alive – an illusion of reality. Life is a moment at a time. Not to waste one precious moment… I try to live by this motto.

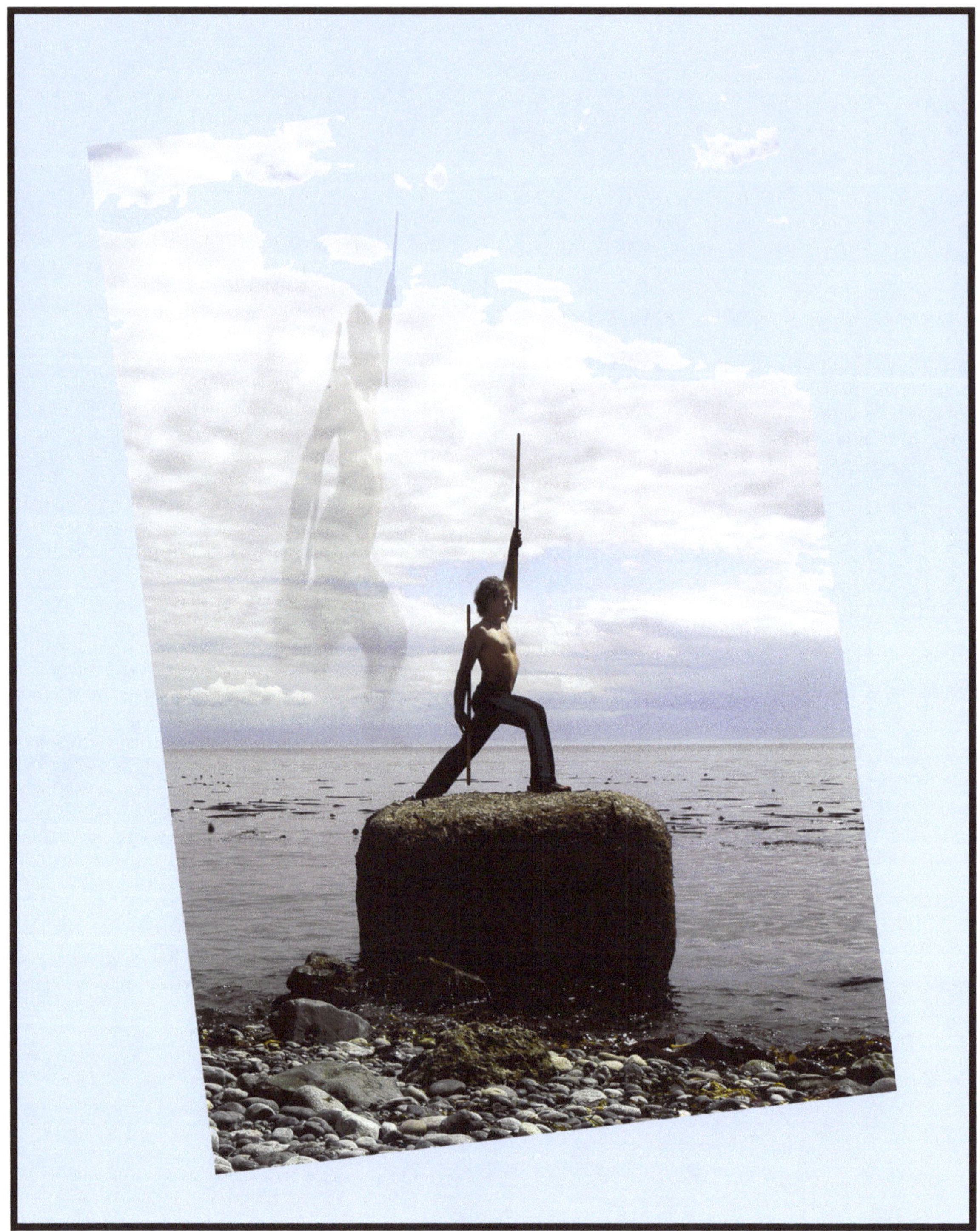

Warrior

I had the privilege to photograph this man, and later he became my instructor. The art of working out and self defence have their origins in the east, and now have great positive influences on us in the west.

<u>Praise received</u>:
"I love the way your photo depicts his warrior spirit and the way you did the image in the clouds as well."

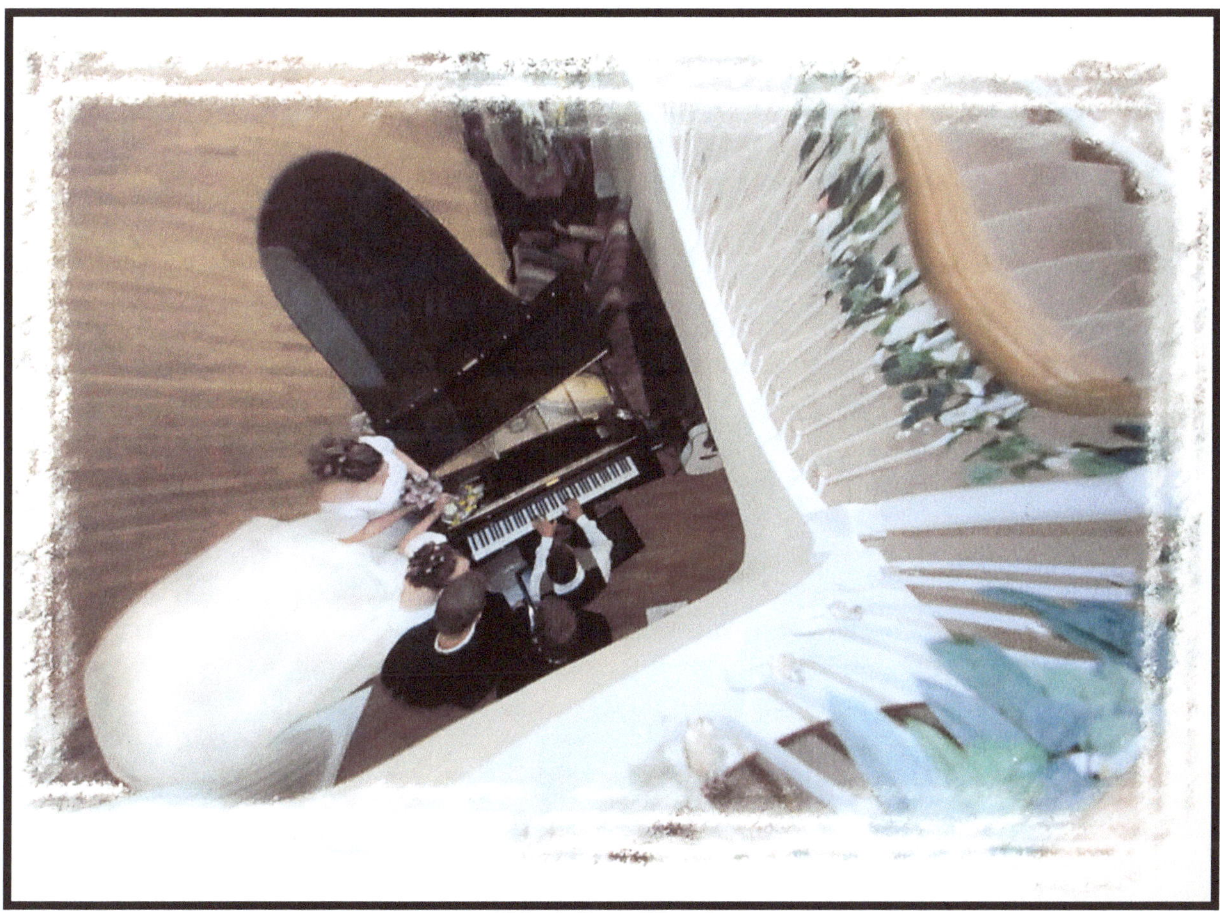

Wedding Music

Wedding Music came about when I was hired to photograph a wedding in Calgary, Alberta. During our consultation the bride asked, “Please make an art piece that I can hang on our wall forever.” Then she said, “For the wedding album, just the normal photos would be fine.” I always feel as though I need to come up with something worthwhile, beyond the normal. I saw the piano and the staircase, all pretty normal. When I asked them to gather around the piano the group wanted to look up, so I told the pianist to play a song that they could sing. That enabled me to keep them looking down at the piano, and then photographed the image. I added a twist to the banister so it looked more artistic, and because the group was singing it gave me the feeling I was trying to create. Some Photoshop work was also added. The image was printed using the giclee method and the printed edges, what I sometimes refer to as sloppy edges, were introduced as well. The couple was very pleased with the finished image and provided a lot of word-of-mouth publicity for my work by sharing the image with friends and family.

Praise received:
"I love this. What a unique and unexpected perspective from you, Klaus."

Photography as Art

To understand photography we must realize that it is in its infancy when compared to painting and other arts. Its beginning was in the early part of the 1800's and took off quickly in the middle and later 1800's. So relatively speaking, we can see photography is still in its early stages.

The growing pains are still being felt. With the development of technology racing ahead of most arts, it has been difficult to mature and survive on its own merits. Photography is a stand alone cousin to the other works of art, especially those that have the capital A, Art. Today we in photography have grown in leaps and bounds; not only because of technology but also since it has given the artistic photographer the privilege to explore more than camera operations.

Now with giclees and the possibility to paint on watercolour paper or canvas, we have the opportunity to make each and every image unique in its own right. When paintings were copied and turned into numbered editions it took on a photographic ability and is now mass produced, whereas photography has now taken on an 'Art of One'. Each piece can be hand embellished to give the image originality which was lacking before in spite of the darkroom manipulations. May our appreciation for the art of photography grow in our mind's eye and touch our heart by *feeling more deeply about photography*, as my brand can reveal.

Structures

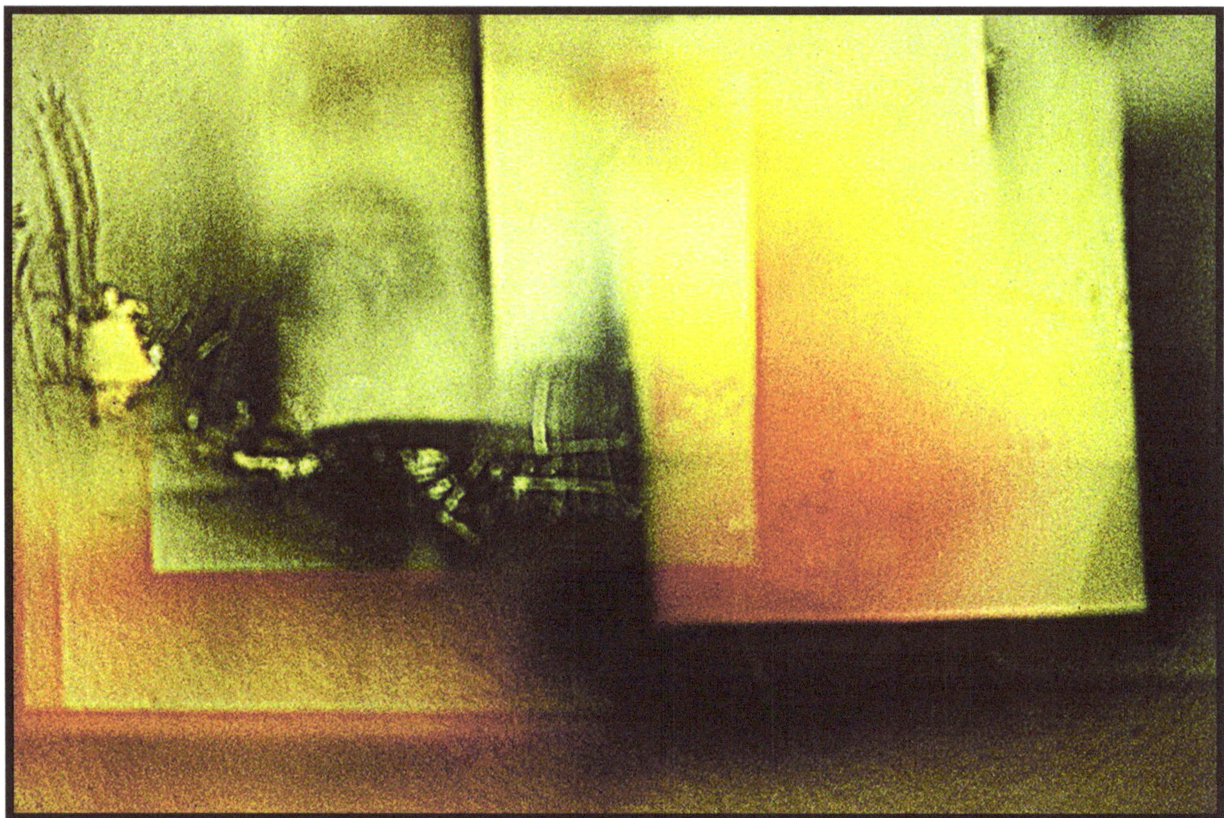

Abstract Painting

Viewing this image I recall where I found the design – in my spray booth. For those who don't know what that is, most studios had a paint spray booth to spray their images. Retouch spray to retouch the image by hand, more or less what we now accomplish with our computer, or spray a lacquer to protect the photograph from ultraviolet rays and from damage such as water or dust. What caught my eye was the colour and design, accidental perhaps, but art and design is where you find it or creativity happens. I will not try to explain this piece; just enjoy the composition as it is.

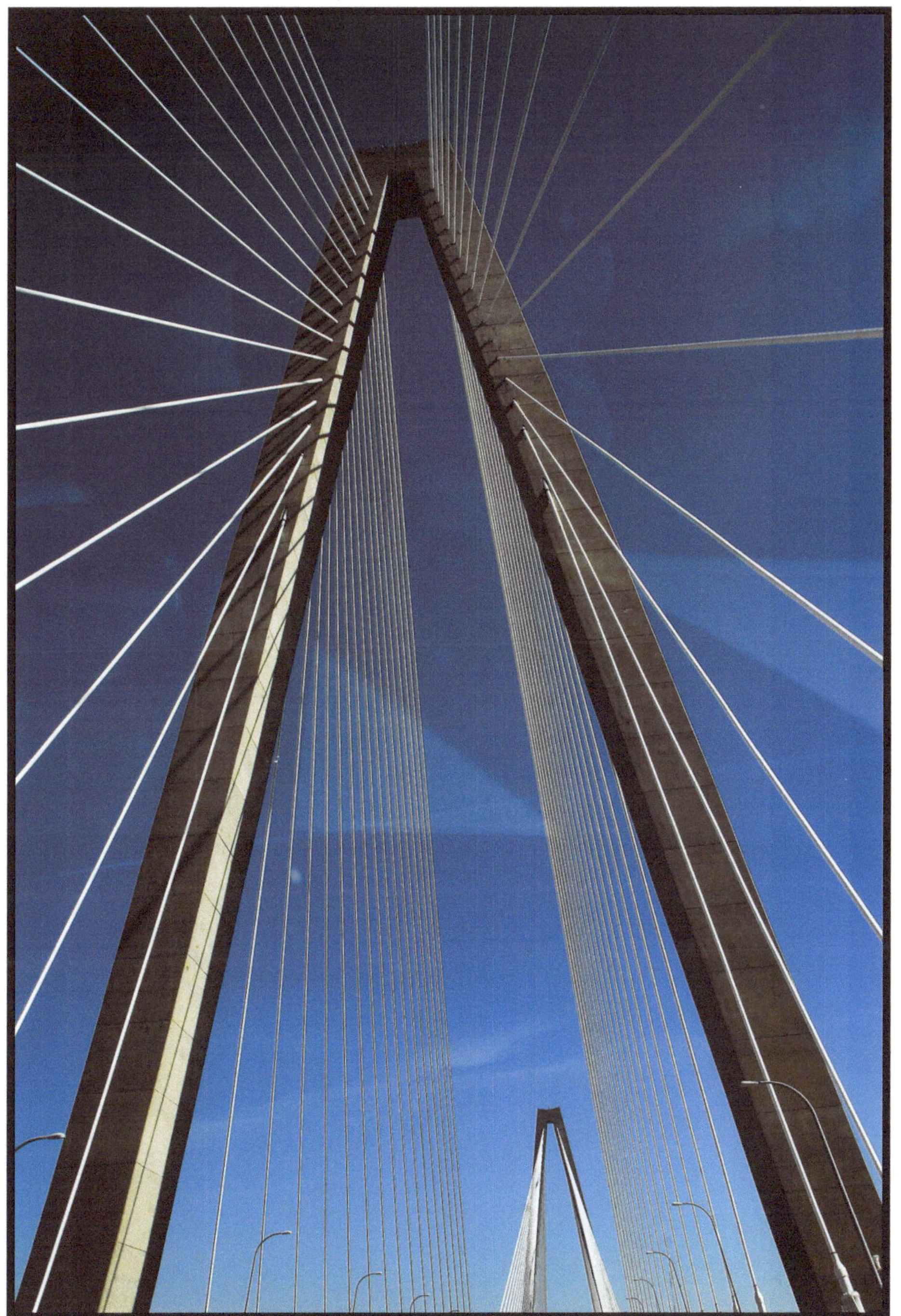

Ashley River Bridge

A visit to South Carolina enabled me to photograph this spectacular bridge.

Praise received:
"You have made a wonderful abstract, Klaus."

"Spectacular photo! Superb lines!"

Joseph: "The POV [point of view] is incredible.
There is an organic element to me. It's as if the structure is rising from the ashes."

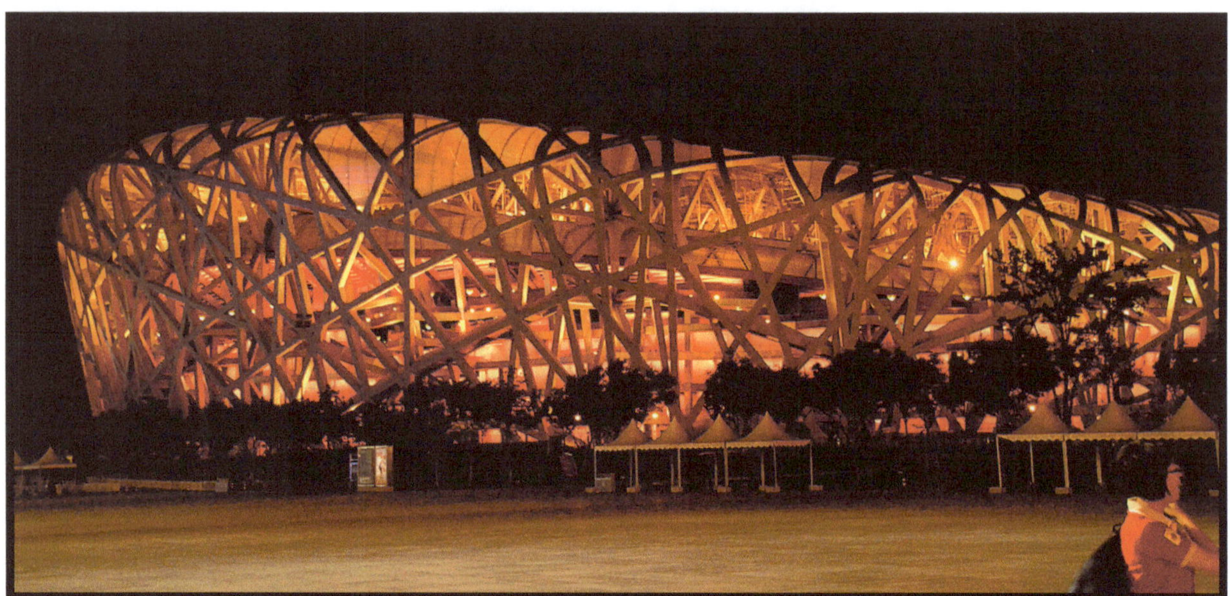

Bird's Nest

I had the privilege to photograph the Beijing National Stadium, nicknamed The Bird's Nest, at night during the 2008 Summer Olympics in China. As it happened a girl walked by wearing a red shirt. I photographed her as she was leaving the photo – telling me that the games were over, but will always be a fond memory and a beacon of reality of the past. There is an open door in the image, seemingly open to our imagination, seeking what we may not have experienced but can imagine.

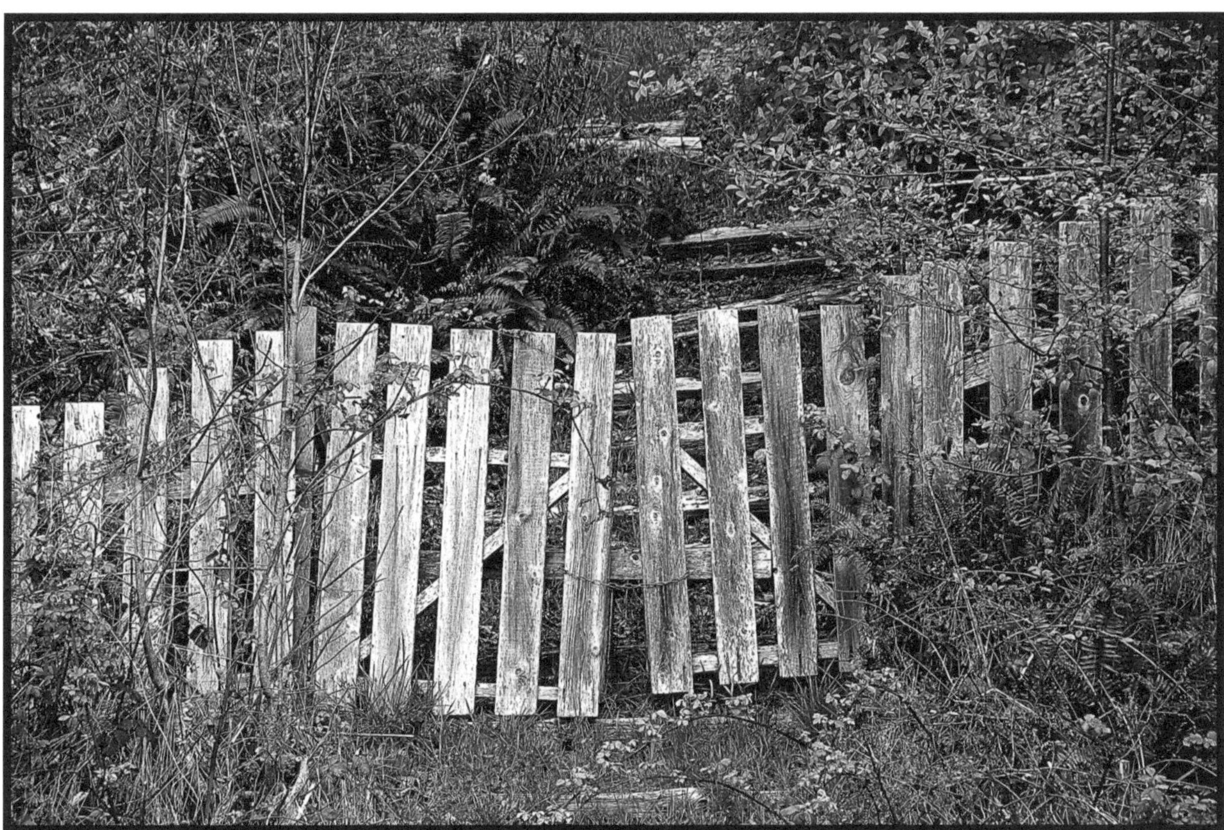

Blocked

Black and white is an abstract concept or illusion to our conscious mind since most of us see the entire colour spectrum. A few amongst us do have colour blindness, meaning the difference between dark red and dark brown and other such combinations may be difficult to see. The absence of colour, reducing what we see in terms of black and white and shades of gray, lends a flavour, an impression appreciated by so many of us who understand the nuances of black and white photography. There is a beauty, an art form, delicate, light, dark, moods, feelings, almost touchable in three dimensions even when displayed on flat paper. The depth is so apparent that we are deluded into thinking and feeling the image is in fact reality. How beautiful and artistic this form of art, photography can take on a life of its own.

Blocked – to get as many gray tones as possible from black to white. Ansel Adams became famous by adding two more gray tones than anyone else was able to produce at that time. I was trying to capture as many as possible because I liked the feeling I had while walking by the fence – just to look and then to see... beyond.

Praise received:
Jeff: "Great! Reminds me of Ansel Adams."

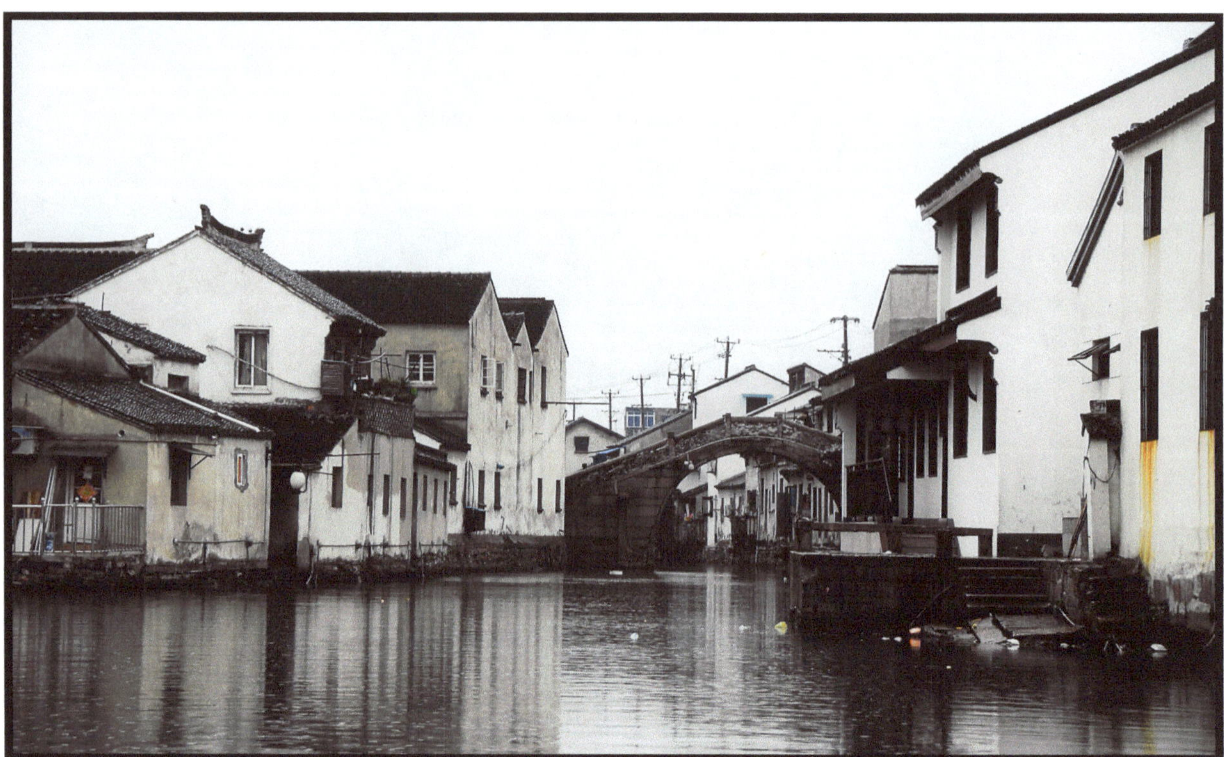

Canal Houses

This is the China River with houses on both sides – what a place to live – like houses by the sea. The colour is almost black and white, yet there are some naturally occurring hints of colour as you can see.

<u>*Praise received*</u>*:*
"A classically composed image,
subtle, evocative, inviting of imagination… very nice!"

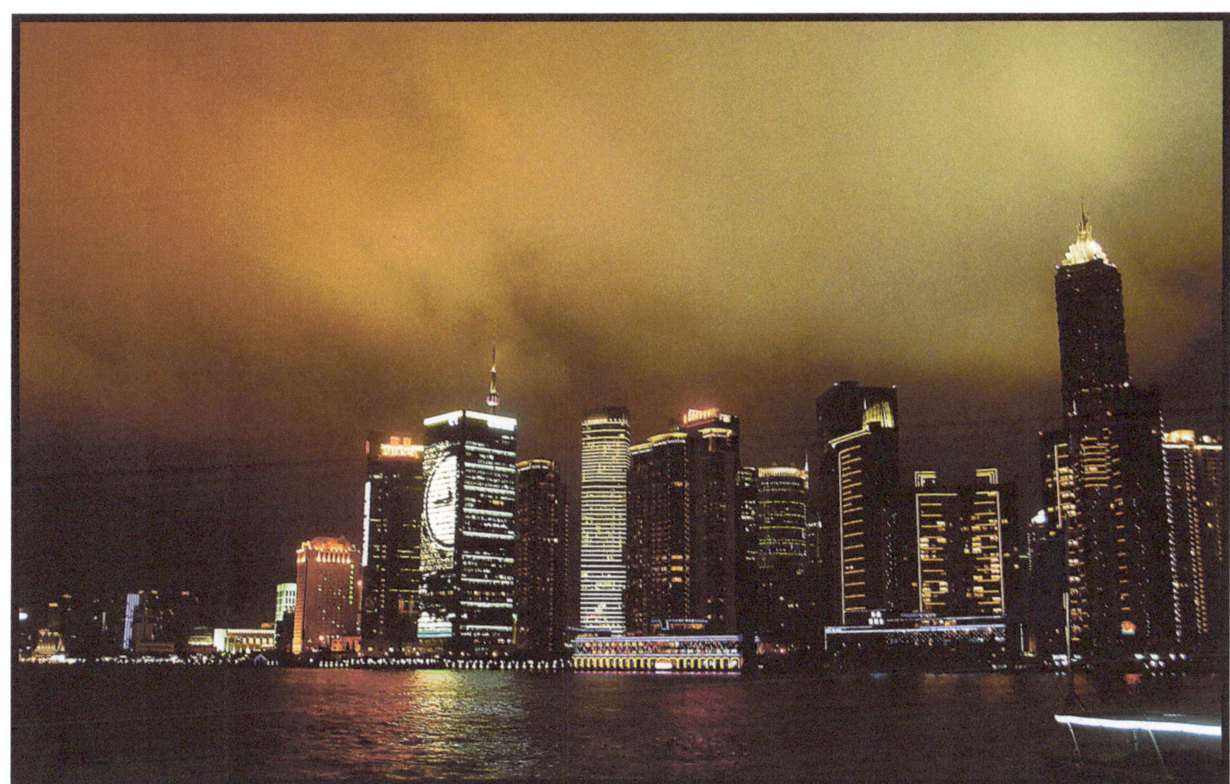

City of Lights

During my trip to China we took a boat and sailed down the river to see the city lights in all their glory at night.

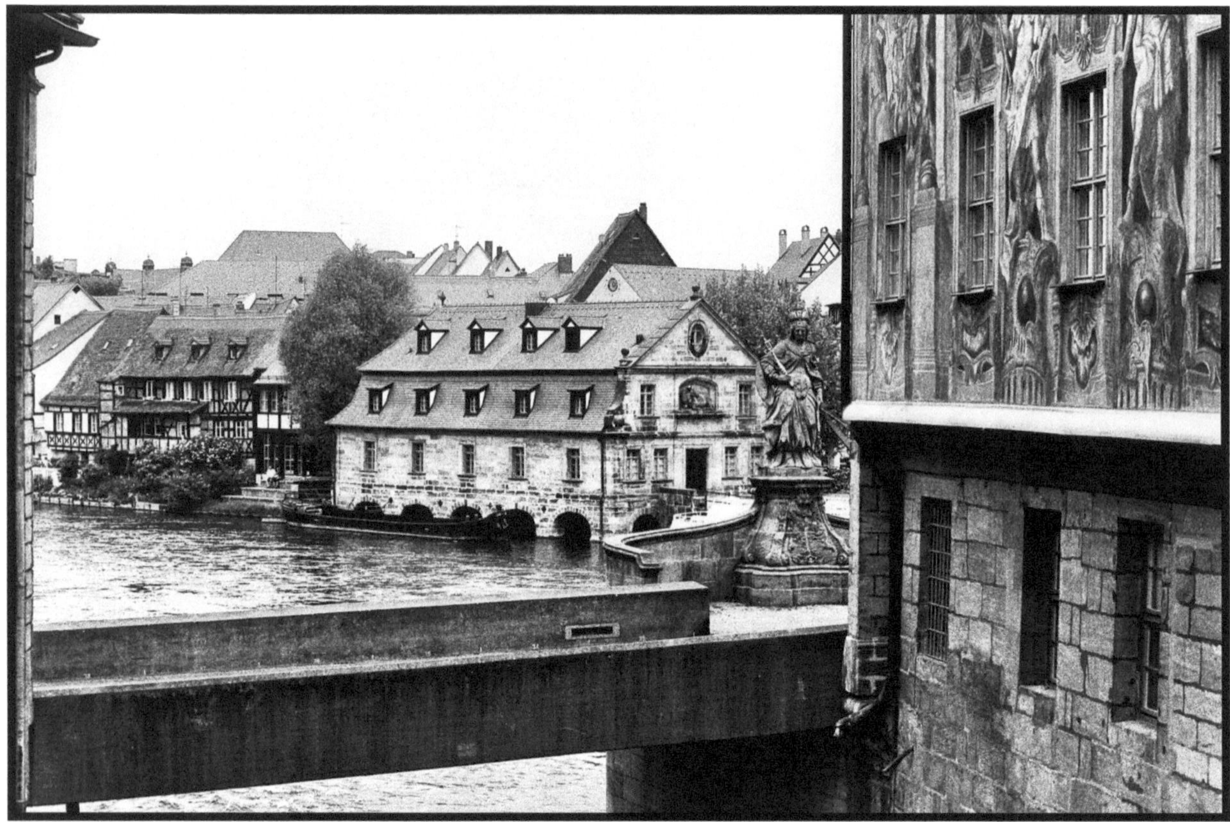

City of Stone

This image illustrates the feeling I had while walking the streets of this old city. That particular day it was cool and raining. The texture and contrast gave me the perspective to choose the composition that expressed what I love about this era and the structure of the buildings erected so may centuries ago.

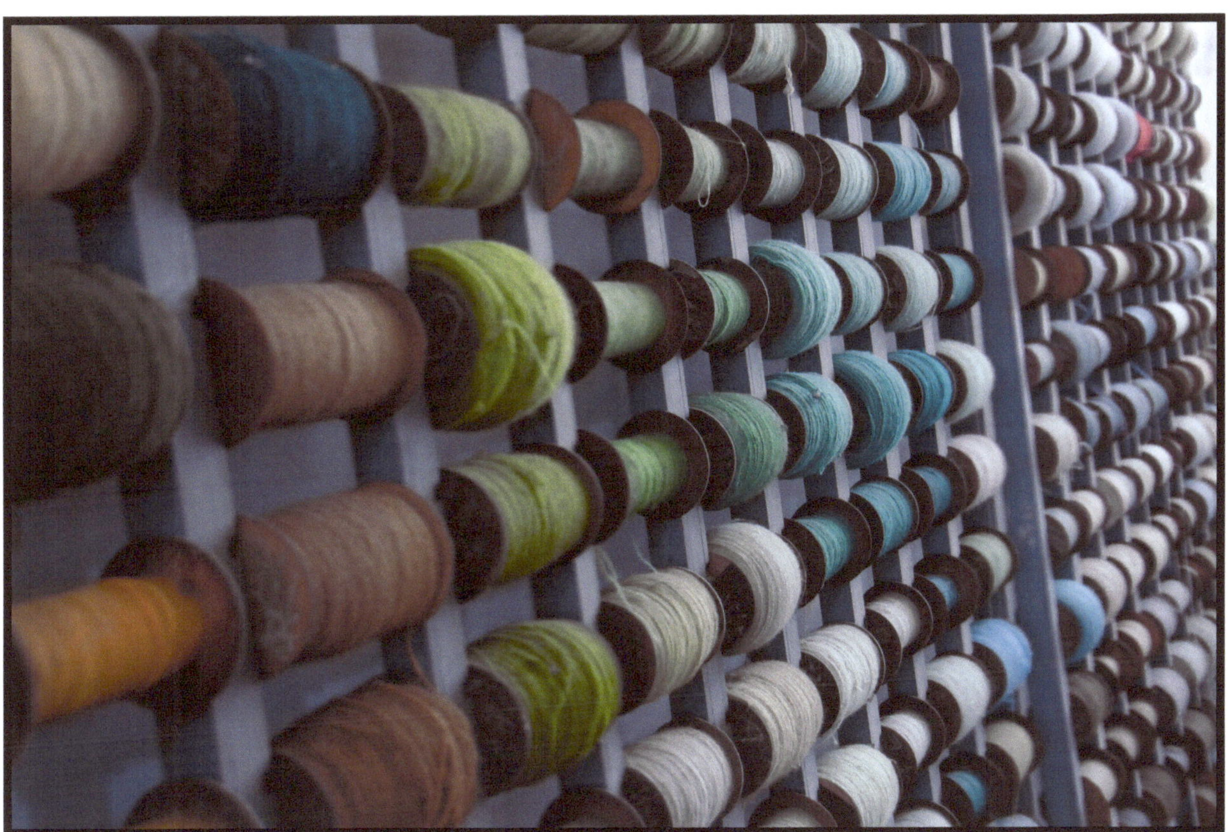

Endless Rolls

When I came upon this sight, a seemingly endless number of woolen rolls, the angle gave me a design that was interesting.

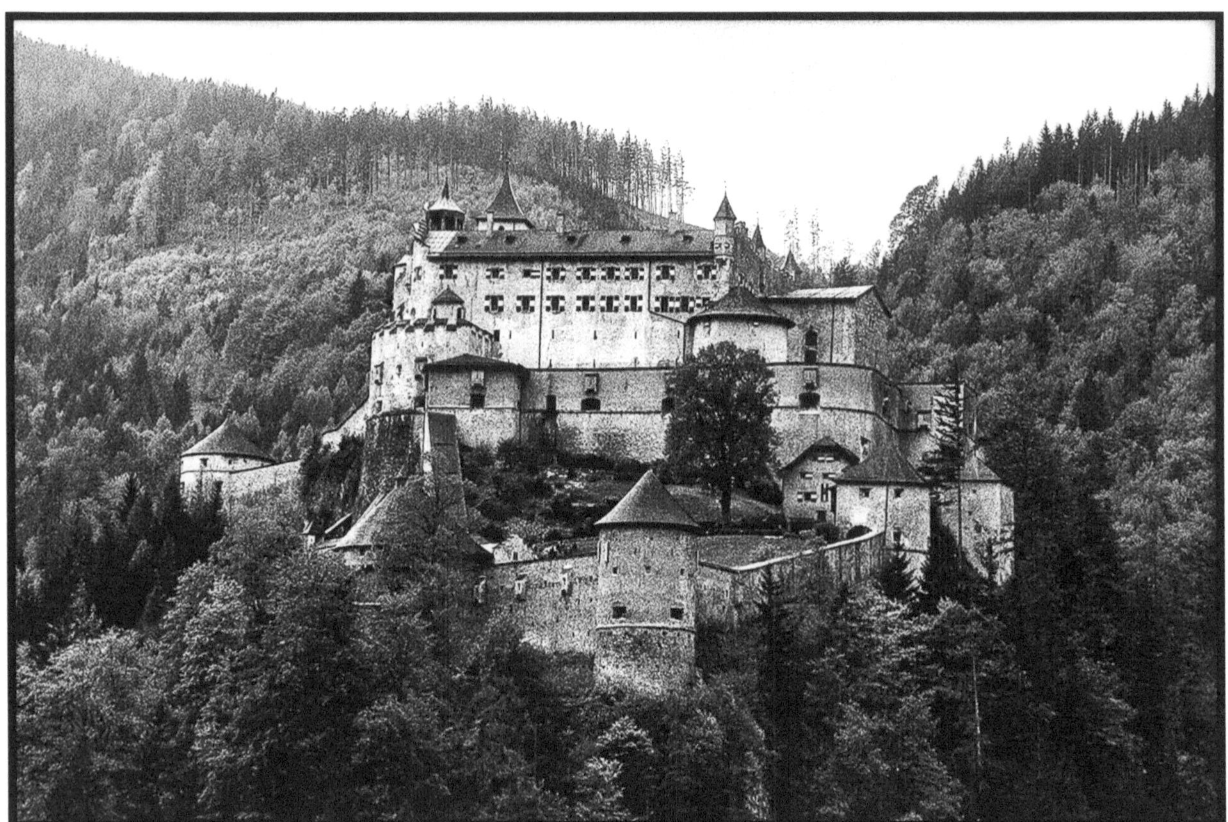

Etched in Stone

We spent two nights way up in the mountains of Austria and had the opportunity to visit this castle. I wanted to photograph it from the other side of the valley; even as we did, the road was so steep we never reached the height I had anticipated, but still managed to climb high enough as can be seen in the image. The feeling of an etching was added by contrast, sharpness and grain. The castle's history is so long and involved, anything I could write here wouldn't do it justice. The etched look gives it a feeling of age and the warm tones are like a Bromoil finish.

<u>*Praise received:*</u>

Joseph: "A wonderful picture. It creates the desire to be there and experience a part of Austrian history. Very nice."

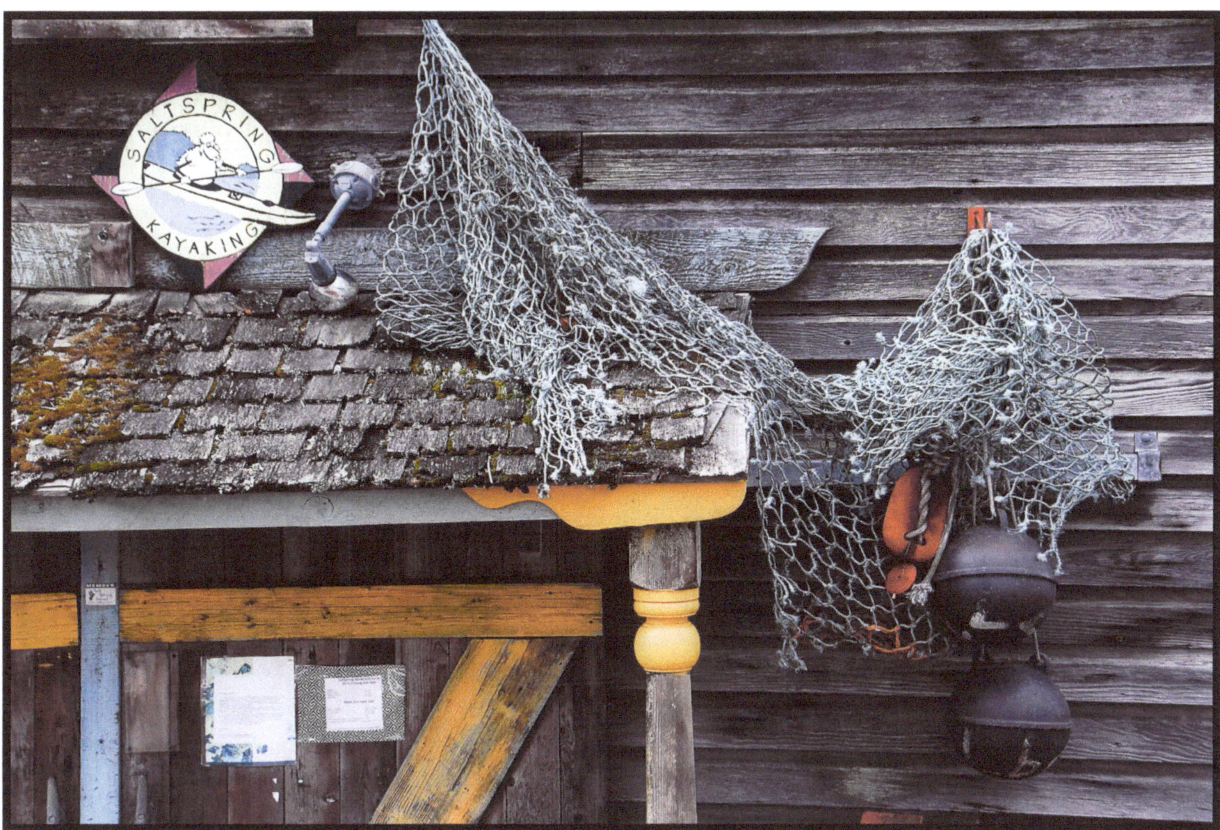

Fishing Shack

It truly reminded me of what I imagined fishing shacks would have looked like 100 years ago. Maybe not the company logo or light fixture, but just the same, photos are there to remind us of the past, where we have been – to imagine and reflect on the past can be given to us in picture form when we find something in our world today.

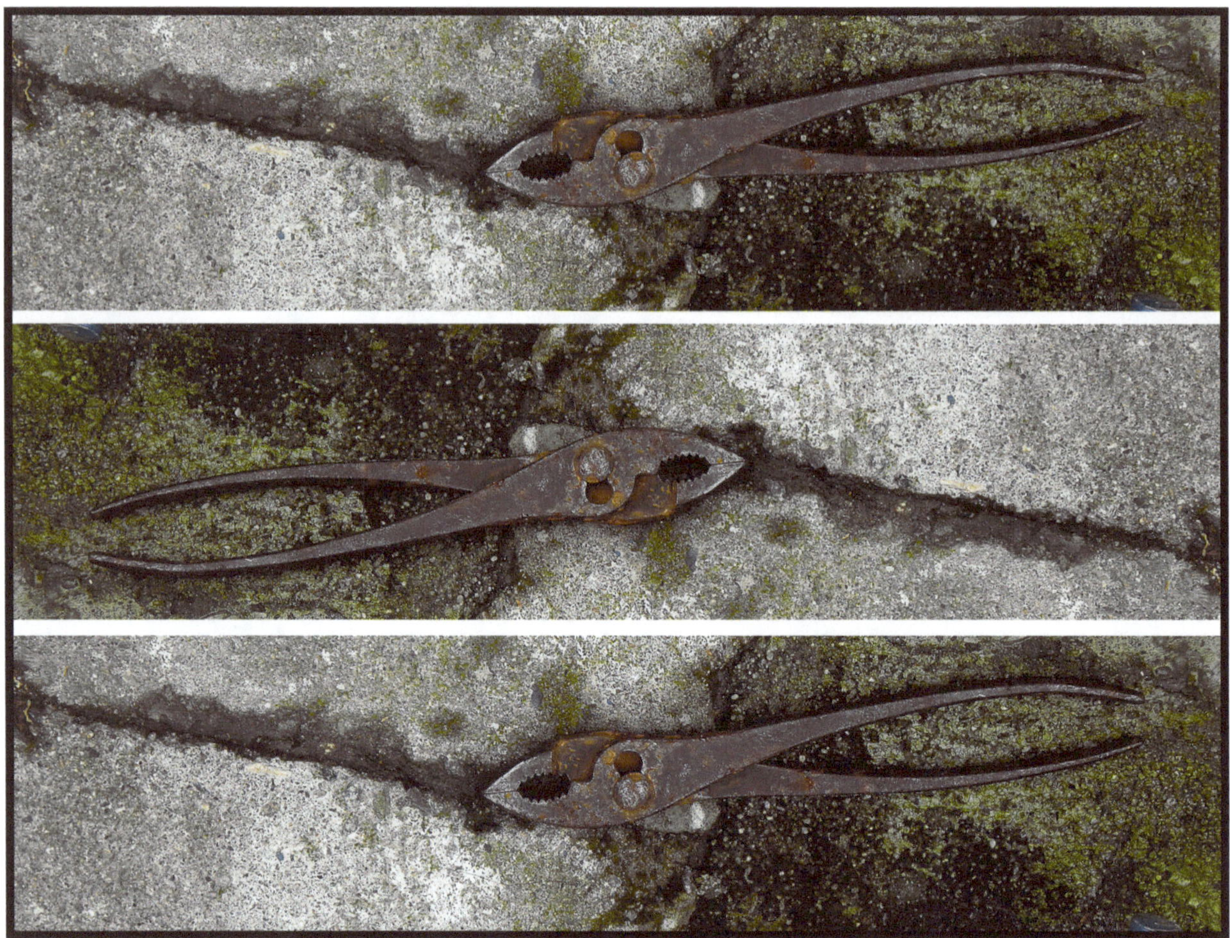

Forgotten

The concept of left behind – “Forgotten” – came when I saw these pliers just lying there on the ground for seemly a very long time. All rusted and old looking, I felt for the poor abandoned tool that served a purpose many years ago. I felt like picking them up and giving them a place in my garage. Then I though there might be a person who needs them more so I left them untouched. I worked with one image, then two, then three, but not until I turned the middle one around, did it feel right. They’ll always be saved in my image even if the pliers were forgotten.

Praise received:
Submitted and approved in the
Inspired Art Group on RedBubble.

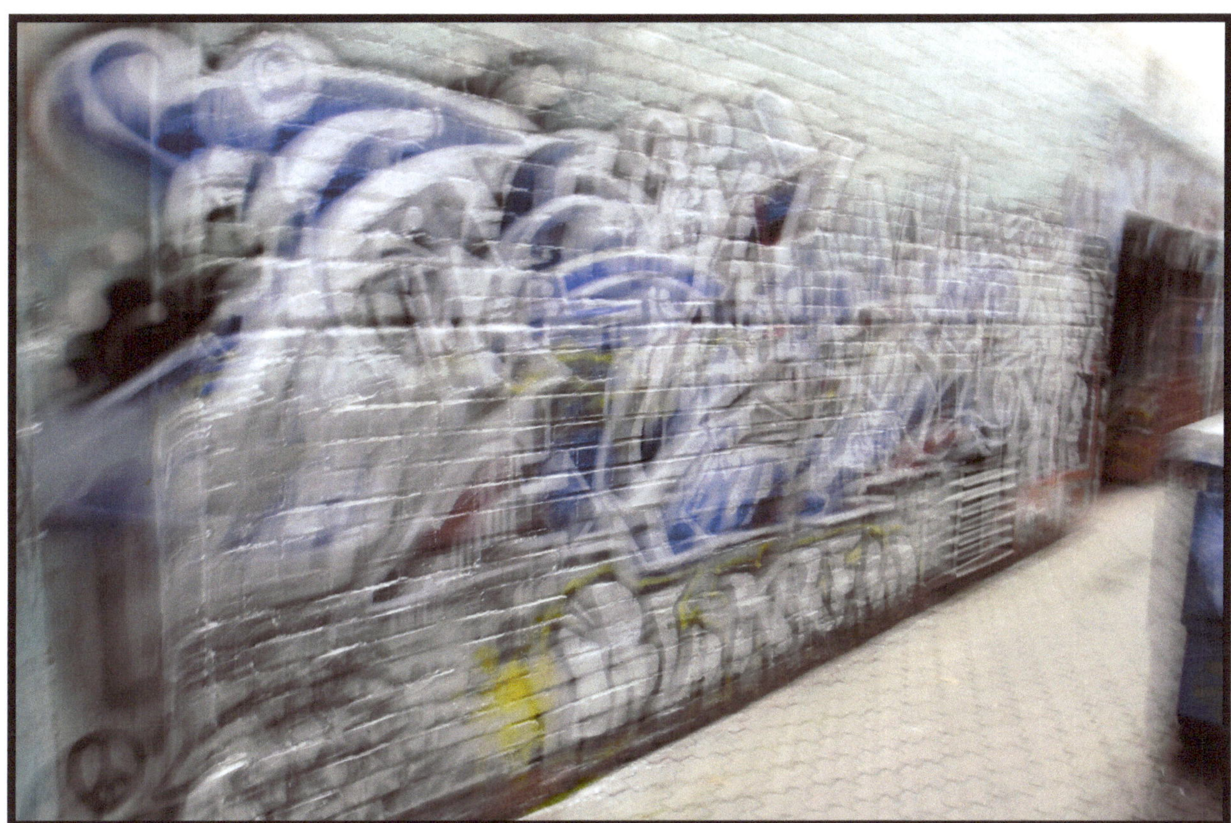

Graffiti

What is real, what is illusion – how do we see this? All art is self-explored and intrepid but the viewer tries to see it in two ways: first, perhaps, is how do I see what I see, and the second is what was the artist trying to show me – not with words – showing me without words…

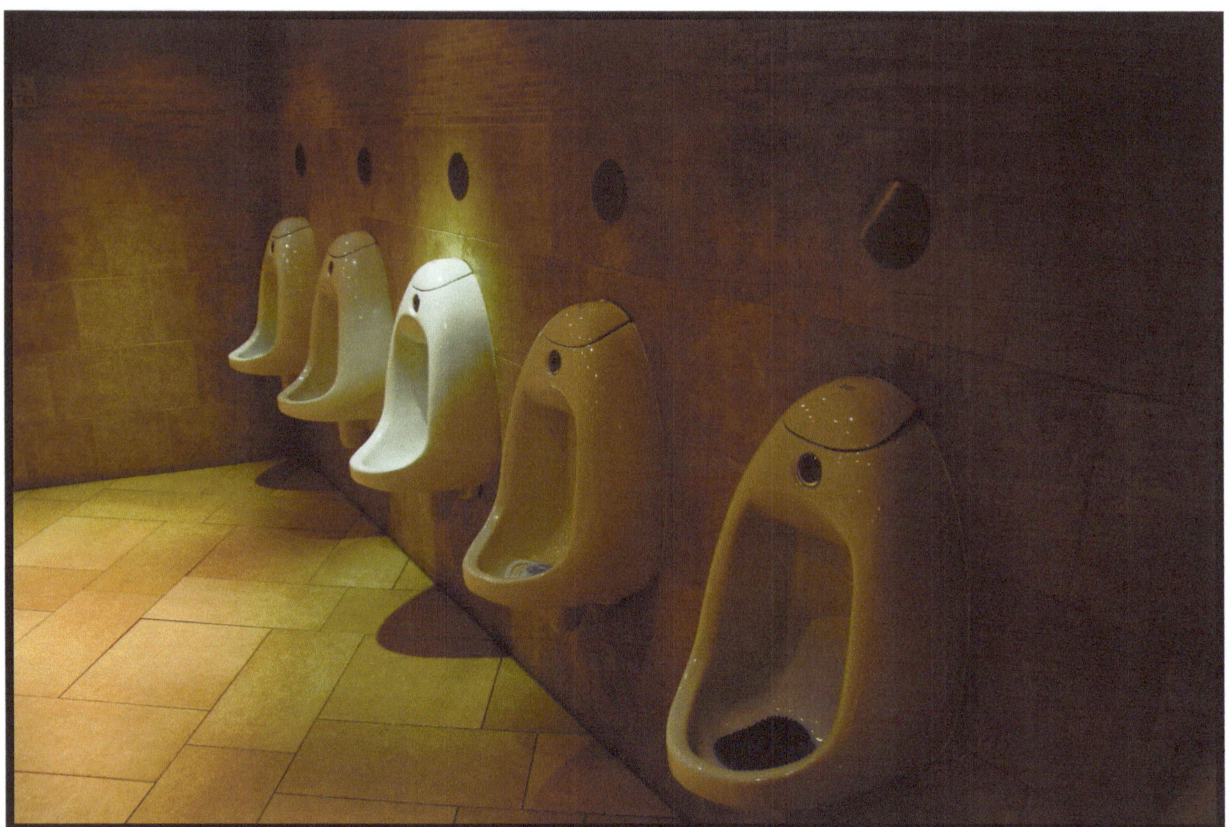

Light Strikes

I was not going to show this image but I sold it, so I thought I would. I was in Niagara Falls some time ago and I walked into the washroom and saw what you see, so I ran back out and got my camera and took this image. Men may relate to this image more, and it was a man who purchased it, he is hanging it in his large washroom. The feeling that the photograph speaks to me is real, and yes, so unreal with just a single light on only one of the urinals. I hope that others can and may see why I took the image, the feeling to go. I want to thank the man who purchased the image for his wall.

Praise received:
Daniela: "Absolutely stunning! A classy shot! Seriously!
Only GREAT photographers can shoot such
ordinary things with such a touch of class!

Photograph featured in "The World As We See it, or as we missed it."

Mimi: "Everyone sees things in a different way.
I can see this hanging in a restroom... very tastefully done!"

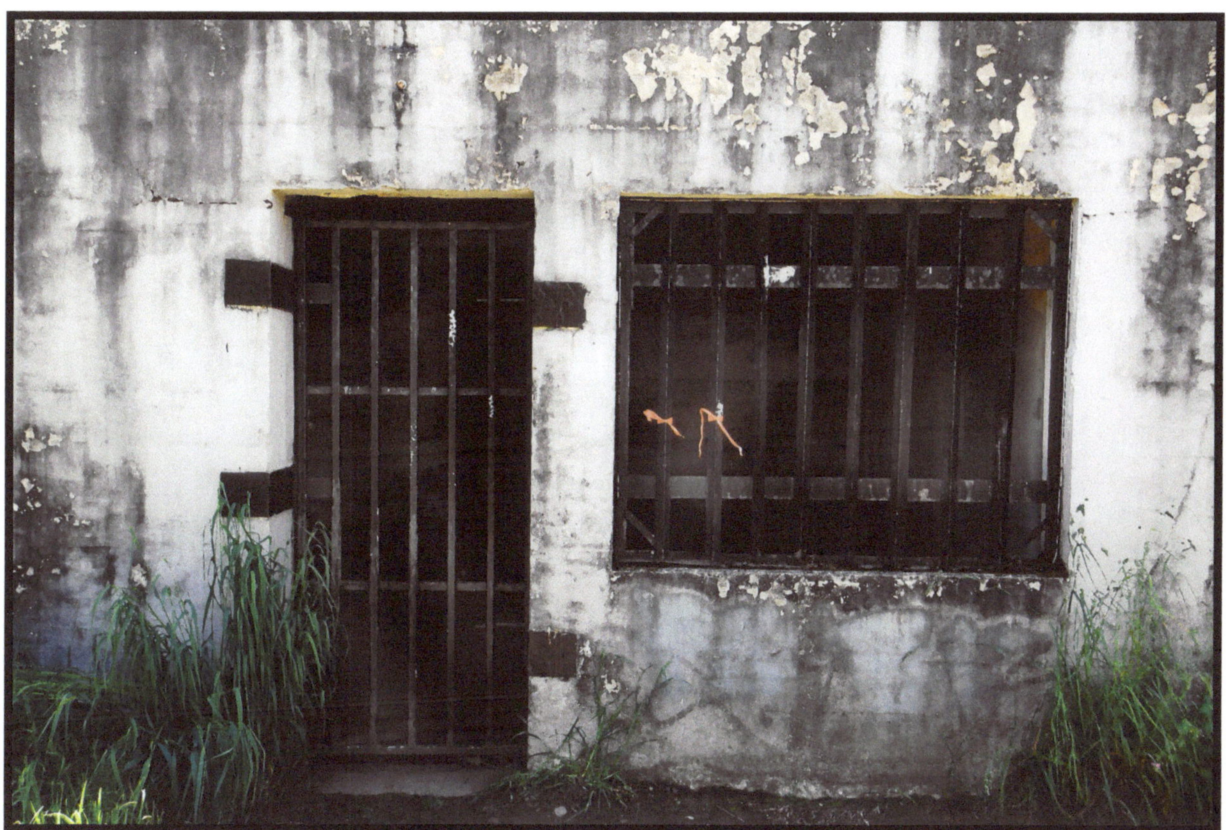

McCauley Point Locked Up

This was a place where the military kept their ammunition and even prisoners, so I was told. This old place felt haunted to me, with the greenery in the foreground and the old peeling cement walls that had been given some whitewash-like paint – peeling away as time had its way. The two little red pieces of ribbon stuck out, as if to say PEACE!

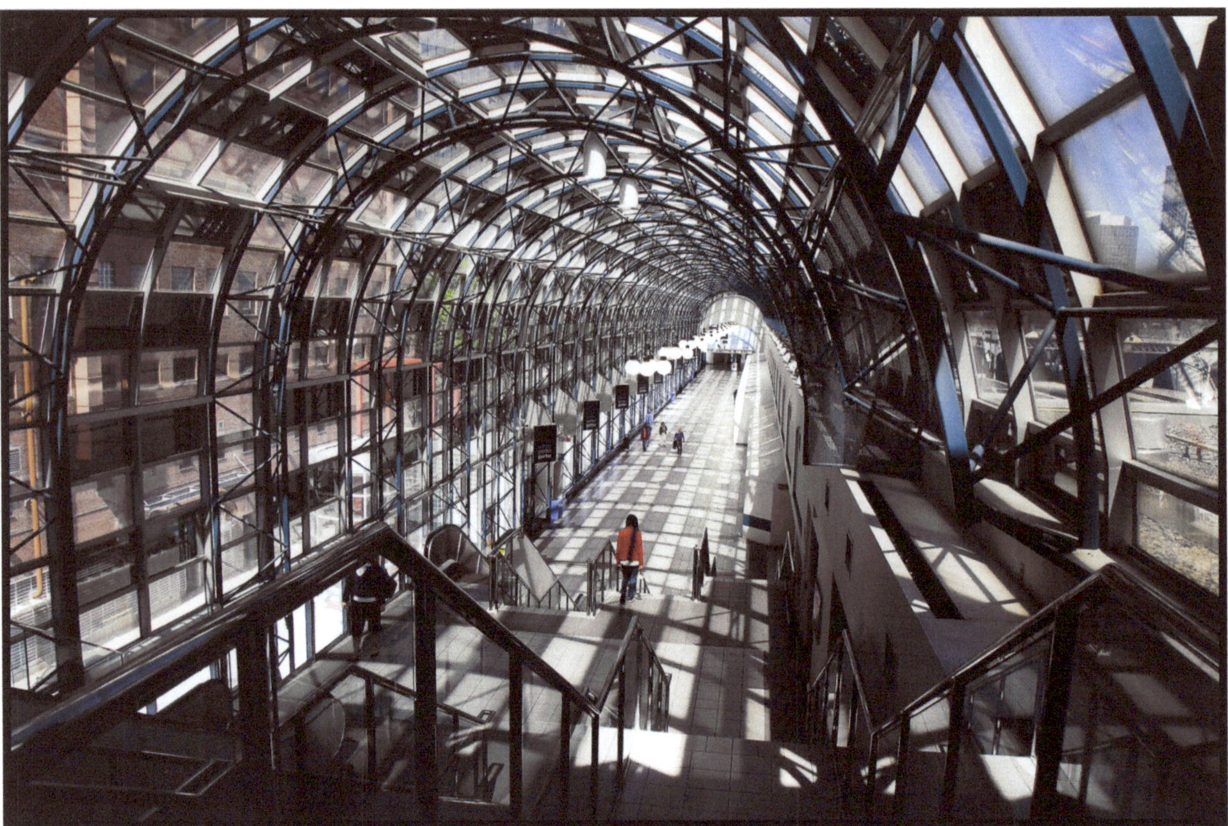

Mosaic

A walkway that extends far into the distance like the future, and seeing how we will get there!

<u>*Praise received:*</u>

Graham: "This is a brilliant shot Klaus. The lighting is perfect and the combination of curves and regular shapes in the light and shadow make it an image to be explored. The focus given by the red jumper keeps pulling the eye in but there is so much around it that you keep wandering off to explore more."

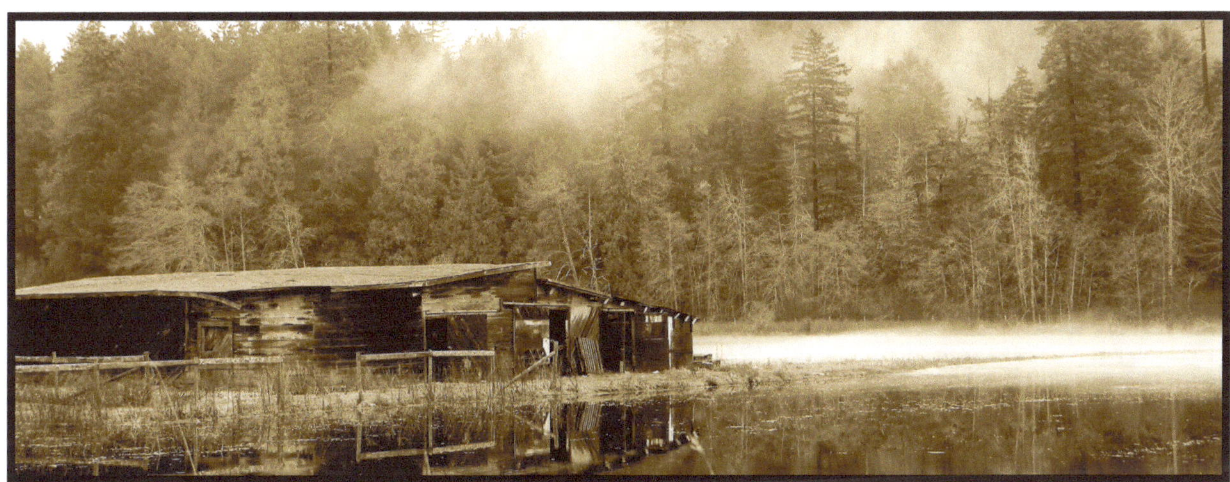

Old Look

A look to the past – in modern times.

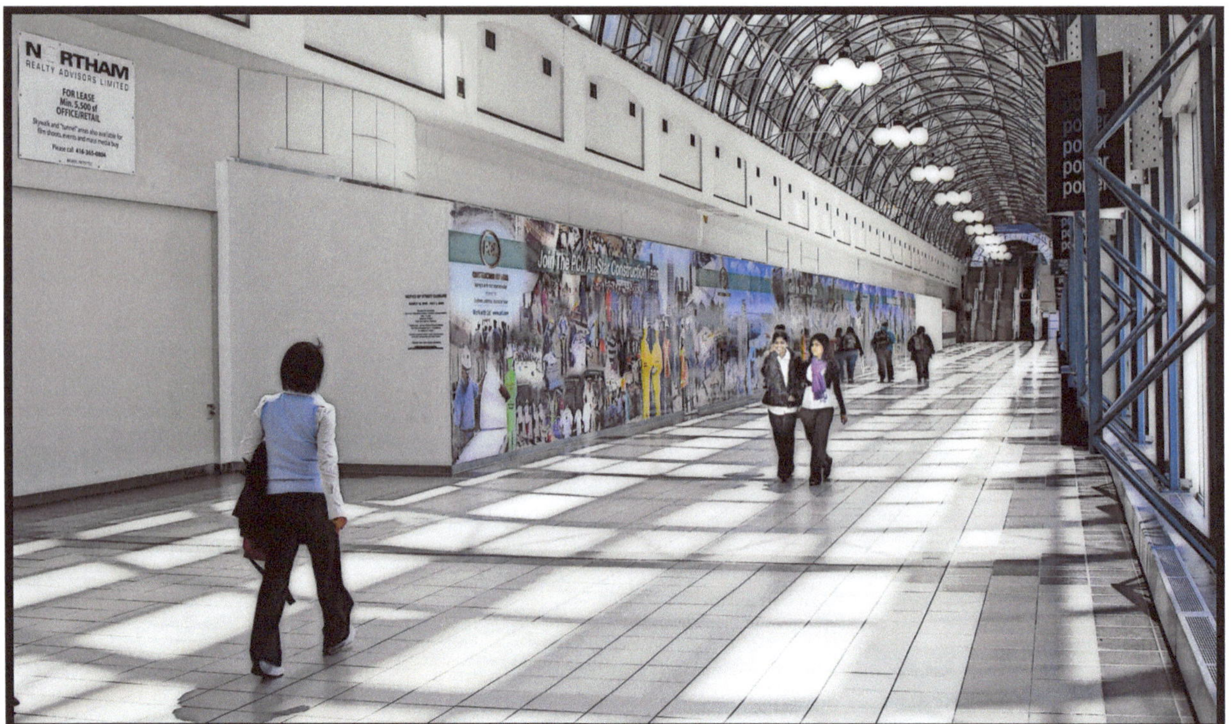

Pastel

The tunnel with the composition as you see it was so interesting, but not there yet. I added a filter to my camera and enhanced the image somewhat with Photoshop as well. I waited a few minutes to capture the spacing of the people to add to the feeling of depth and movement. Pastel was dictated by the environment. I felt that with a soft blue tint, it added more to the uniqueness of the image.

Praise received:

"There's much to enjoy in this one, from the treatment, colours, perspective, focus… and more."

Sandy: "Great framing and use of depth of field to lend a great perspective of distance! Wonderful lines and shades. They compliment and add extra interest to the person walking in the foreground. Lovely work!"

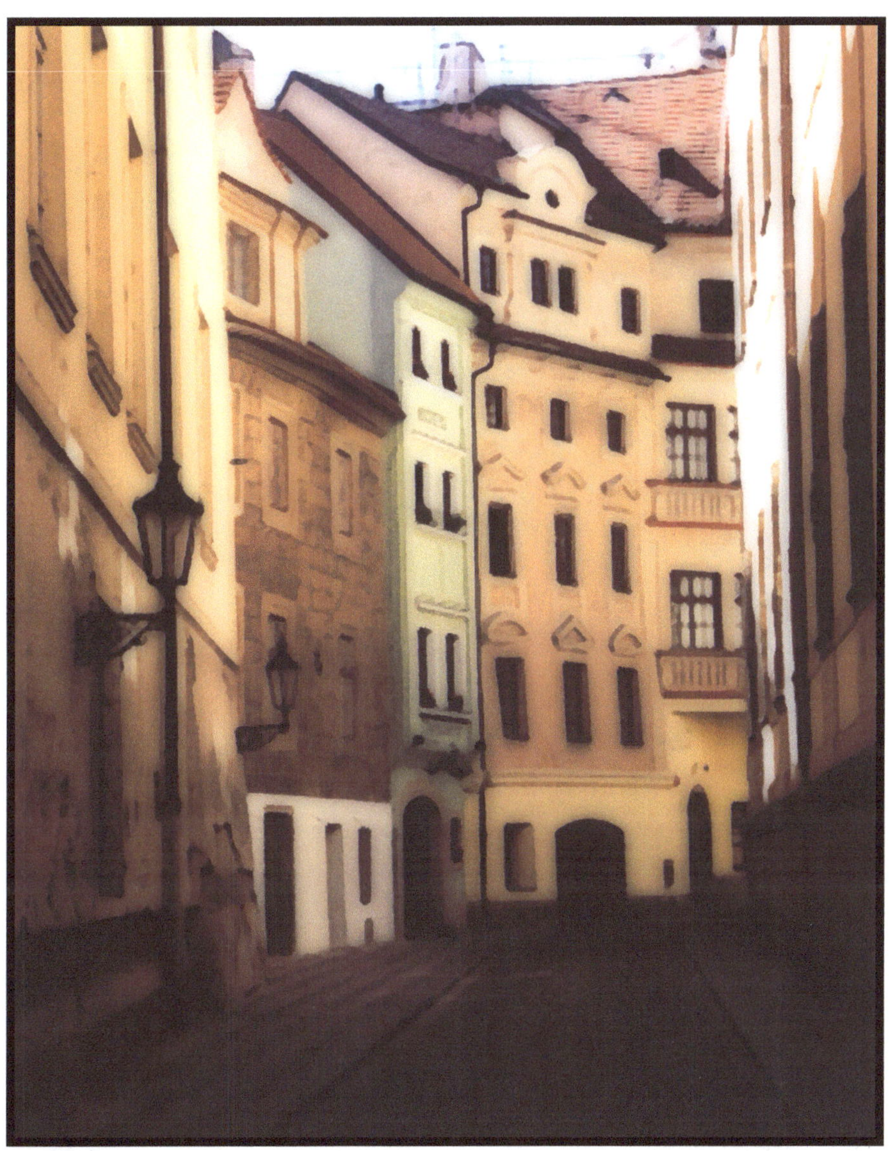

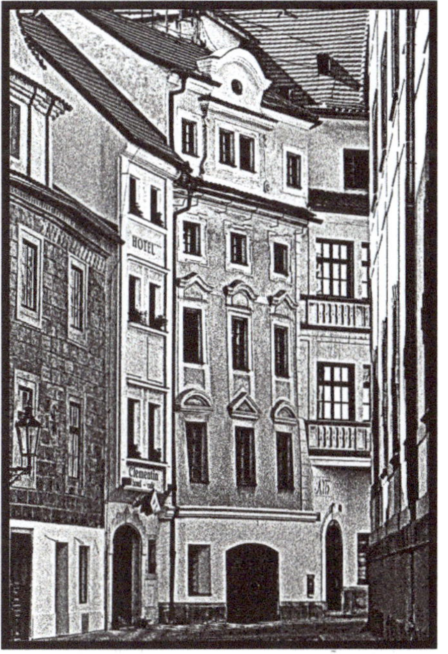

Prague Sketched

I found the buildings in Prague to be particularly interesting. When I looked at the photo I wanted to show the feeling, as a painter might have painted it many years ago. I also wanted to show it as a pencil sketch for a companion piece. Two visions of how an artist centuries before may have shown this part of the city.

Praise received:

"Fabulous version of your Prague image Klaus! I am very impressed with this as I have tried sketching several of my photos, but yours are outstanding when compared to mine."

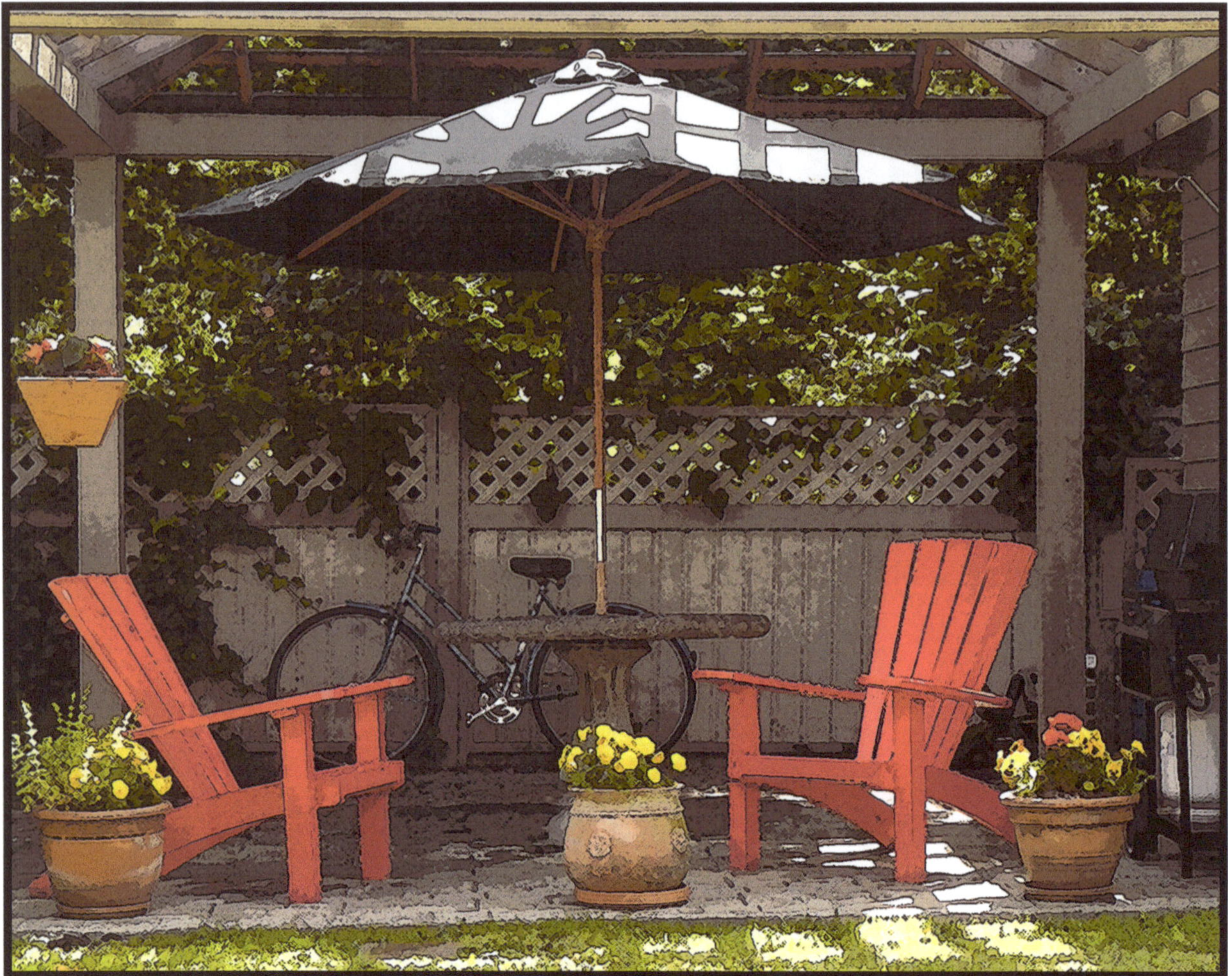

Red Chairs

My client loved this image that was part of the back yard where they entertained and relaxed. They asked me if I could capture the feeling of this area that may represent their style of living. Being artists in their own right, it was a challenge for me to produce something that exceeded beyond a mere photographic image while keeping the feeling of their place.

The background of what enabled me to create Red Chairs: The photography was the least challenging because of the years of practice in operating my cameras and learning about lighting, and how to manipulate both successfully. When I invited two photographers from the western provinces to my studio and hired an expert in Photoshop in 1998, their lectures and hands-on approach proved very helpful. We were encouraged to name each layer we used to make the image more painterly, but I always feel the need to approach each image from a fresh perspective; so I don't have an easy formula to fall back on and produce the same look over and over again. My lab printed the image on canvas. Then I added oil paints by hand to make the image unique and personal to the buyers, to purchase a one of a kind art piece.

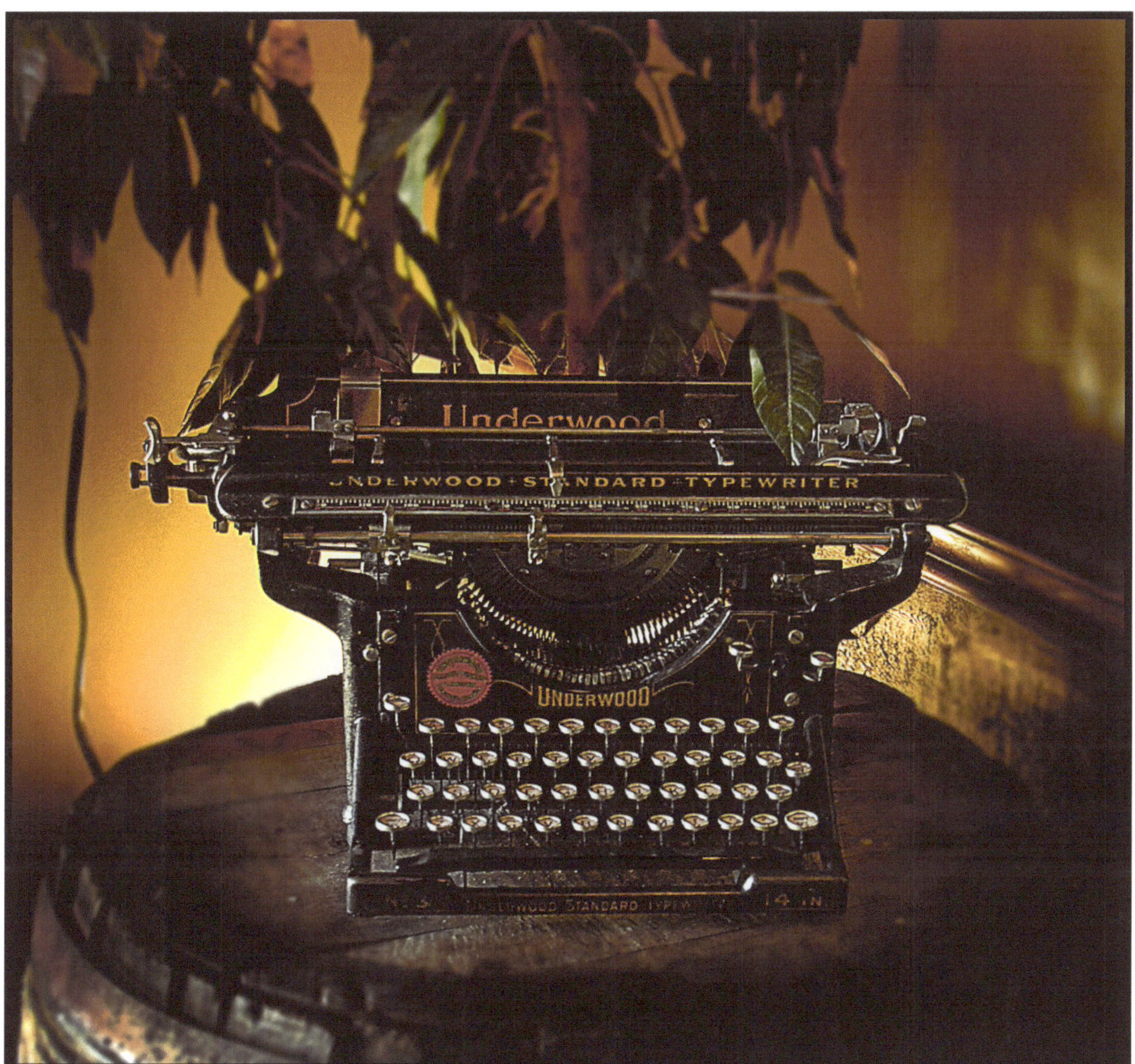

Retired

Typewriter retired – I saw this and got my camera to record just what you see here. It felt so old and yet so much a part of our history. I wanted to capture the past and preserve it for the future and the NOW! I like the way they lit the environment – the typewriter sitting on the old barrel with a glow of focus – well done – it worked hard for many years and is now being showcased in its retirement.

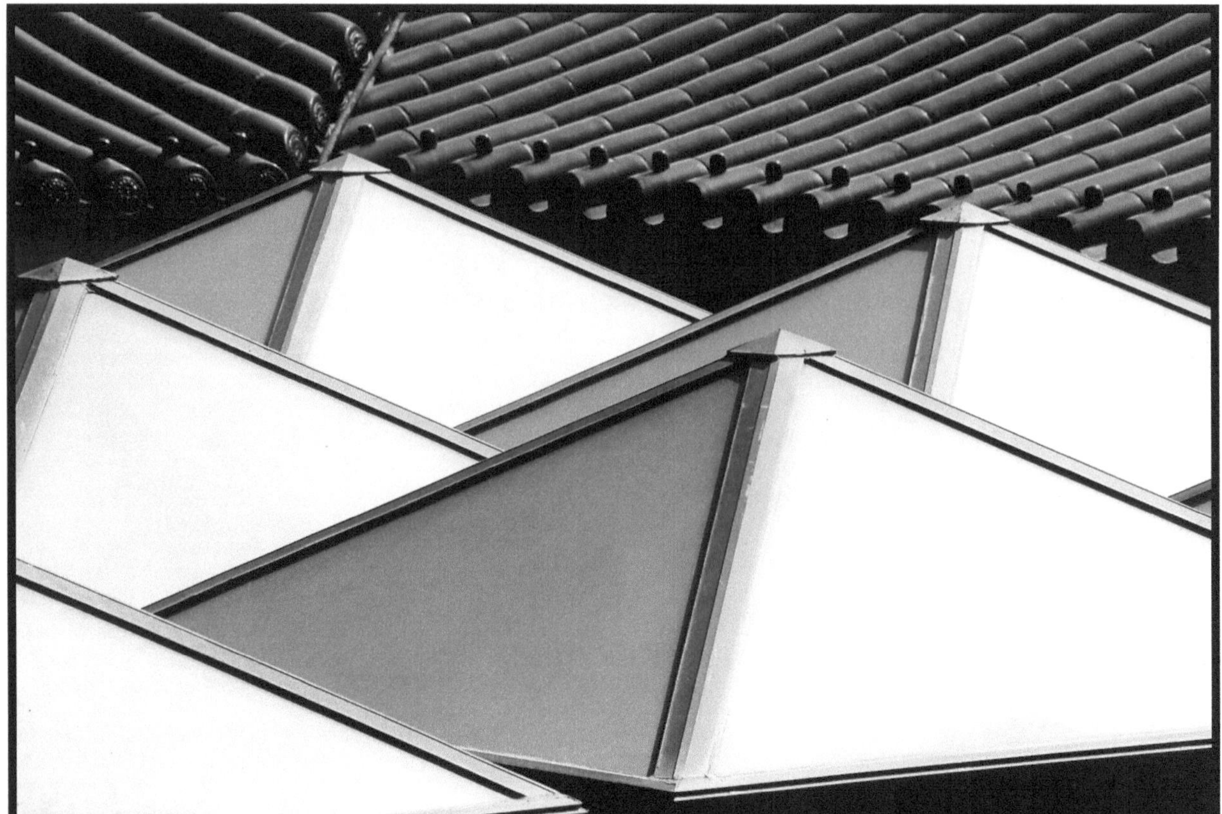

Roof Tops

The roof tops were there as I walked downstairs in a building during my visit to China. Little pyramids lined up and were contrasted by black lines of roughness designed by rows of pipes. The shape and texture appealed to me. Black and white seemed to express what was there in the overcast light. Contrast from the background enabled the windows to have their rightful place.

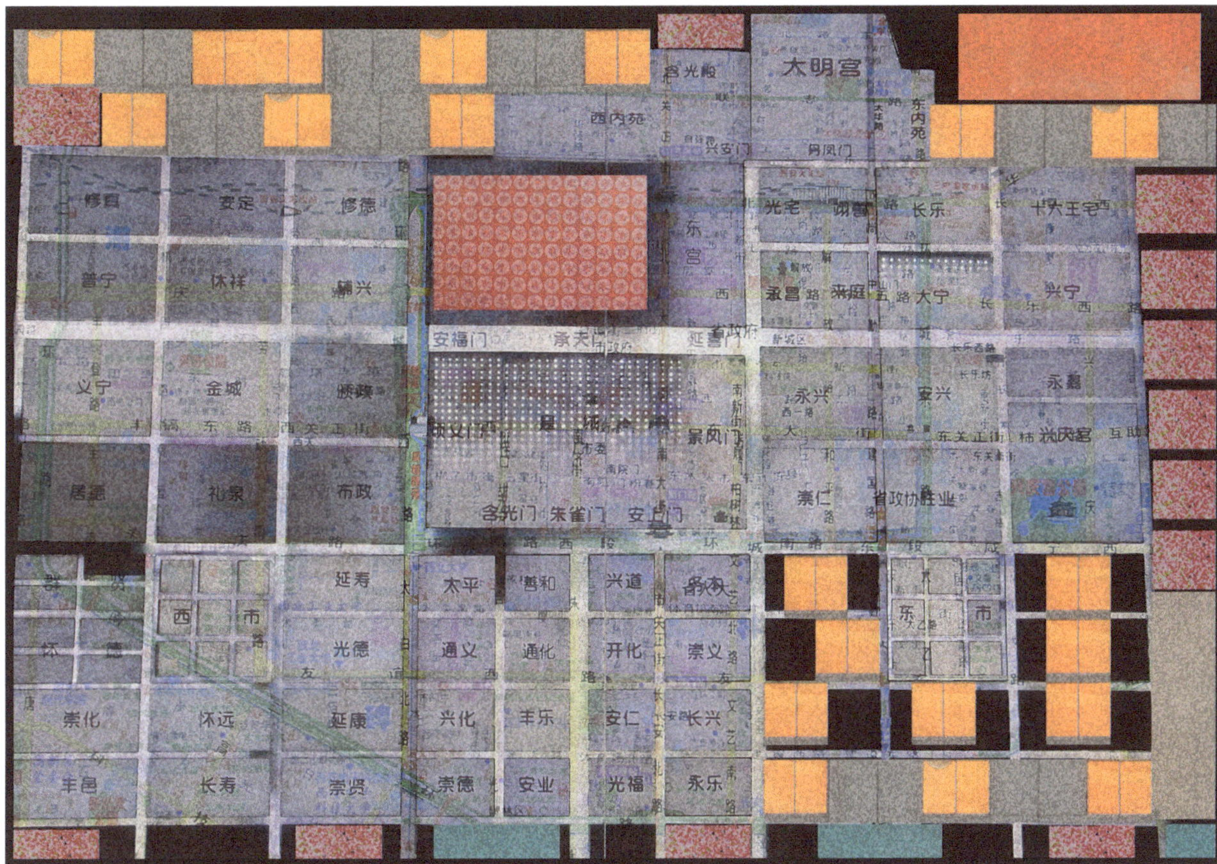

Squares

I think patterns can bring to light design and interest even if it is illusive and maybe not what we are used to seeing.

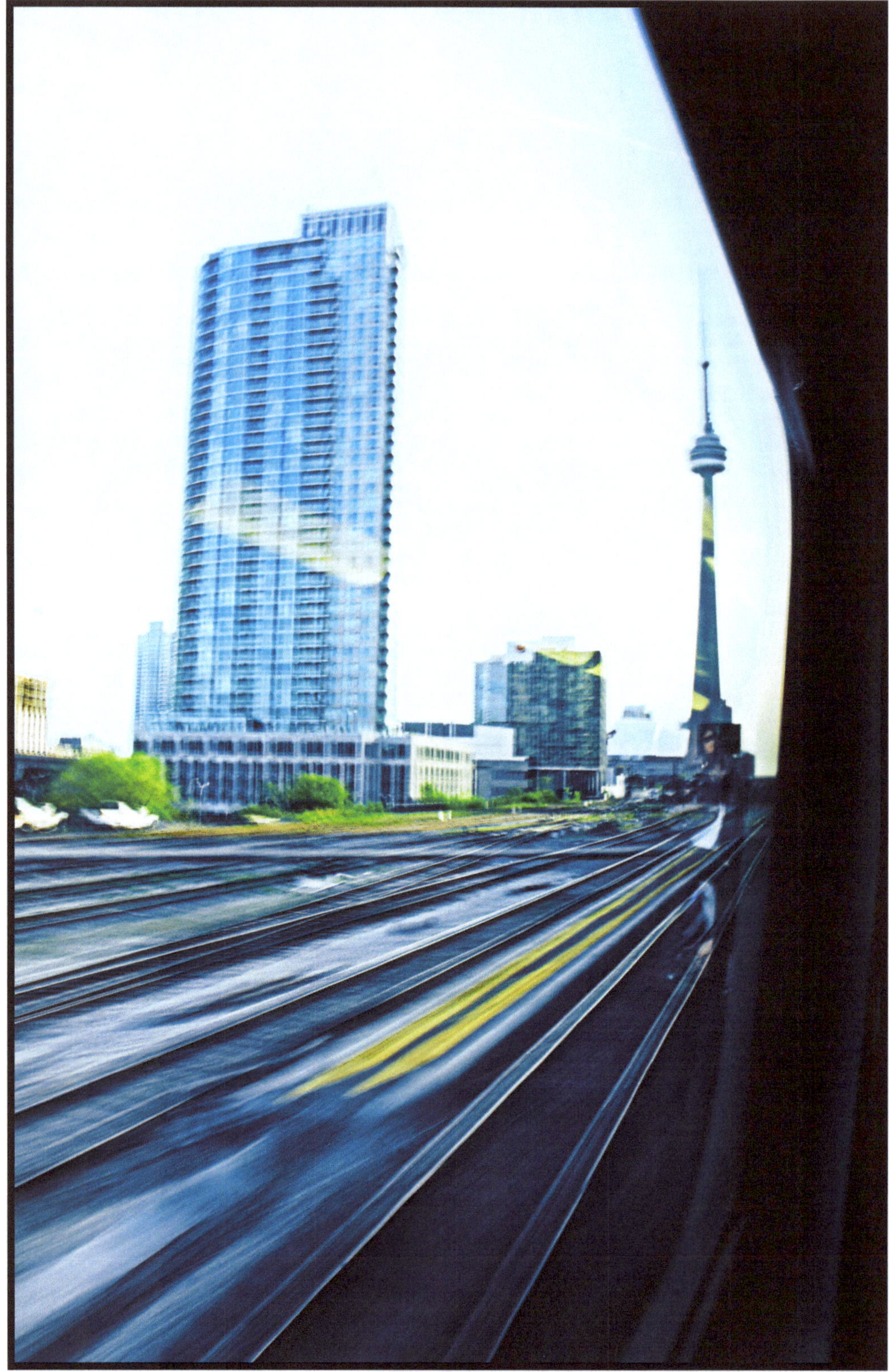

Streaking

The streaking was made while in a moving train and using a slower shutter speed. I wanted to capture the tower in a meaningful way. The illusion of speed and sound – playing a trick on our senses – the eyes are the doorway to reality as we see it.

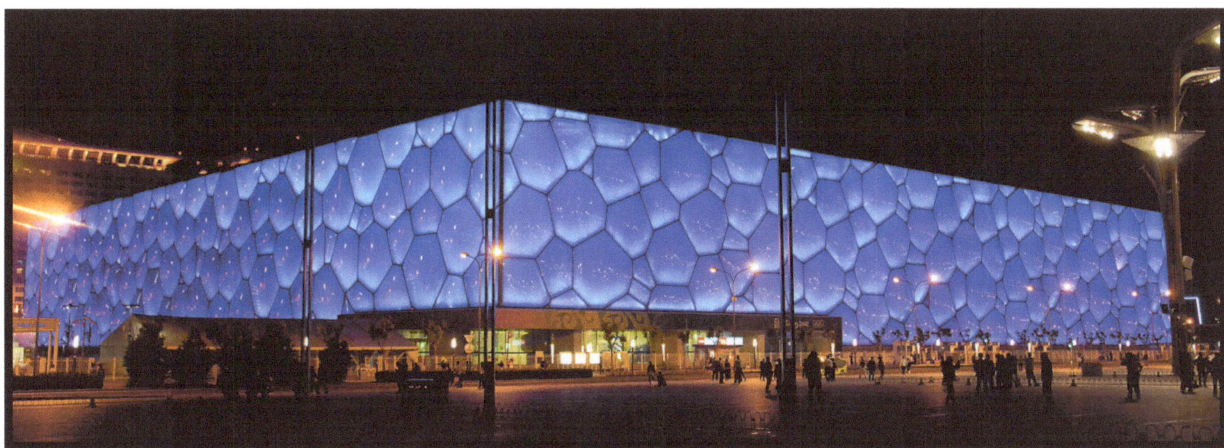

Swimming Pool

This modern structure is where all the swimming competitions were held during the 2008 Summer Olympics in China. I was worried that I wouldn't be able to capture the entire building but managed to do so. This memento will be there for the visitors and the ones who couldn't be there. Most beautiful and impressive!

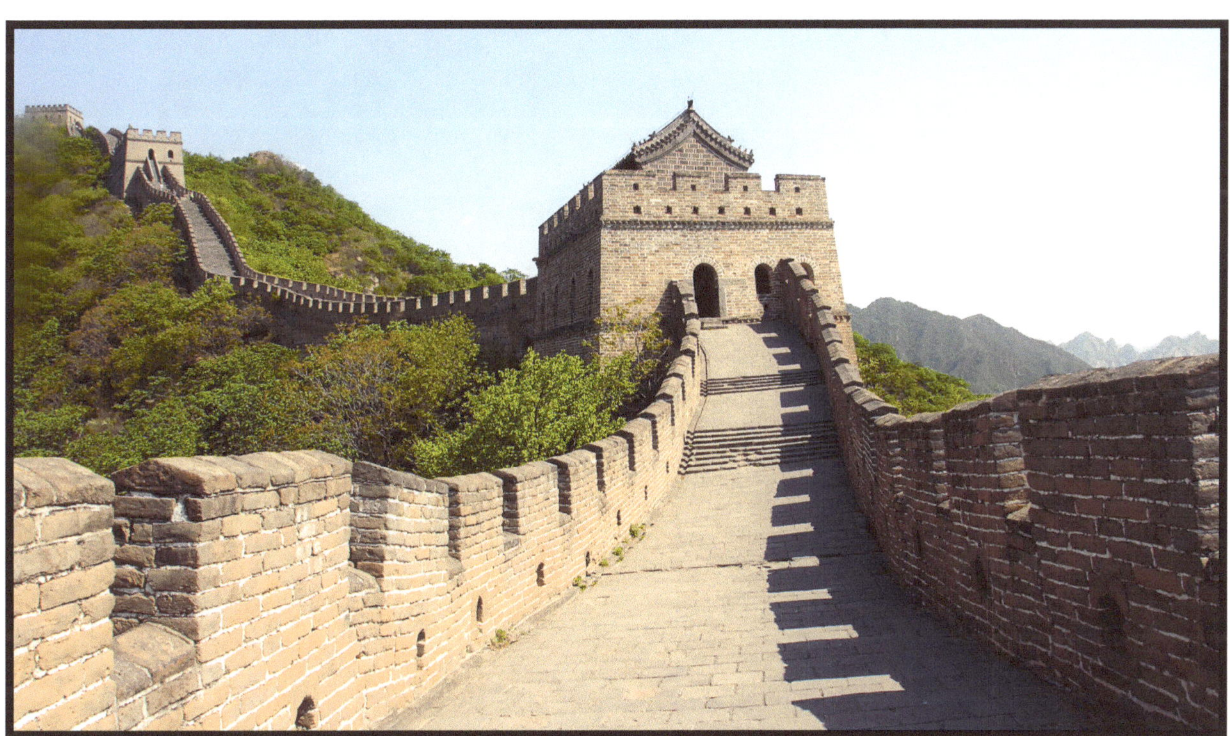

The Great Wall of China

It thrilled my soul to walk all the way to the old part of the wall and even to walk on it. This was my greatest privilege. I had been in China before but missed going to the wall.

<u>*Praise received:*</u>
"Beautiful photography, I love the way you captured
the wall as it climbs up the winding hill."

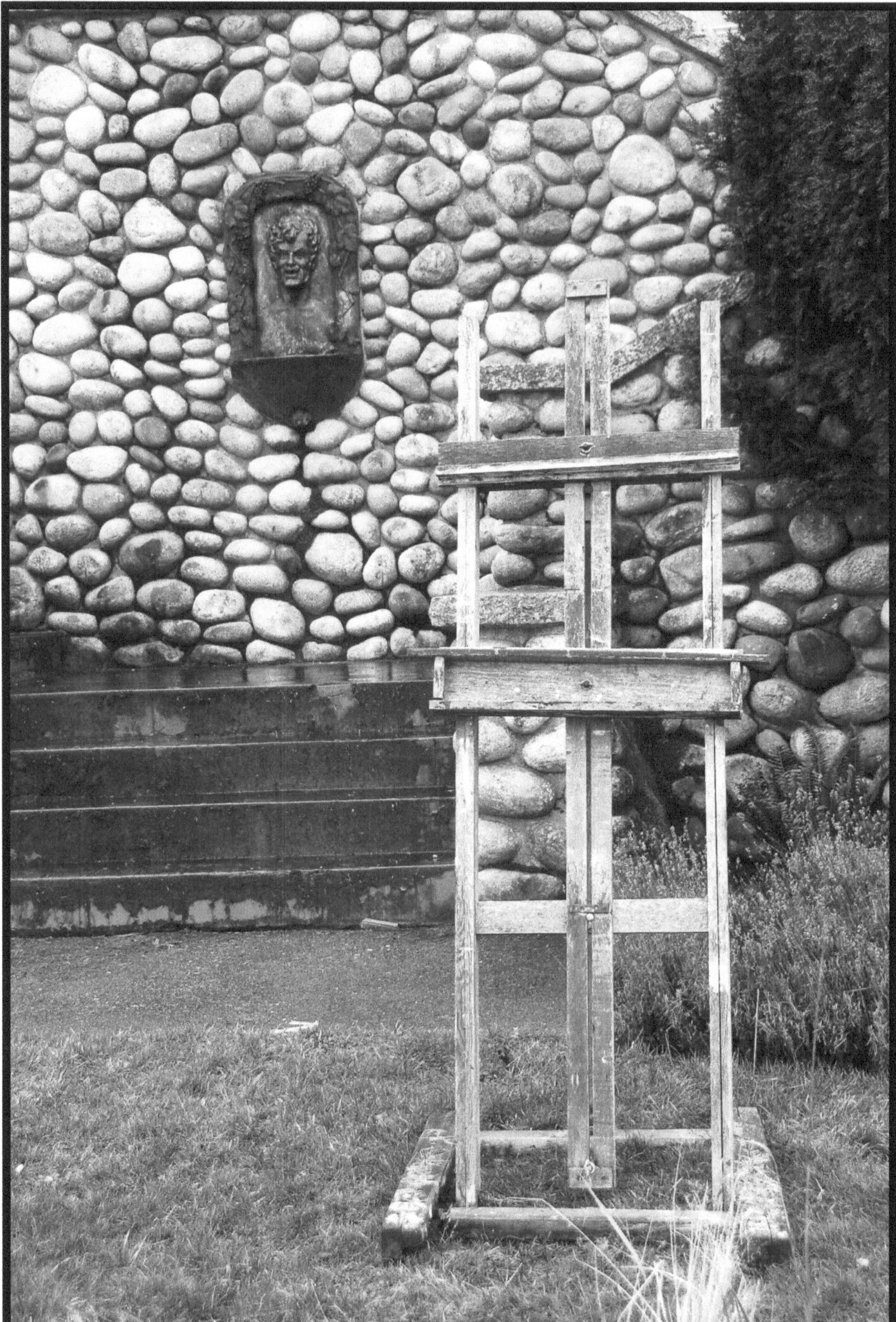

Time Passed

I found this old easel where I teach photography at Coast Collective – it was abandoned so I moved it over and propped it up. The feeling is that the easel wants to be used – at least one more time. The stone sculpture embedded in the rocks is there to be photographed or painted – just waiting. I felt for both the easel and this sculpture in the rocks. It is my rendition of loneliness and the forgotten…

<u>*Praise received:*</u>
"I agree with you Klaus, a touch of melancholy there.
Sadly, the passage of time is the eventual winner."

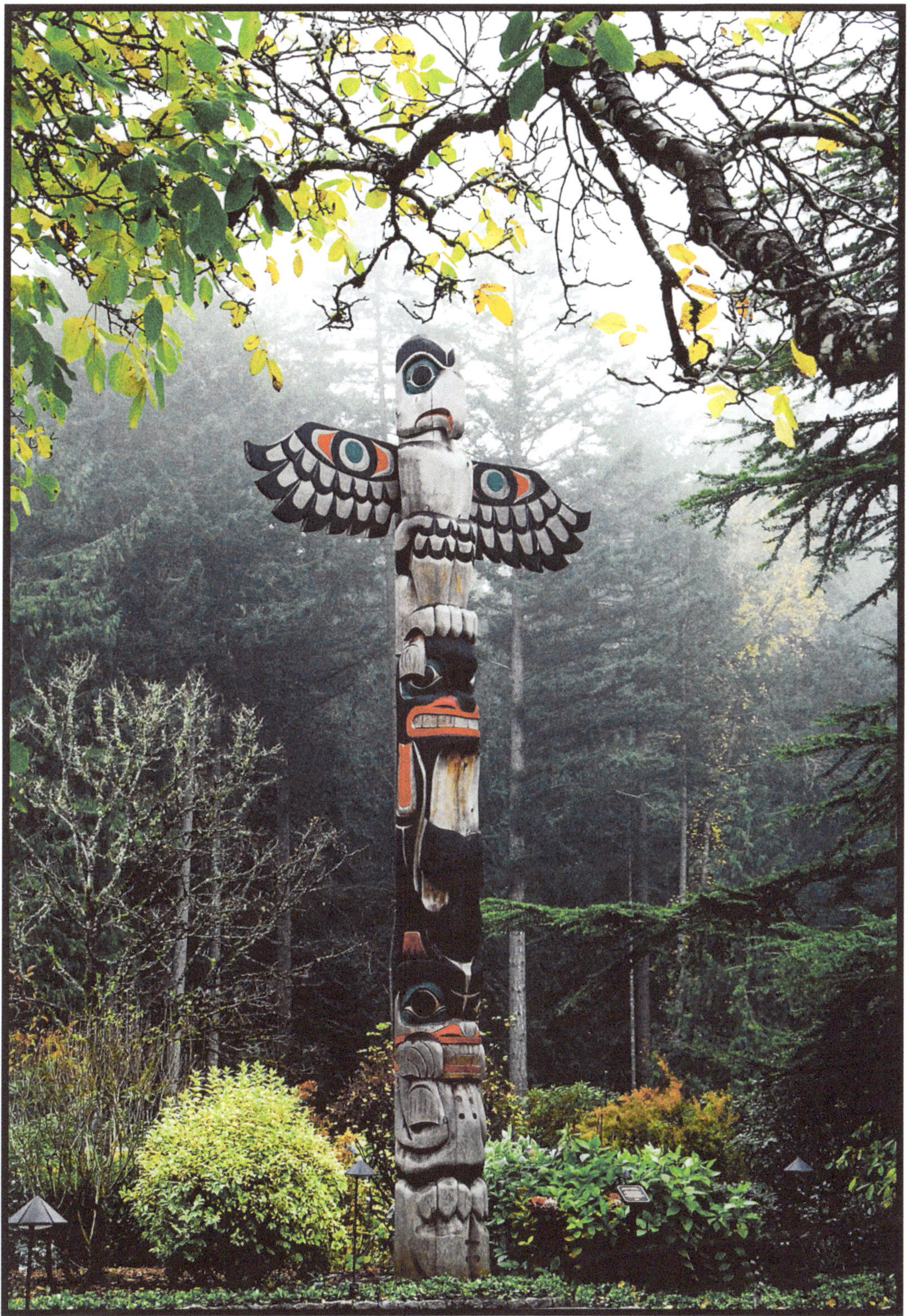

Totem Pole

I have wanted to photograph totem poles even before I reached Vancouver Island, and now I am putting some effort into doing so. This particular totem pole is centred to give it respect and honour, the colours adding beauty of their own to be admired. The trees in the background assist in the storytelling, slightly bent in reverence and giving space while also creating depth in the image – the lighting and atmosphere were perfect. The telltale carving of history and what it says is beyond my ability to understand its language.

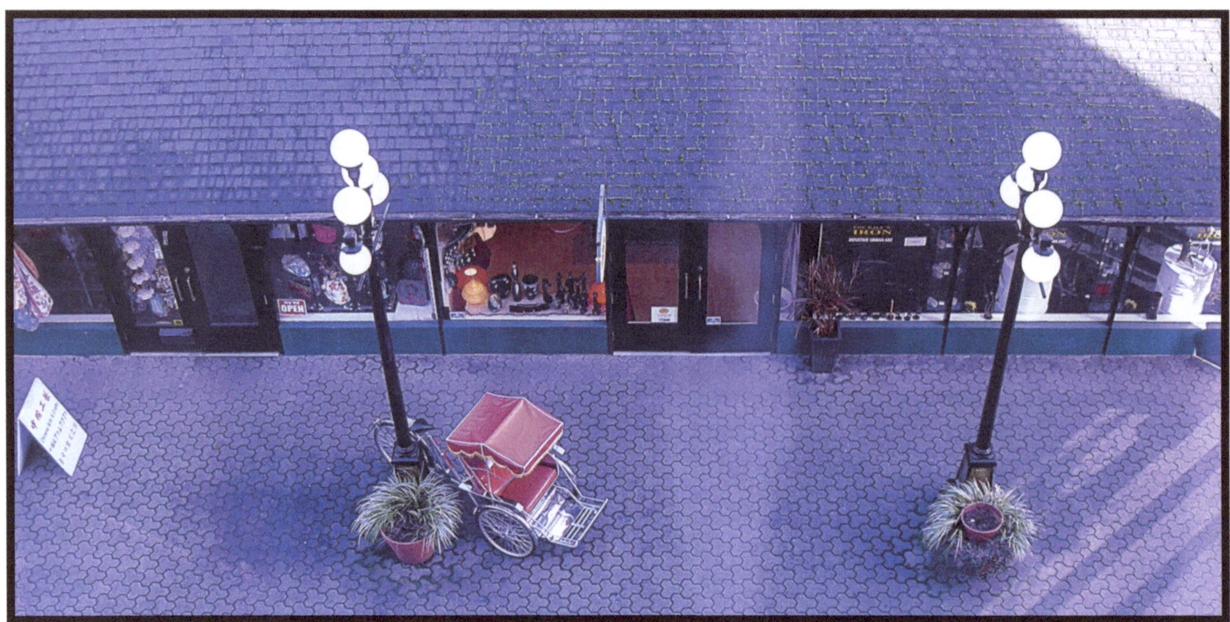

Unreal

Peering out of my friend's window I saw something that for Victoria, British Columbia, Canada seemed unreal to me – a rickshaw attached to a bicycle. I embellished the image by adjusting the colours to my liking.

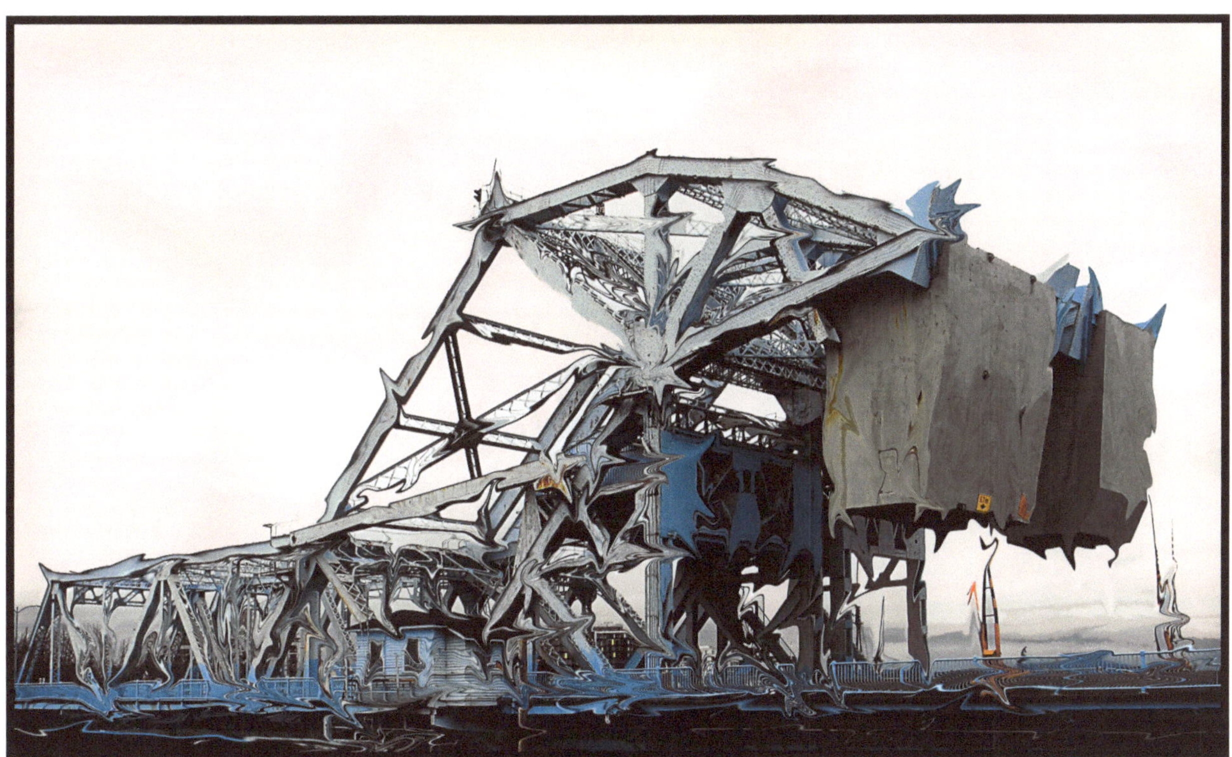

Weeping Blue Bridge

Most people refer to the Johnson Street Bridge as the blue bridge. I had a studio downtown for two years only two blocks from the blue bridge. It is one of the oldest bridges in Victoria, British Columbia. Many people are upset that they are tearing it down and building a new bridge. This blue bridge has been a landmark since its opening in 1924. I would walk over to the bridge at least once a week or more when I had my studio downtown. I photographed the blue bridge and wanted to add feelings; to show its demise. I saw an art piece that the bridge was all twisted and out of shape. This gave me the inspiration to make my photograph unreal. It's weeping because it is going to be torn down, done away with – laid to rest…

Praise received:

"I like what you did. Maybe what comes after can be tied to what you have once it's done... like a phoenix. Great photo work as always."

"I too get upset when they destroy a part of history. Sorry for your loss my friend. Things like that can be upsetting."

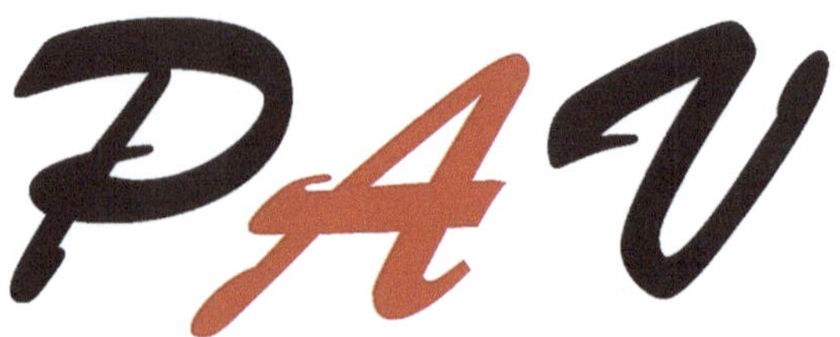

My Brand:
P stands for what I do, Photography

A stands for what I make, Art

V stands for where I live, Victoria

My Slogan:
Feeling more deeply about photography

What my photography means to me:
Photographs, spoken words, written words and body language

Concluding Remarks

Photography has always been an expression of my vision – not merely documentation.

The Art in photography goes beyond what is in front of the camera – it's what has been within the photographer's imagination. How to accomplish this with an apparatus we call a camera is the key.

What is real art? Whatever it is, we need to pursuit it – for it is a world of discovery. We need to discover the artist first by following our passion, then we can appreciate the cost of the artist, not the price of the art.

In photography people don't ask the photographer to show their credentials, degrees, who they've studied under or even with whom they've apprenticed. What do you really know about photography and the art of photography? Is it because you have a good camera? Let me tell you about a man who uses a very old inexpensive camera and puts filters in front of the lens – he admits he knows very little about his camera – just that it works – this man is... David Hamilton, a world renowned British-born French photographer. He is a true artist because it is not about the equipment, but rather about the individual, the heart, his evolution, growing inside – it is life, it is what he lives for.

When I started to teach I had no degrees and that was a hindrance for me to speak in the United States. When I received my Masters and my Fellowship and was accredited, things changed but I was still the same person in my soul. Why should that matter? Well it doesn't unless you want to fit into a mold. Bill Macintosh once told me he learned to disassociate himself from his association degrees because the clients who wanted his work weren't interested, and made him feel closed in, as if within a box.

I think art needs to be mysterious in development, but real in its outcome – not shining, overly perfect, too unreal... instead, believable. I hope the images contained within this book provide a small lesson of my development. I have tried to keep it short, but as always, there is so much more I could say.

About the Author

Klaus Bohn graduated from the Winona School of Professional Photography in 1972 and over the years has attended private classes from well known photographers who have lectured throughout the world including Joe Zeltsman, Monte Zucker, Linda Lapp-Murray, Donald Jack, Rocky Gunn, Yousuf Karsh, Arnold Newman, and many more.

Over the years he has worked to develop his unique style and received his Fellowship (F/SPPA) and Craftsman (CPA) in 1987 and his Masters of Photographic Arts (MPA) in 1989. He has also received his Accreditation in Child Photography (A) along with many other awards for Excellence in Photography.

He has been an active executive member of the Saskatchewan Professional Photographer's Association and held the title of Education Chairman as well as other positions. Klaus has also been a member of the Professional Photographers Association of British Columbia, Professional Photographers of Canada, the Professional Photographers of America and the Royal Society of Great Britain.

Klaus has taught professional photography since 1984 across Canada and the United States. Always trying to assist amateur and professional photographers alike, Klaus has also judged at many National and Regional photography competitions.

He has authored many magazine articles and has had his photos published in Range Finder Magazine, the Professional Photographers of Canada (PPOC) Magazine and others, as well as a series for Briar Patch Magazine.

Presently residing in Victoria, British Columbia, Klaus owns his own studio business, ***Photographic Art*** and has completed two previous books, *50 Principles of Composition in Photography* (2006) and *The Art Within Portrait Photography* (2007). His current endeavours include writing and exploring new unique forms of photographic art. Klaus may be contacted directly through his Photographic Art web site:

www.photographicartvictoria.com.

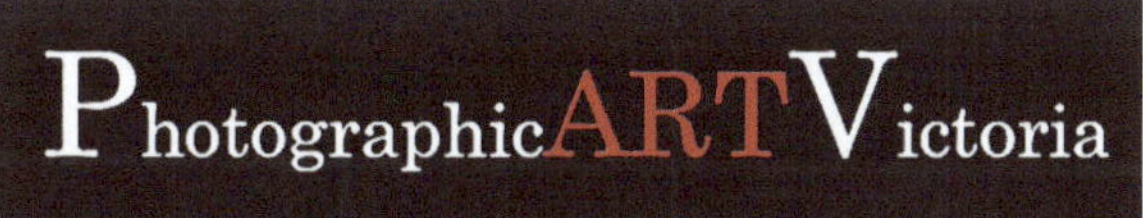

www.ingramcontent.com/pod-product-compliance
Lightning Source LLC
LaVergne TN
LVHW070125110826
845147LV00002B/187
* 9 7 8 1 9 2 7 3 6 0 1 9 4 *